GREENWOOD
G U I D E S

First published in 2000 by Greenwood Guides,
Cornhall House, Cranbrook, Kent, TN17 3DT, UK.

Twelfth edition

Copyright (c) June 2013 Greenwood Guides Ltd

Simon Greenwood has asserted his right to be identified as the author of this work.

ISBN 978-0-9575715-0-1

Printed in China through Colorcraft Ltd., Hong Kong.

THE GREENWOOD GUIDE TO
SOUTH AFRICA
hand-picked accommodation

Including Swaziland and Lesotho
twelfth edition

www.greenwoodguides.com

Acknowledgements

Series Editor: Simon Greenwood

Writing collaboration and inspections: Hannah Sheppard and Ben Balfour.

Map data provided by Collins Bartholomew Ltd.

Production, DTP and Design: Tory Gordon-Harris and Jo Ekin

Printing: through Colorcraft Ltd, Hong Kong

UK Distribution: Quiller Publishing Ltd
SA Distribution: Sula Sales and Marketing

Cover main photo courtesy Black Leopard Camp, entry number 241
Front cover small photos from left to right: The Bush House, entry 225,
Woodcliffe entry number 158, Ben Balfour, Les Hauts de Montagu entry
number 137, Papkuilsfontein Farmhouse entry number 213
Back cover images from left to right: Villa Tarentaal entry number 47,
Jaci's Lodges entry number 226, Angala Boutique Hotel entry number 65
Cover design and digital manipulation by Tory Gordon-Harris.

Title page image: Ben Balfour

Province intro images: all by Ben Balfour except Soweto by Ollie Smallwood.

The Team

Simon Greenwood

Hannah Sheppard

Ben Balfour

Contents

Symbols
and what they mean

 No credit cards accepted.

 Meals can be provided, often by prior arrangement.

 Rooms all have TVs.

 Wild game can be seen.

 Wireless Internet access.

 Children are welcome without proviso.

 Working farm.

 Off-street car parking.

 Access only for wheelchairs.

 Full wheelchair facilities.

 Swimming available in pool, sea, dam or river.

 No smoking inside the buildings.

 Good hiking or walking direct from the house.

Introduction

Welcome to the Greenwood Guide to South Africa, edition 12!

GG has been going for so many years now that it is probably time to update the photo of myself on the team page... take a shot from even further away.... maybe next year.

Meanwhile, this edition represents business as usual for GG with some inspiring new places to visit. I hope that you find the Greenwood Guide an indispensable and trustworthy help in finding wonderful places to stay.

The GG Approach

I receive a great deal of email from travellers, which I encourage. It gives us a good idea of how our choices are being received out there in the field. And since we live or die on the happiometer of our travellers, i.e. you, then this information is vital. Our aim is to choose places that more-than-just pass muster. We will always be judged by the worst, not the best, of our choices.

We have made genuine human hospitality our common denominator rather than the sterile but safe judgement of a place's worth according to its facilities. We do not therefore distribute stars or tiaras. A place is either right for the guide or it isn't. Beyond that each traveller will need to look at location, rates and exactly what sort of place it is and make their own decisions.

First and foremost we assess the people running the accommodation and choose only those for whom looking after others, whether they be friends, family or paying guests, is an innate pleasure. Taste, furnishings, facilities, views, food, beds, bathrooms… all these things are important too, but only if they are provided by friendly, caring hosts.

Thank you for choosing our guide. We do put in an enormous amount of effort each year, revisiting each place each edition, weeding out places that have lost their energy - as often happens in the world of accommodation - and sounding out all the new great, good and ordinary places that open each year. The standard rises continually in South Africa and this does mean that new places emerge at the top and old places drop off the bottom too. We seriously recommend therefore that you make sure that this is a latest edition of the guide. It is published annually in June.

As I always say, we would be delighted to hear from you when you get back from your travels. One request though: emails (to simon@ greenwoodguides.com) are definitely preferable to letters or faxes.

The GG Website

www.greenwoodguides.com

Much is happening on our website these days. It is well worth a visit, even if you prefer having the book in hand for convenience when actually on the road.

MAPS

We have now transferred to Google maps so you can pinpoint exactly the location of each place to stay.

CURRENT SPECIAL OFFERS

We publish a monthly list of specials being offered by GG places. These change every month. Go to the website and click on the 'SA specials' button and you will be able to take advantage if you happen to be booking your trip and your itinerary coincides with what's being offered.

BLOG OF UPCOMING EVENTS

We have a continually updating and highly eclectic blog of upcoming events written by Mark Bland, called An Ear to the Rail. Here are some wildly different recent items so you have an idea of what it's all about:
* A steam train ride.
* A tour of the under-city tunnels in Cape Town.
* A rickshaw ride round Durban
* The Darling Music Experience.
* A re-enactment of the Battle of Isandlwana.
* The Clarens beer fest.
* The Outeniqua farmers' market.
* The rugby world sevens tournament.
* The Ficksburg cherry fest.
* The Tokai Forest 15km fun run.
* Apricot picking at De Krans
Etc etc. Check out An Ear to the Rail at www.greenwoodguides.com.

RESTAURANT OF THE MONTH

Mark (who is a budding chef himself) also picks one or two restaurants each month that he is particularly keen on.

Some info on travelling with this book in South Africa

ARRIVAL

Make sure that you have two clear pages left in your passport. I am told that they are very strict about this and it would be a crazy way to be refused entry.

DRIVING

There is nowhere in South Africa that would make a 4-wheel drive a necessity.

CAR HIRE

Make sure that you have considered the amount of daily mileage your car hire company gives you. 100km or even 200km a day is virtually nothing and the final cost can be far higher than you estimated. Try and work out roughly what distances you will be covering and ask for the correct daily allowance. Or ask for unlimited mileage. There is usually a surcharge for taking your car across the border from SA into other countries.

N.B. Also make sure you are insured to drive the car on dirt roads.

We highly recommend Comet Car Rental, owned and run by Dave Halley and Cathy Heyburgh, on 021-386-2411 or info@cometcar.co.za. They are very friendly and helpful and we use them ourselves. Airport pick-ups and drop-offs are no problem. They have offices in Cape Town, Johannesburg, Durban and Port Elizabeth and are small enough to offer a friendly and efficient service where you are not just an unknown number. Dave and Cathy are also very experienced with over 20 years in the car rental industry and offer a professional service with no hidden costs like most of their larger competitors.

Also they are offering all GG travellers a discount of 10% on their car hire. Just mention that you are travelling with the Greenwood Guide if you decide to use Comet.

MOBILE/CELL PHONES

Airports all have shops that provide mobile phones. They are invaluable and we recommend that you get one. You can buy a cheap handset or just rent one for the duration of your stay and then pay for calls as you go with recharge cards.

TELEPHONE NUMBERS

The numbers printed for entries in SA in the book are all from within South Africa. To call South Africa from the UK dial 0027 then drop the 0 from the local code. To call the UK from South Africa you now dial 0044 - it used to be 0944 but this changed recently.

Another change is when dialling a local number you now always have to dial the full number including the area code.

TORTOISES

Look out for tortoises. They are slow, but seem to spend a lot of time, completely against the tide of advice put forward for their benefit, crossing roads.

TIPS on TIPPING

• In restaurants we tend to give 15%.

• At a petrol station my policy is to give no tip for just filling up, 3 rand for cleaning the windows, and 5 rand for cleaning the windows and checking oil and water. If you really don't want the attendant to clean your windows you need to make this a statement when you ask for the petrol… or they will often do it anyway.

• At a guest-house I would typically give R30 per person staying for up to two nights. If you are staying longer than two nights then you might feel like adding more. If there is obviously one maid to whom the tip will go then give it to her direct. If there are many staff members who will be sharing the tip then give it to your host.

* Tipping game rangers at game lodges: often these highly-qualified people are the main reason why you have such a great stay at a particular lodge. I suggest around R100 per guest per day depending on the quality of service you receive.

THE GARDEN ROUTE

Many people imagine, not unreasonably, that the Garden Route is a bit like a wine route where you can go from garden to garden, smelling roses and admiring pergolas and rockeries. Not so. The Garden Route is so named for its lushness and greenery. The area is covered in forests and rivers, which spill into the sea. And, although many people there surely do have lovely gardens, the name is a little misleading. A fantastic area for walking though.

TIME OF YEAR

I got in a bit of a tangle in the first edition trying neatly to package up what is really quite complicated. So I will limit myself to one observation. It seems to me that most Europeans come to South Africa in January, February and March to avoid their own miserable weather and write taunting postcards home from a sunny Cape.

However, the very best time of year to visit the Northern Cape, Mpumalanga, Limpopo, North West Province, KwaZulu Natal and the Karoo, i.e. the whole country except the southern Cape, is from May to October. The air is dry and warm, game viewing is at its best and there are fewer tourists keeping the prices higher.

PAY FOR ENTRY

We could not afford to research and publish this guide in the way we do without the financial support of those we feature. Each place that we have chosen has paid an entry fee for which we make no apology. It has not influenced our decision-making about who is right or wrong for the guide and we turn down many more than we accept. The proof of this is in the proverbial pudding. Use the book and see for yourself. It is also impossible for us to write up a place that we are not enthusiastic about.

THE MAPS SECTION

The maps at the front of the book are designed to show you where in the country each place is positioned and should not be used as a road map. There are many minor and dirt roads missing and we recommend that you buy a proper companion road atlas. Each place is flagged with a number that corresponds to the entry number below each entry.

Some have complained that it is hard to find detailed road maps of South Africa in the UK, so I suggest you buy one at the airport when you arrive in SA. Or try Stanfords in London on Long Acre in Covent Garden, 020-7836-1321.

CANCELLATION

Most places have some form of cancellation charge. Do make sure that you are aware what this is if you book in advance. Owners need to protect themselves against no-shows and will often demand a deposit for advance booking.

PRICES

The prices quoted are per person sharing per night, unless specifically stated otherwise. Every now and then complications have meant we quote the full room rate. Single rates are also given.

We have usually put in a range within which the actual price will fall. This may be because of fluctuating prices at different times of year, but also we have tried to predict the anticipated rise in prices over the book's shelf life. Obviously we cannot know what will happen to the value of the rand and prices might fall outside the quoted range.

Most game lodges quote an all-in package including meals and game activities.

Although South Africa has become substantially more expensive since the first edition of this guide came out 11 years ago, it is still great value on the whole. The value-for-money increases significantly the more off-the-beaten-track you wander.

CHILDREN

We have only given the child-friendly symbol to those places that are unconditionally accepting of the little fellows. This does not necessarily mean that if there is no symbol children are barred. But it may mean chatting with your hosts about their ages, their temperaments and how suitable a time and place it will be. Most owners are concerned about how their other guests will take to kids running wild when they are trying to relax on a long-anticipated holiday... from their own children. Places that are fully child-friendly are listed in the activities index at the back of the book.

DISCLAIMER

We make no claims to god-like objectivity in assessing what is or is not special about the places we feature. They are there because we like them. Our opinions and tastes are mortal and ours alone. We have done our utmost to get the facts right, but apologize for any mistakes that may have slipped through the net. Some things change which are outside our control: people sell up, prices increase, exchange rates fluctuate, unfortunate extensions are added, marriages break up and even acts of God can rain down destruction. We would be grateful to be told about any errors or changes, however great or small. We can make these edits at any time on the web version of this book.

DON'T TRY AND DO TOO MUCH. PLEASE.

It is the most common way to spoil your own holiday. South Africa is a huge country and you cannot expect to see too much of it on one trip. Don't over-extend yourself. Stay everywhere for at least two nights and make sure that you aren't spending your hard-earned holiday fiddling with the radio and admiring the dashboard of your hire car.

PLEASE WRITE TO US

My email address is simon@greenwoodguides.com for all comments. Although we visit each place each edition many of the places featured here are small, personal and owner-run. This means that their enjoyability depends largely on the happiness, health and energy of the hosts. This can evaporate in double-quick time for any number of reasons and standards plummet before we have had a chance to re-evaluate the place. So we are also very grateful to travellers who keep us up to date with how things are going. We are always most concerned to hear that the hosting has been inattentive.

THANKS

So that's about it for another year. My great thanks this year go to Hannah (Sheppard) and Ben (Balfour) for all their efforts in researching and updating this 12th edition of the guide. I wish them well in their new lives in Australia. Also my thanks to Mike (Munro) for his work on the monthly specials. And to Mark (Bland) for his excellent web blogs. And finally to Richard Albion who works tirelessly on the website and all other matters technical that keep the good ship GG under sail!

I hope that this book will be seen as the main reason why you enjoyed your holiday as much as you did. Please feel free to write to me with praise or criticism for individual places that you visit at simon@greenwoodguides.com. And, once again, it really is worth having a look at www.greenwoodguides.com before you set off. Have a fantastic trip whether it is a major 4-week extravaganza or just a weekend break.

Simon.

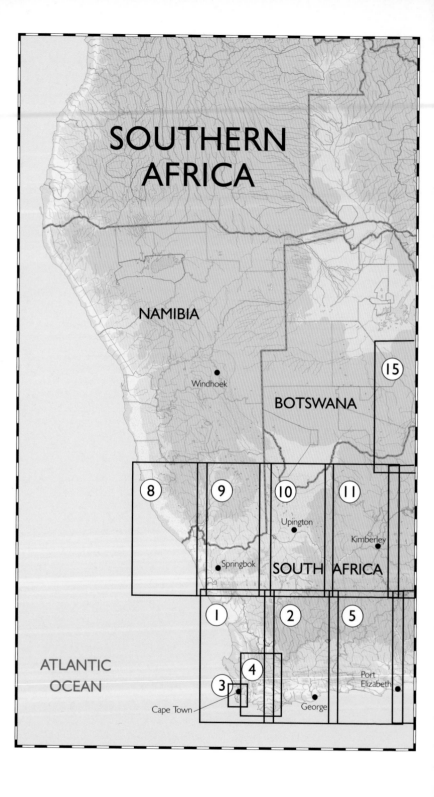

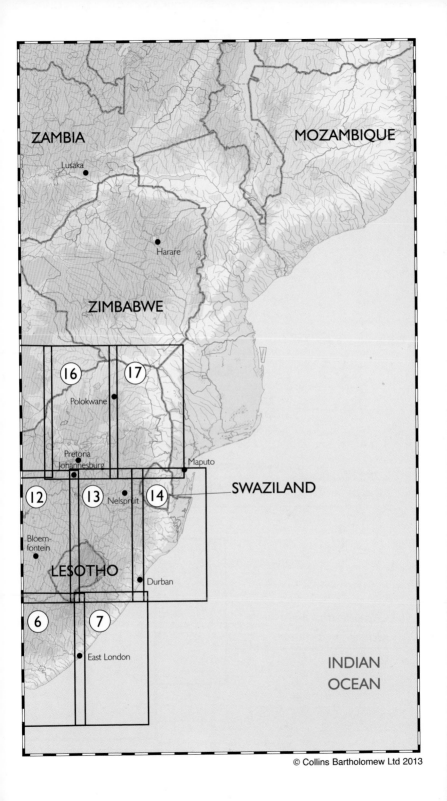

ZAMBIA

Lusaka •

Harare •

ZIMBABWE

MOZAMBIQUE

16   17

Polokwane •

Pretoria •
Johannesburg •

12   13   Nelspruit •   14

Maputo •

SWAZILAND

Bloem-
fontein •

LESOTHO

Durban •

6   7

• East London

INDIAN
OCEAN

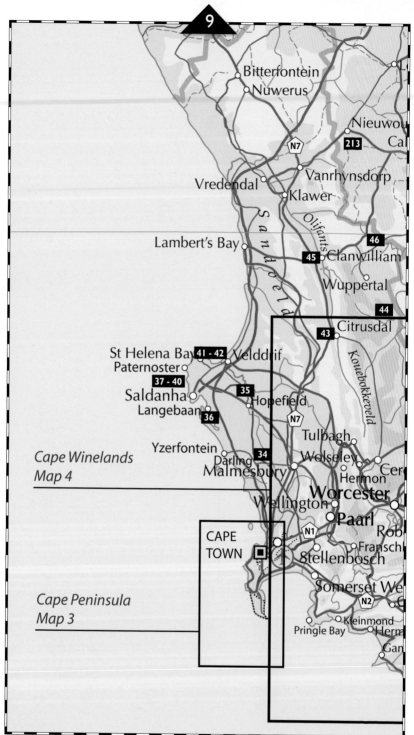

MAP I

© Collins Bartholomew Ltd 2013

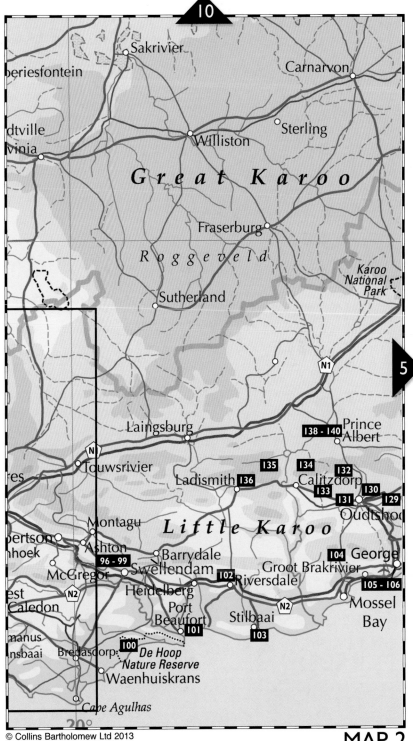

Sakrivier

beriesfontein

Carnarvon

dtville
vinia

Sterling

Williston

Great Karoo

Roggeveld

Fraserburg

Karoo
National
Park

Sutherland

5

N1

Laingsburg

Prince
Albert

138 - 140

N

135

134

132

Touwsrivier

Ladismith

136

Calitzdorp

133

131

130

129

Oudtshoo

Montagu

Little Karoo

104

George

bertson
hoek

Ashton

96 - 99

Barrydale

Groot Brakrivier

105 - 106

McGregor

Swellendam

102

Riversdale

N2

Mossel
Bay

est
Caledon

N2

Heidelberg

Port
Beaufort

Stilbaai

manus
nsbaai

Bredasdorp

101

103

100

De Hoop
Nature Reserve

Waenhuiskrans

Cape Agulhas

20°

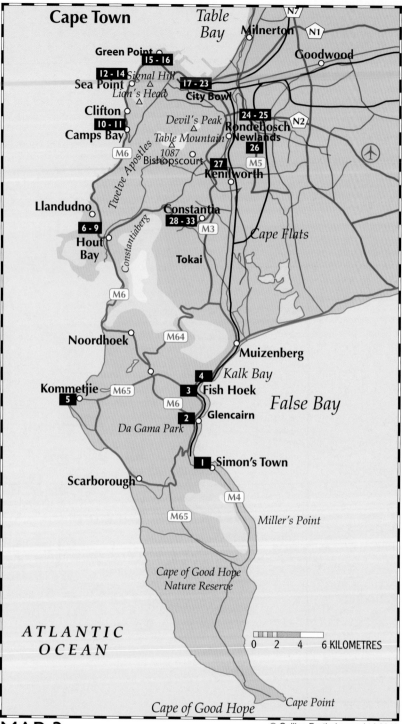

MAP 3

© Collins Bartholomew Ltd 2013

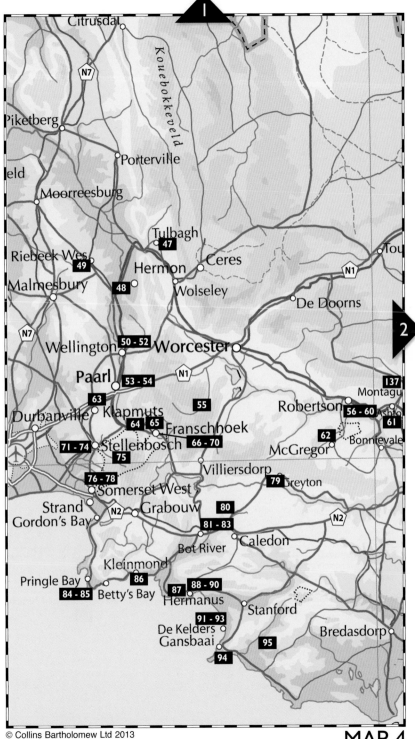

© Collins Bartholomew Ltd 2013

MAP 4

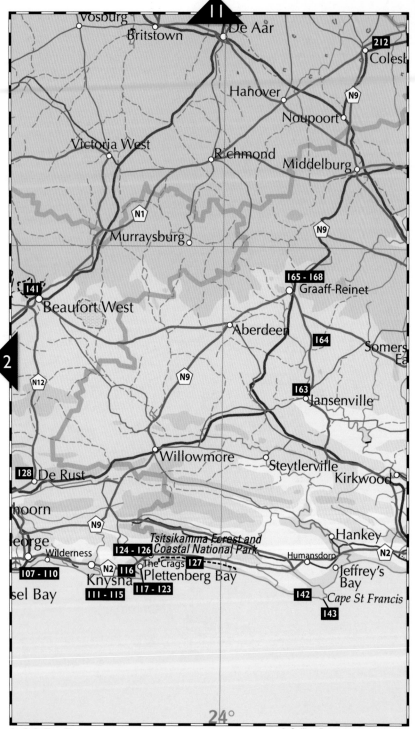

MAP 5

© Collins Bartholomew Ltd 2013

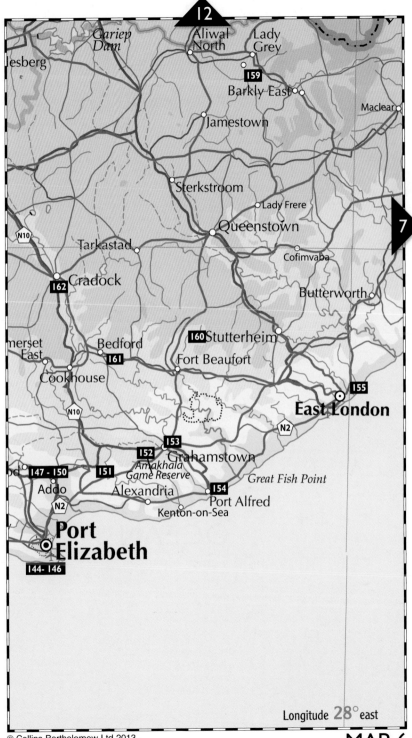

12

Gariep
Dam

Jesberg

Aliwal
North

Lady
Grey

159

Barkly East

Maclear

Jamestown

Sterkstroom

Lady Frere

Queenstown

7

Cofimvaba

N10

Tarkastad

Cradock

162

Butterworth

merset
East

Bedford

161

160 Stutterheim

Cookhouse

Fort Beaufort

East London

155

N10

N2

152 153

Grahamstown

147 - 150

151

Amakhala
Game Reserve

Great Fish Point

Addo

Alexandria

154

N2

Kenton-on-Sea

Port Alfred

Port
Elizabeth

144- 146

Longitude 28° east

© Collins Bartholomew Ltd 2013

MAP 6

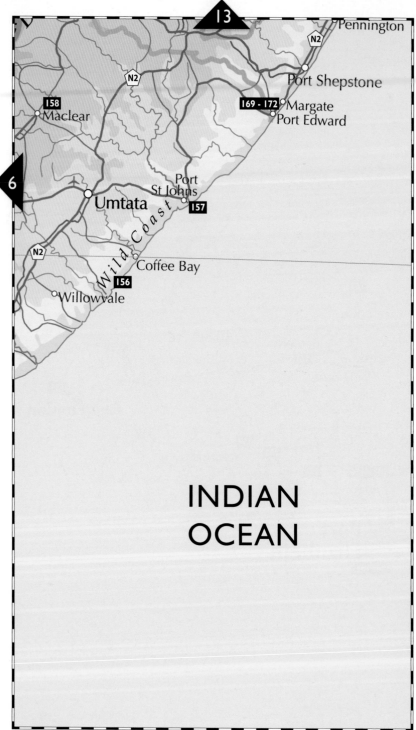

INDIAN
OCEAN

MAP 7

© Collins Bartholomew Ltd 2013

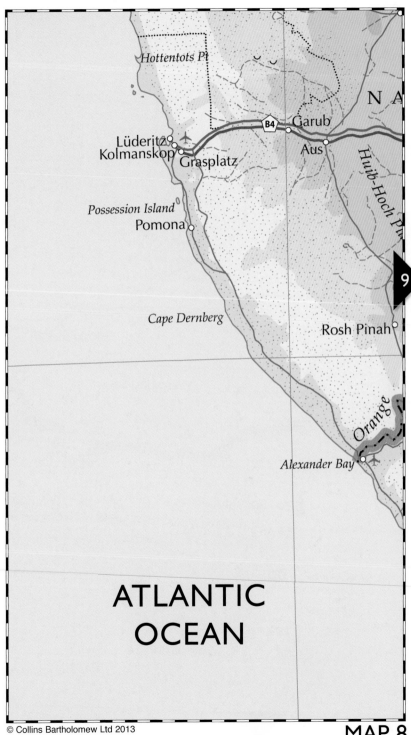

Hottentots Pt

B4 Garub

Lüderitz
Kolmanskop Grasplatz
Aus

N A

Huib-Hoch Plu

Possession Island
Pomona

9

Cape Dernberg

Rosh Pinah

Orange

Alexander Bay

ATLANTIC
OCEAN

MAP 8

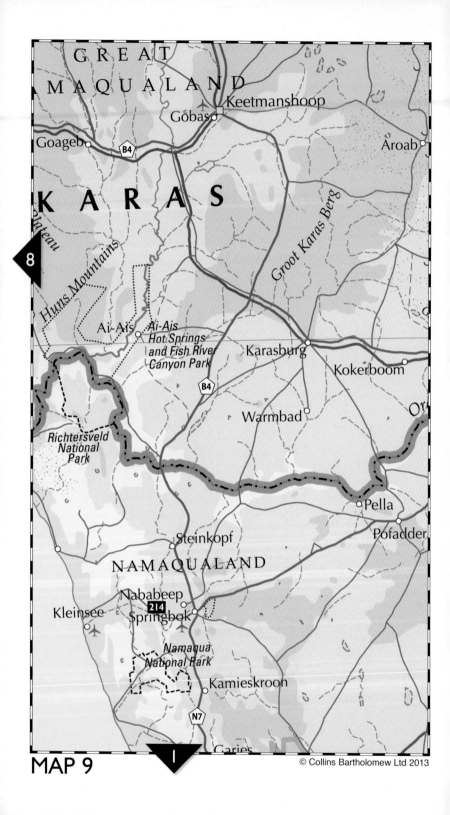

MAP 9

© Collins Bartholomew Ltd 2013

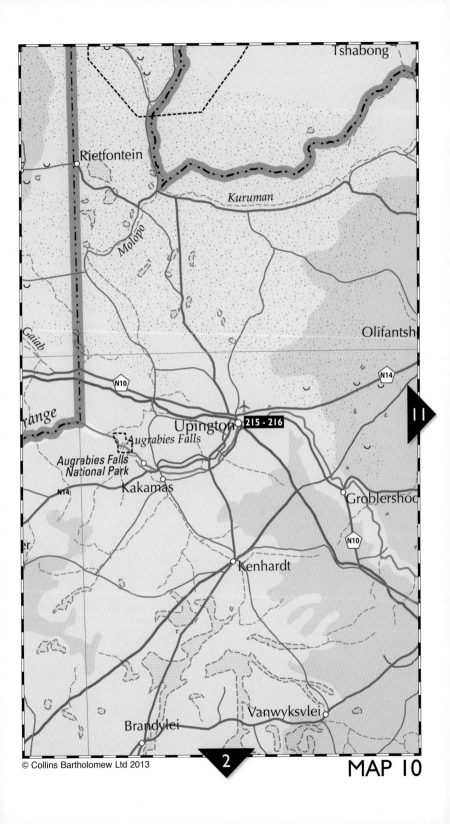

Tshabong

Rietfontein

Kuruman

Molopo

Gaiab

Olifantsh

N10

N14

range

Upington · 215 - 216

II

Augrabies Falls

Augrabies Falls
National Park

N14

Kakamas

Groblershoc

N10

Kenhardt

Vanwyksvlei

Brandvlei

2

MAP 10

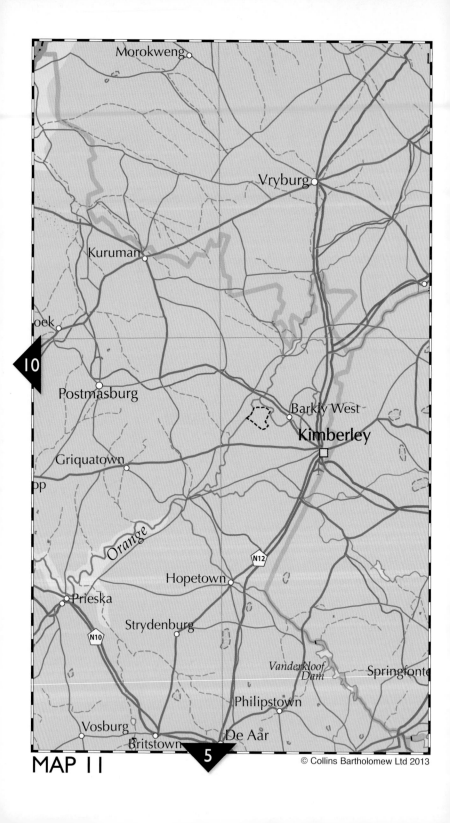

Morokweng

Vryburg

Kuruman

oek

10

Postmasburg

Barkly West

Kimberley

Griquatown

pp

Orange

N12

Hopetown

Prieska

Strydenburg

N10

Vanderkloof Dam

Springfonte

Philipstown

Vosburg

Britstown

De Aar

5

MAP 11

© Collins Bartholomew Ltd 2013

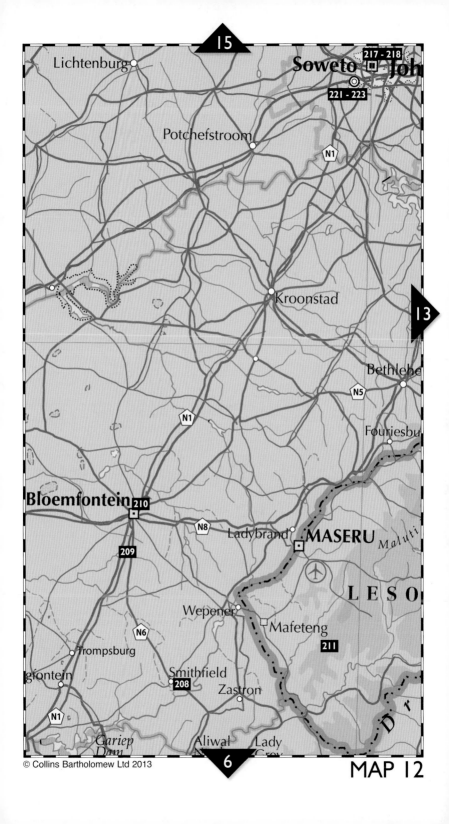

MAP 12

MAP 13

© Collins Bartholomew Ltd 2013

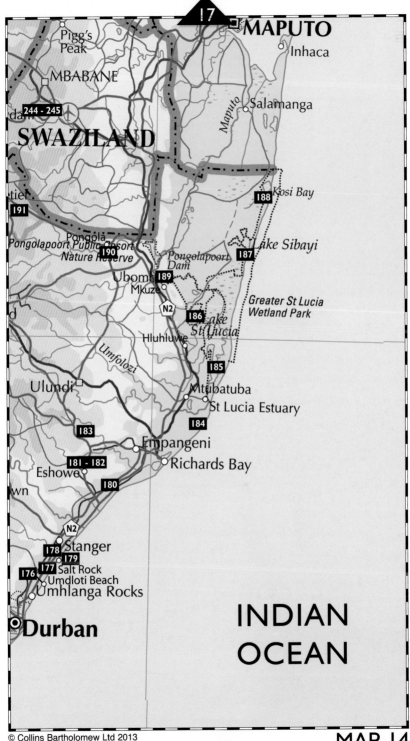

!7

▪️MAPUTO

○Inhaca

○Pigg's
Peak

□MBABANE

244 - 245

SWAZILAND

Salamanga

Maputo

tiel

191

Kosi Bay

188

Pongola

Pongolapoort Public Resort
Nature Reserve

190

Lake Sibayi

187

Pongolapoort
Dam

Ubom

189

Mkuze

N2

186

Lake
St Lucia

Greater St Lucia
Wetland Park

Hluhluwe

Umfolozi

185

Ulundi □

Mtubatuba

○St Lucia Estuary

184

183

Empangeni

181 - 182

○Richards Bay

Eshowe○

180

wn

N2

178 ○Stanger

179

176 177 Salt Rock

○Umdloti Beach

○Umhlanga Rocks

◉Durban

INDIAN

OCEAN

MAP 14

MAP 15

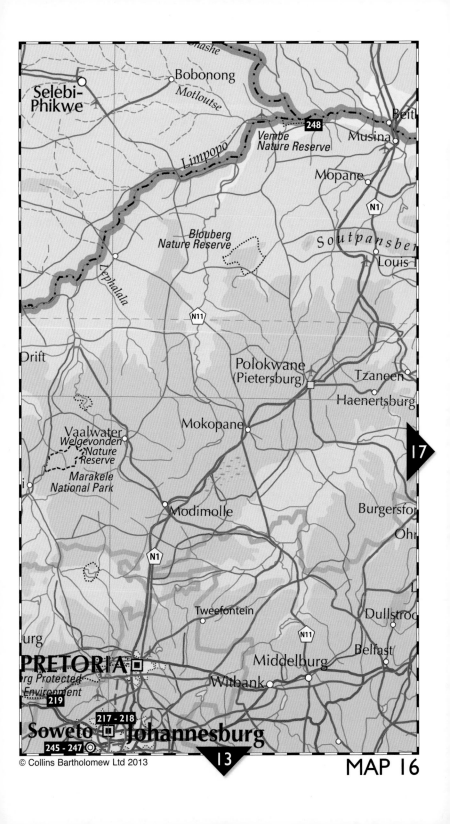

MAP 16

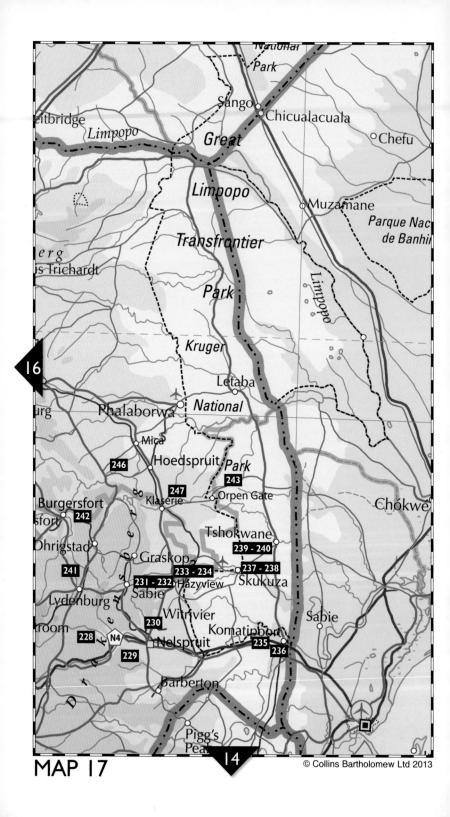

MAP 17

© Collins Bartholomew Ltd 2013

Western Cape

Albatross House

Leon and Sandy Strydom

37 Victory Way, Simon's Kloof, Simon's Town
Tel: 021-786-5906 Fax: 021-786-4297
Email: albatrosshouse@lantic.net Web: www.albatrosshouse.co.za or
www.facebook.com/Albatrosshouse Cell: 082-363-6449

You can see the sea from every room. Despite this, you'll probably want to spend most of your time outside on the terraces overlooking False Bay ("a 360-degree view, HD!" as Leon puts it), keeping an eye on the movement in the harbour or studying the water for whales during season. Inside, décor is fresh and summery throughout with wooden panelling in the bathrooms that lends them a boathouse feel. With private sitting rooms and connecting terraces (lightly screened off if privacy is preferred), dotted with deep wooden chairs, this is a perfect place to relax with friends. I was quite envious of three ladies who, as Sandy explained, had been chatting, laughing and playing bridge into the early hours. The Garden Apartment offers the addition of an amply-equipped kitchen for those wishing to self-cater, with separate parking and entrance; Leon invites you to "come and make this your second home". But don't fret. Leon and Sandy won't abandon you. Breakfast is available, even on the odd (lazy) day for self-catering guests, courtesy of Sandy and tailored to your wishes. As a member of a weekly hiking group, Leon knows the hiking trails, birds, fauna and flora well and can give good tips on where to go, relative to the time of year and weather. There are stunning jaunts just minutes from the house. If you'd rather soak up some history in Simon's Town, take the path below the house, specially constructed by Leon and Sandy, through their indigenous fynbos garden and down into the town. Just remember, the view awaits you on your return... a sundowner anyone?

Rooms: 3: 1 king en-s bath & 1 twin/dble en-s shr (sharing lounge & kitchenette); 1 self-catering apartment (sleeps 4 + 1 adult or 2 small kids on sleeper-couch): 1 qu en-s bath & sh'r & 1 twin/dble en-s sh'r.
Price: B&B R440 - R650 pp sh. Room only (i.e. no breakfast) or self-catering R380 - R575 pp sh. Discounts for longer stays.
Meals: Full breakfast included with B&B. Breakfast: R75 pp (room only or self-catering).
Directions: From Simon's Town station on L go past Admiralty House on L. Move to R lane. Turn R then L up Soldiers Way. R into Arsenal, L into Cornwall, becomes Runciman. Go past 3-way stop, R into Simon's Kloof, follow signs.

Moonglow Guest House

Gillian O'Leary

7 Bennett Close, Cairnside, Glencairn, Simon's Town
Tel: 021-786-5902 Fax: 021-786-5903
Email: seaview@moonglow.co.za Web: www.moonglow.co.za
Cell: 082-565-6568

"We've been here ten and a half years now but I still get goose-bumps every time I see the moon hanging over it," Gillian confides to me as we stare out over the smooth expanse of False Bay. I challenge you to find a better view of the bay than this one. Unsurprisingly most of the rooms at Moonglow take full advantage - even the ones that don't still get their own private seating areas round at the front. With Jess the dog staring lovingly at the succulent blueberry muffin that was supplied with my tea, I could have happily stayed for an eternity ensconced on the sofa of the bar-lounge… but an ever-enthusiastic Gillian (who says she will attempt her basic French for French-speaking guests) was keen to show me more and I had a job to do. Throughout this house you'll find original artworks everywhere, including a stunning leopard print and four-foot-high figurines hewn from solid granite. If it catches Gillian's eye she's got to have it. Vibrant oil paintings add a splash of colour to creamy rooms, all drenched in sunlight from large picture windows or glass doors. Beds and tables have been individually designed, and a multitude of mohair blankets and the finest quality linens have had Gillian's hand-embroiderers busy detailing them with intricate dragonflies and bumblebees "… just so the colours match." Moonglow shines.

Rooms: 6 double rooms, all en-suite.
Price: R525 - R615 pp sharing. Singles on request.
Meals: Full breakfast included. Lots of restaurants nearby.
Directions: Map on website or directions can be emailed on booking.

Blue Yonder

Sally and Bruce Elliott
14 Hillside Rd, Fish Hoek
Tel: 021-782-0500 Fax: 021-782-0500
Email: info@blueyondercape.co.za Web: www.blueyondercape.co.za
Cell: 082-441-9589

For those of you on the self-catering trail this is a must. A three-storey house converted into flats, Blue Yonder is a luxury ocean liner of a place. When Sally opened the door to an invading GG team the sun was blasting through the wall-to-wall windows. She was keen to show me around, but I spent the first ten minutes standing out on the enormous silver-railed balcony, transfixed by the view. From all three apartments here you can watch the full arc of the sun, rising over a glittering False Bay, and finally sinking behind the red-tiled roofs of the Fish Hoek bungalows below. Excellent for whale-watching. Once the trance wears off (which it won't) head inside and make the most of the stainless steel and cream kitchens, complete with all mod cons (including my personal favourite: the dishwasher). Sally grew up in this house, but after a huge conversion job the Rhodesian teak floors are the only reminder of her family home. Now, gloriously indulgent queen-sized beds look out on the bay and cool, beige armchairs are just waiting to be lounged in. Once you summon the energy for a dip in the ocean, your own private steps lead down to the beach, just a stone's throw away. My advice? Bring the whole family, light up a braai on the balcony and settle in for at least a month. *5 mins to food shops. All apartments have braais.*

Rooms: 3 self-catering apartments: Upper: 1 queen with en-suite shower & 1 twin with en-suite bath & shower; Middle: 1 queen en-s b & sh, 2 twins en-s b & sh; Lower: 1 queen en-s sh only. Serviced every week day.
Price: R265 - R445 pp sharing dependent on season and number of persons per unit.
Meals: In fridge on arrival: tea, coffee, milk, sugar. Full kitchen.
Directions: Head to Muizenberg from Cape Town, go south along main road through Fish Hoek. At roundabout at end of Fish Hoek main rd turn L towards Simon's Town. 1 km further take 1st R at lights up Hillside Rd. Blue Yonder c. 300m up on R.

The Mountain House

Miles and Carin Hartford

7 Mountain Road, Clovelly
Email: info@themountainhouse.co.za Web: www.themountainhouse.co.za
Cell: 083-455-5664

Welcome to your very own private mountain realm. You do not have to share The Mountain House with anyone, so you have total privacy and the freedom to come, go and do as you please. Miles and Carin are passionate about 'their mountain', known as Trappieskop, and have managed to clear out all the alien invaders and restore the indigenous flora. In the process much of the local fauna has returned too, much to the delight of all their nature-loving guests (such as I hope we all are!). The house is a simple organic space where everything fits and works perfectly. Clever innovations such as clerestory windows, Japanese sliding screen doors and a kitchen island on wheels ensure maximum use of both natural light and space. You have the option of taking 1 or 2 rooms depending on the make-up of your party. Both are gorgeous, uncluttered and supremely functional. Considering your surroundings, inside-outside living is a must and the jewel in the crown here is the sheltered deck. Protected from the prevailing south-easter, this outside living space is designed for use and with views over Fish Hoek Bay, the wetland below, the mountains and Clovelly golf course I can't see any reason not to take every meal, numerous drinks and extended bird-watching breaks right here. The Mountain House is exactly as its name suggests and is perfect for couples who enjoy being close to all things natural.

Rooms: 1 self-catering apartment with optional second bedroom.
Price: R600 - R1,200 per couple. Add R250 per additional adult.
Meals: Self-catering
Directions: See website for directions and a virtual tour.

The Olive Garden

Annette White

36 Mountain Road, Kommetjie
Tel: 021-794-4594
Email:
annette_rwhite@yahoo.co.uk

Olive Garden is a secret treat hidden in a jungle of trees and plants at the foot of Slangkop Mountain with views stretching along Noordhoek Beach, to Chapman's Peak, Hout Bay and up the back of Table Mountain. This is Annette's holiday home and, fortunately for us, she is more than happy to share it. Annette (who also owns 'Beluga of Constantia') has always had a nostalgic soft spot for Kommetjie after memorable years living here when she first moved to South Africa. She proudly gave me the grand tour. To be honest, I was sold on the place at the front door. This opens into the large, open-plan living room, centralised around the lime-green sofa with its quilted throw, made all the more enticing by a soft light pouring in through large windows and doors that lead out to a wooden balcony. This in turn is furnished with a long table and chairs (an additional set also indoors by the open fire). As the tour led us down the balcony steps to the garden, I saw my perch, the cushioned pergola within jumping-in distance of the pool. The kitchen is fully equipped with all essential mod cons and more. Bedrooms open onto a large wooden deck overlooking olive trees and the pool. Shops, delis and cafés are all within walking distance, not to mention Kommetjie's famous Long Beach (with good waves for surfing… so I'm told) and Slangkop Lighthouse. Lying halfway down the west coast of the Cape Peninsula, Kommetjie is a prime position from which to explore Cape Point or Cape Town central. And it is just seven minutes to the beach. We're lucky Annette hasn't kept this a secret.

Rooms: 1 (sleeps up to 4 adults + 2 children): 1 king with bath & shr; 1 king/twin shr only; extra double futon in study, plus 2'6" bed downstairs outside bedroom 2.
Price: R2,750 - R3,500 pn rental for house, min 5 nights high season.
Meals: Self-catering. Basic provisions on arrival.
Directions: From airport: N2 to Cape Town. Take M3 turn-off to Muizenberg. At end of M3 R onto Steenberg Rd. Bear L at 2nd lights onto Ou Kaapse Werf. Turn R at 2nd lights onto Kommetjie Rd. After passing Wireless Rd L into Rubbi Rd, 2nd R into Mountain Rd Nos 36 on RHS.

Frogg's Leap

Jôke Glauser and Stewart McLaren

Baviaans Close, off Baviaanskloof Rd, Hout Bay
Tel: 021-790-2590 Fax: 021-790-2590
Email: info@froggsleap.co.za Web: www.froggsleap.co.za
Cell: 082-493-4403

The huge Frogg's Leap verandah, with its impressive views of the Hout Bay mountains and sea seems to be the focal point of life here. At breakfast the house springs to life with Jôke (pronounced *yokie*) and Stewart engaging in easy banter with all who emerge and chiding guests for sitting at the long wooden table inside when the parasol-shaded tables outside are so enticing. Then, in the evening, with the sea breeze swinging the hammocks and a sundowner in your hand, it is not hard to get to grips with being lazy and on holiday. I can't remember a place where guests made themselves so at home. Jôke and Stewart used to run charter boats in the West Indies and Frogg's Leap has a breezy Caribbean feel with many open French doors and windows. Bedrooms are cool ensembles of natural materials: painted floors, seagrass matting, palms, natural stone in bathrooms, lazy wicker chairs, reed ceilings, thick cotton percale linen and old wooden furniture. Hout Bay itself is a fishing harbour enclosed by mountains and is within minutes of beaches and hiking trails with spectacular whale-watching when whales are in town. This is a place that has been consistently recommended both before and since the first edition and it is a continued pleasure to recommend it myself. *Guest phone 021-790-6260.*

Rooms: 6: 5 doubles/twins and 1 double, all with en-suite bathrooms; 2 with shower, 4 with bath and shower. Plus extra single room.
Price: R375 - R495 pp sharing. Single supplement: +50%.
Meals: Full breakfast included and served until 10am. There are 20 restaurants nearby for other meals.
Directions: A map will be faxed to you on confirmation of booking.

Paddington's

Di and Don Lilford

3 Lindevista Lane, Hout Bay
Tel: 021-790-1955 Fax: 021-790-1955
Email: dlilford@telkomsa.net Web: www.paddington.co.za
Cell: 083-259-6025

Standing in Di's garden, I sighed with satisfaction, gazing across a valley and beach bathed in late-afternoon sunshine. Well away from the hustle and bustle of Cape Town proper, Hout Bay runs at a pace of its own... and Paddington's and the Lilfords are right in step. After years on their valley-floor farm, they have moved up onto the hillside accompanied by a gaggle of visiting guinea fowl (impatiently tapping on the French doors for their tea when I arrived) and their steady stream of guests. There's a relaxed feel of country living here and while the building itself may be new and square, it's full of old prints, family furniture and well-trodden rugs. Visitors have the run of the tiled ground floor, with both bedrooms just two yawns and a stagger from breakfast, tacked onto the drawing room and kitchen. One room gets the morning sun, the other the afternoon rays and both are blessed with gigantic beds. A deep and enticing claw-foot bath in the one and a power shower in the other. If you feel up to it, Don and Di (both journalists - Don is the editor of the *Hout Bay Sentinel* no less) will point you in the direction of the best restaurants, golf courses and the beach. While for the lethargic loungers among you there's pétanque on the gravelled French courtyard or a book on the vine-covered verandah. With a Kronenbourg in hand, you could easily be in St Tropez. Oh, and there's always the dark and minimalist, heated jet-pool behind the house. Choices, choices.... *Email for self-catering options.*

Rooms: 2 king/twins, I with bath, I with shower.
Price: R400 - R450 pp sharing. Single rates on request.
Meals: Full breakfast included.
Directions: Faxed or emailed on request.

Dreamhouse

Ivanka and Luis Frasco

53 Mount Rhodes Drive, Hout Bay
Tel: 021-790-1773 Fax: 021-790-4864
Email: dreamhouse@yebo.co.za Web: www.dreamhouse.de
Cell: 082-547-7328

You cannot fail to be inspired by Dreamhouse and its mountainous harbour-view setting. The staggered garden contains many intimate leafy places that envelope both you and the landscape in the foliage. This is an artist's oasis and, if the mood takes you, Ivanka will dish out brushes, watercolours, canvas and frame so you can paint your own memories and take them home. The house and rooms reflect your host's own creative flair in colour, texture and line, with sweeping-armed suede sofas (it's always handy when your other half deals in furniture), a heavy wooden-beamed fireplace and high ceilings. The rooms are all different and named after their predominant colour, my favourite being the red luxury suite at the heart of the house where I imagined star-gazing from bed or rocking in the balcony-bound hammock for two. Hand-made mirrors, draped sarongs from Pakistan and an abundance of shells adorn the daily-different table décor. "Everything has its own story," according to Ivanka. Devoted to her guests, she applies attention to detail and impeccable yet unobtrusive service at all times. Whether it's a picnic basket you need, a cocktail at the pool lounge or directions for a sunrise walk up Little Lion's Head, she'll be there. Also trained in reiki, aromatherapy, reflexology and various massages there are a multitude of blissful experiences available at her hands. As we used to say at university (for some reason), "live the dream!"

Rooms: 11: 10 king/twin with en-suite bath/shower, 2 with en-suite kitchenette, 1 queen with en-suite shower.
Price: R450 - R900 pp sharing. Singles on request.
Meals: Full breakfast included. Dinner and light lunches on request (preferably with 24-hours notice as only fresh produce used).
Directions: Emailed or faxed on request. GPS: 34 01 05 10S - 18 20 54 90E.

Hout Bay Hideaway

Sue and Martin Collins

37 Skaife Street, Hout Bay
Tel: 021-790-8040
Email: info@houtbay-hideaway.com Web: www.houtbay-hideaway.com
Cell: 082-332-7853

The Hout Bay Hideaway, painted ivy green, literally disappears into the thick foliage of its delightfully overgrown garden. Smart meranti shutters lead you out of the rooms onto the long winding verandah that wraps around the house. Making my way along the tree-lined platform, where a jacaranda tree draped its purple flowers over the rail, I ogled at mountain, pool, garden and beach (which is only a five-minute walk down the hill). I'm sure most of the action takes place outside here, round the pool or rambling up buried garden paths to find the hammock platform. Inside, the rooms are a treat too, big, elegant and cosy with Turkish rugs decorating the floors, leather armchairs, palms in large pots, mohair blankets, giant wooden wardrobes, old trunks and original artwork, not to mention hard-working fireplaces for those less well advertised Cape Town winters. Skylight Suite is my favourite, with prime access to the outdoor Victorian bath buried in the shrubbery. Despite being rather exposed, outdoor bathing is apparently very popular. "They don't care, they're on holiday," laughed Sue and that's exactly the atmosphere she and Martin encourage – carefree and relaxed. One of the perks is breakfast in bed (or served to the room at least). "Couples love it. They're still wandering around in their dressing-gowns at midday," adds Martin. Thick fluffy gowns are provided, by the way.

Rooms: 4: 3 king/twin suites with en-suite showers and kitchenettes. 1 ground floor apartment with kitchenette, king/twin beds, bath and separate double cabin shower.
Price: R450 - R850 pp sharing (depending on season and length of stay), singles on request.
Meals: Full breakfast included, 5-10 mins walk from restaurants and the beach.
Directions: On the website and can be emailed on request, or just call.

Ambiente Guest House

Marion Baden and Peter Forsthövel

58 Hely Hutchinson Ave, Camps Bay
Tel: 021-438-4060   Fax: 086-670-5975
Email: info@ambiente-guesthouse.com
Web: www.ambiente-guesthouse.com Cell: 072-460-1953

Marion and Peter's affair with Ambiente Guest House began with a holiday. An initial joke to buy from the previous owners became a reality that ended in signatures on more than one dotted line: they not only bought the place, but also got married here. Many years later and they're still going strong. So what does Ambiente have to sustain such marital harmony? A base of sturdy functionality is hidden beneath a layer of exciting features and continual surprises. Original native masks, chairs and colour schemes are fused with a Mediterranean feel to produce an effect of African-themed modernity. Choose from beds suspended by chains or with wavy topless posts. Immerse yourself in the big luxurious bathrooms where showers are powerful, sinks are exciting (trust me, sinks can be exciting, you'll see) and baths cry out for a glass of champagne. Amidst these mirror-filled havens things aren't always what they seem. Is that an African spear disguised as a towel rail? A boulder in the shower? This place has playful passion. It has the drama of half the mountain in the breakfast room, the shock of sand beneath your feet in the loo. If that's not enough to keep you amused, the views of mountain and ocean will make you gawp, the pool and garden will refresh and the paintings, if you look long and hard enough, will make you blush.

Rooms: 4: 3 king suites, all with en-suite bath and shower; and 1 double room with en-suite bath/shower. Separate toilets in all bathrooms.
Price: R720 - R990 pp sharing.
Meals: Full breakfast included. BBQs possible by arrangement.
Directions: Take the N1 or N2 to Cape Town and follow signs to Cableway/Camps Bay. Remain on M62, Camps Bay Drive, with the 12 Apostles to your left and Camps Bay down to your right. Turn Left into Ravensteyn Ave then first right into Hely Hutchinson Ave. Ambiente is number 58.

Map Number: 3

Entry Number: 10

Ocean View House

Katrin Ludik
33 Victoria Road, Bakoven
Tel: 021-438-1982 Fax: 021-438-2287
Email: info@oceanview-house.com Web: www.oceanview-house.com

Tucked in between the Twelve Apostles mountain range and the turquoise Atlantic, Ocean View House is the perfect place to be mesmerised by humpback and southern right whales frolicking among the white horses that roll into Camps Bay (in season, of course.) There's no end to Ocean View's eccentric delights with its Russian marble and award-winning gardens. Everyone has either a balcony or a terrace with fabulous views of sea, pool deck, mountain or garden. It is a hotel, but such a personal one with huge wooden giraffes hiding behind every corner and the friendliest staff who smile and sing while they work (which is always a good sign). There's also a great pool and how many hotels run an honesty bar? To cap it all, Ocean View has its own nature reserve, a tropical garden that ushers an idyllic river from the mountains to the sea. They have placed tables and sun-loungers on the grassy river banks, a sort of exotic *Wind in the Willows* scenario with rocks, ferns, trees, tropical birds, succulents, waterfalls and butterflies. If you ever feel like leaving Ocean View, Camps Bay is a 20-minute stroll away with its string of outdoor restaurants and zesty atmosphere. It's a good place to watch trendy Capetonians at play. Tired out long before they were, I walked back to the hotel. The nightwatchman was expecting me and escorted me to my room, which was also expecting me, tomorrow's weather report by my bed.

Rooms: 17: 8 Suites; 7 Luxury Rooms & 2 Pool Deck rooms.
Price: R385 – R1,450 pp sharing. Single rates available.
Meals: Full breakfast is included and served until 10am. Light lunches and picnic hampers on request.
Directions: On the coast road a mile out of Camps Bay towards Hout Bay.

Antrim Villa

Jonas Sandstrom

12 Antrim Road, Green Point
Tel: 021-433-2132 Fax: 021-433-2133
Email: stay@antrimvilla.com Web: www.antrimvilla.com
Cell: 072-106-8844

It was pure pleasure to walk into Antrim Villa's cool interior after a long day on the road, and to savour the quadruple rewards of a bounteous welcome from the manager, Joy (by name and nature), a fresh, scented towel, a fresh orange juice and the comforting aroma of baking bread. Jonas arrived from Sweden in 2003, fell in love with Cape Town and promptly and enthusiastically opened his first guest-house. This was a success, more rooms were needed and so Antrim Villa was born. With Jonas's interior design background, he has taken this old English Victorian-style house and created a fresh and modern oasis in the heart of Green Point. With its high old metal sheet ceilings and original wood floors, harmonious colours and natural fabrics, you'll feel calm and relaxed in this tranquil, tropical-African villa. In the garden, you'll find a gorgeous, highly-enticing pool area, decked out with palm trees and sun-loungers. If you feel like going for a wander, then you really couldn't ask for a better location either. Antrim Villa is within walking distance of the ocean, the new stadium, the Victoria & Alfred Waterfront and Green Point Main Road, with its abundance of trendy bars and restaurants. It is all on your doorstep. For those of you with real wanderlust who want to venture completely out of the 'neighbourhood', talk to Joy. She is a certified tour guide and knows a great deal about Cape Town and other areas. Antrim Villa (which is also Fair Trade certified) really does have it all.

Rooms: 8: 5 luxury doubles, 2 standard doubles and 1 standard single. All with en-s shower, 1 with en-s bath and shower. Luxury includes the following additions: flatscreen TV, mini-fridge, iPod docking station.
Price: R425 - R925 per person sharing. Singles R550 - R1,100.
Meals: Continental breakfast included. Lunch and dinner available on request.
Directions: Follow Strand Street which will turns into High Level Road. Turn right into Hill Road and then turn left into Antrim Road. Antrim Villa is on L.

Map Number: 3   Entry Number: 12

The Villa Rosa

Lynn Stacey and Heather John
277 High Level Rd, Sea Point
Tel: 021-434-2768 Fax: 021-434-3526
Email: villaros@mweb.co.za Web: www.villa-rosa.com
Cell: 082-785-3238

How I managed to drive straight past the Villa Rosa I'll never know. With dramatic red- and white-tinged walls the villa is hardly a shrinking violet. But I did anyway…. I wandered up the front path through mingled scents of wild jasmine, chives and roses and was met at the stained-glass door by Lynn, who emits the same bright warmth as her villa walls. As we chatted over a juice in the kitchen we were interrupted by Ruby (Maltese) and Schumi (Maltese) who had come to give me a warm barking welcome! The villa continues its rosy persona within. Soft rose pinks are set off with hints of contrasting greens and dark wooden furniture. Most rooms are lit by enormous bay windows and intricate chandeliers, each one unique in its delicate hanging flowers, gems and metalwork. I soon discovered that Lynn had had a chandelier 'binge' at some point. And that chandeliers were just one of many such undeniable urges; the 'bathroom binge' resulted in a complete bathroom overhaul producing the fresh stone-floored en-suite beauties now in place. The metal leaf-chairs in one room (literally chairs that look like giant leaves) were "so wacky we just bought them," says Lynn. The art binge is ongoing and the walls continue to fill up with local talent. Looking at Ruby and Schumi, I wondered if Lynn would ever consider an 'adoption binge'. If so I'll be volunteering myself as the next eligible stray. *Synagogue is a two-minute walk away and a kosher breakfast is available.*

Rooms: 8: all doubles, 4 with en-suite bath and shower, 4 with en-suite shower. Possibility of joining two rooms to form a family suite. 1 self-catering unit.
Price: R380 - R595 pp sharing. Singles R530 - R775.
Meals: Full breakfast included.
Directions: Emailed or faxed on request. Also on Villa Rosa website. GPS: S 33° 55' 7.2" E 18° 23' 26.9"

Blackheath Lodge

Antony Trop and John Stewart

6 Blackheath Road, Sea Point
Tel: 021-439-2541
Email: info@blackheathlodge.co.za Web: www.blackheathlodge.co.za
Cell: 076-130-6888

Over tea and cake on the white-wood verandah, protected from the elements and warmed by the fire – essential and welcome on a crisp winter's morning - Antony and John advised us on the finest eateries and best excursions that the city has to offer. They are both passionate about Cape Town and they even have a convertible Mini Cooper for hire, so there's no excuse not to go exploring. (Although, maybe in summer you could make a case for hanging out by the pool, on a sun-lounger and with a cocktail!) The rooms are all individually decorated and come with their own eccentricities. My personal favourite contains a huge sofa that's too big to move; rather than banishing this Behemoth to a skip in many sections, the room has been lovingly designed around it. The eclectic mix of furniture, art, decadent light fittings, colours and curios go into making each room unique, comfortable and enticing. The latest addition, a beautiful converted loft suite up in the eaves, has self-catering facilities and an amazing sun-deck complete with louvered roof, sofa and outdoor shower overlooking the Beverly Hills of Cape Town - Sea Point Promenade. As we explored the rooms I noted the many intricate touches that make Blackheath so special: personalised welcome bundles, the ambient soundtrack, magnetic picture frames for house-keeping, fresh flowers, complimentary tea and coffee.... Blackheath is the perfect base from which to extract the most from a trip to this wonderful city.

Rooms: 11: all air-con doubles/twins with en-s showers. Loft Suite also has outdoor shower.
Price: R475 - R1,475 pp sharing. Singles on request.
Meals: Breakfast included. Specials include quiche, French toast, cinnamon pancakes & full English. Evening meals on request from about R150.
Directions: Follow signs on N1 or N2 to Cape Town then Sea Point. At end of Table Bay Bvd turn R at second lights onto Helen Suzman Boulevard. At ocean merge L, then turn L at traffic lights into Three Anchor Bay Rd, continue over lights into Glengariff Rd, then turn R into Blackheath Rd – No. 6 is on R.

De Waterkant Cottages

Tobin Shackleford and Richard Gush

40 Napier Street, De Waterkant
Tel: 021-421-2300 Fax: 021-421-2399
Email: book@dewaterkantcottages.com
Web: www.dewaterkantcottages.com Cell: 072-457-4387

Now here is something a little bit different, the chance to have your own home (albeit only for the period of your stay), right in the centre of one of Cape Town's trendiest neighbourhoods. De Waterkant Cottages is a constantly-evolving array of brightly-painted former slave cottages (some dating from the 18th century) and more modern, but sympathetically-styled, homes in the National Preservation site that is De Waterkant Village. Each is individually owned, but all are run on a day-to-day basis by Tobin, Richard and their team. Only the best are selected, assuring you of high-quality fixtures, fittings and furnishings. All have standardised luxury linen, plates, knives, forks etc, in fact everything you could ever want or need to make your stay here a pleasure. The concept is all about choice (which, trust me, will be no easy thing). First you'll have to choose between traditional and contemporary, but then you'll need to choose your exact cottage. Tobin and Richard used to live in one – could there be a higher recommendation? This particular home has furniture made from car parts, speakers are embedded in the walls and the shower has a glass roof, allowing you to gaze up at the stars while you wash. There are too many to go through them all, but I also witnessed roof decks galore, exposed wooden floors, luxury leather sofas, private gardens, roof-top jacuzzis, rain-head showers, flat-screen TVs, real fires, amazing views, plunge pools… the list goes on. (See, I said it wouldn't be an easy choice). *All accommodation serviced daily except public holidays. Property flowers, pre-stocked fridges and airport pick-ups available.*

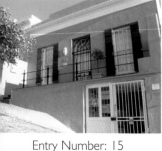

Rooms: 18 fully-serviced cottages, with one, two, three & four bedrooms (queen, king & twin). All main bedrooms with en-suite bathrooms, showers and air-conditioning. Online bookings and availability.
Price: R840 - R3,300 two persons per night per cottage. Additional persons R300 - R500. Under 2s stay free.
Meals: Kitchen can be stocked on request.
Directions: See website for map and instructions.

Cheviot Place Guest House

James and Brooke Irving

18 Cheviot Place, Green Point
Tel: 021-439-3741 Fax: 021-439-9095
Email: cheviot@netactive.co.za Web: www.cheviotplace.co.za
Cell: 082-467-3660

Cheviot Place is something fresh for the Cape Town accommodation scene. This was apparent from the moment James opened the front door, dressed in Hawaiian shirt (sunny) and trainers (trendy), Jamie Cullum (jazzy) wafting out behind him. I was just in time for sundowners. Impassioned tips for a tour of the vineyards were aptly passed on around the wine barrel. The verandah looks out over a perfect cityscape incorporating St Margaret Mary's church, the splendid new Green Point stadium and on to the glittering waters of Table Bay. And let's not forget the immediate gardens bursting with bright pink hibiscus and yesterday-today-tomorrow. There is something of the San Francisco vibe about this venerable, turn-of-the-last-century house, with its high ceilings, pillars and arches. New wooden floors, natural hemp-style rugs and black metal light fittings have been added to set off the original marble fireplaces. Cheviot Place is a contemporary home retaining the best of its Victorian heritage. James made me feel like an old friend over my Cheviot Scrambler breakfast (carefully selected by me the previous evening – I spurned the 'healthy morning' breakfast). The self-catering unit below the main house is surely the ultimate in 21st-century living, reminding me of the troglodyte homes carved out of the rocks deep in the Sahara. Apart from the bed there is no free-standing furniture: everything has been sculpted from the stone. Original? Yes. Cool? Very.

Rooms: 6: 4 queens, 2 twins/kings. All en-suite. Ask about the self-catering option.
Price: R400 - R650 pp sharing. Single rates on request.
Meals: Full breakfast is included. Picnics provided on request. Braai on request from R150 - R300.
Directions: Ask when booking.

Acorn House

Bernd Schlieper and Beate Lietz
1 Montrose Avenue, Oranjezicht
Tel: 021-461-1782 Fax: 021-461-1768
Email: welcome@acornhouse.co.za Web: www.acornhouse.co.za

Bernd and Beate can barely contain the happiness they derive from Acorn House and their enthusiasm rubs off quickly on all but the stoniest of their visitors. I was a pushover. The listed building, designed by busy Sir Herbert Baker in 1904, sits on the sunny, sea-facing slopes of Table Mountain with tip-top views to Table Bay. (You can 'try before you buy' as there is a niftily-positioned webcam that uploads Acorn's views hourly to the website.) The house is typical Sir Herbert with timber colonnade and huge double-fronted verandah. There is an immaculate garden with black-slate swimming pool and a sun-lounging lawn, cleanly demarcated by agapanthus and lavender bushes. Breakfast, often served by the pool ("until the last guest comes down", i.e. you can sleep in), is a no-holds-barred display of meats, cheeses, eggs and freshly-squeezed fruit juices; "probably the second-best breakfast in Cape Town" is Beate's carefully-worded claim! I smiled my way around Acorn as I noted the personal touches: fresh mint water (with mint from the garden) and upstairs in your bedroom you will find notes of welcome or farewell, chocolates and sprigs of lavender. Wine-lovers are also well served: Bernd is pazzo for the stuff and regularly visits local vineyards to ensure that his house wines are up-to-the-moment (just for his guests' benefit, of course). Having lived in South Africa for several years now, Bernd and Beate are still awash with excitement about their surroundings; a stay in Acorn House will leave you feeling much the same.

Rooms: 9: 1 king, 3 twins and 3 queens all with en-suite bath; 1 family suite with twin; 1 private family cottage with king.
Price: R500 - R690 pp sharing. Singles R490 - R900. Family suite and private family cottage as double R1,000 - R1,380 + R320 for up to 2 kids.
Meals: Full breakfast included and served until you're ready for it. Free coffee & tea available all day. Finally at Acorn House: Nespresso!
Directions: See website or ask for fax.

Lézard Bleu Guest House

Chris and Niki Neumann
30 Upper Orange St, Oranjezicht
Tel: 021-461-4601 Fax: 021-461-4657
Email: welcome@lezardbleu.co.za Web: www.lezardbleu.co.za
Cell: 072-234-4448

It's going to be hard to book the treehouse, particularly when word gets round, but you have got to try! Surely the most wonderful bedroom in Cape Town. The trunks of two giant palm trees spear through a wooden deck at vertiginous heights and a tiny balcony is in among the topmost fronds and spikes. Lézard Bleu was a great house anyway, so this latest extravagant addition represents one huge cherry on a mouthwatering cake. Niki is an actress and Chris is a chef, although he has hung up his hat now... no, don't even ask! They are still young and humorous and the house remains sleek and modern with solid maplewood bedframes, white pure cotton, sandy shades and tones, bright splashes of local and modern art on the walls. Breakfast is the best beanfeast in Cape Town (and that's the opinion of other guest house owners). The Blue Lizard snakes pleasingly from area to area, each room with its own doors out to a patio and to the large pool, where deck loungers take it easy on a surrounding timber deck. There are real fires in winter, an honesty bar, free ADSL Internet access - mere details, but typical. Individual, creative, very comfortable, but most importantly this is somewhere really natural and friendly. *Children welcome from the age of 6 years old.*

Rooms: 7: 1 family room; 5 doubles/twins; 4 with en/s bath and shower; 1 with en/s shr; 1 tree-house double en/s bath and shower.
Price: Double: R540 - R780 pp sharing. Treehouse: R660 - R780 pp sharing. Single occupancy: R780 - R970.
Meals: Full (enormous!) breakfast included and served till 10.30am.
Directions: Ask for directions when booking.

Map Number: 3

Entry Number: 18

Redbourne Hilldrop

Jonny and Sharon Levin

12 Roseberry Avenue, Oranjezicht
Tel: 021-461-1394 Fax: 021-465-1006
Email: info@redbourne.co.za Web: www.redbourne.co.za

One of the happiest and most humorous guest houses in Cape Town, so it always seems to me. Many of Jonny and Sharon's guests refuse to stay elsewhere and gifts arrive daily from overseas… well almost. It's a small, intimate place and you are spoiled: free-standing baths, fluffy duvets, big white pillows, unflowery good taste in mirrors and wood floors, magazines, African artefacts, great showers. One room has a spiral staircase down to its bathroom. You eat breakfast at a diner-style bar stretched along a wall of pretty windows with incredible city views. Guests are treated as far as possible as friends and each time I visit I notice the easy rapport that Jonny and Sharon have generated with them – probably overnight. After a mere five minutes in their company I felt all the formality of my visit slipping away like a coat in hot weather. The wall-enclosed pool comes complete with a mini-waterfall spanning the length of it and Table Mountain looming above. From here you can see if the cable car is working and for the more adventurous you're not far from the start of one of several routes to the top. Otherwise it's an easy ride down to the city bustle, the Waterfront and the Atlantic beaches. Perfect location, great hosts, GSOH!

Rooms: 5: 3 doubles with en/s showers; 1 twin with en/s bath and shower and 1 twin family room with en/s bath and shower plus a sunroom (can fit 4/5 beds).
Price: R450 - R600 pp sharing. Singles on request.
Meals: Full breakfast included. Dinners by prior arrangement. Restaurants nearby.
Directions: On website.

MannaBay

David Ryan
1 Denholm Road, Oranjezicht
Tel: 021-461-1094 Fax: 021-461-8915
Email: res@mannabay.com Web: www.mannabay.com

"I've never seen anything quite like this", was the sole thought occupying my dazzled mind as butlers Shadrak and Simon kindly tended to my luggage. David, the bustling and convivial owner (whom you might catch about town shouldering an African grey parrot, name of Preston), certainly went to town with the interiors. Each room is wildly unique, from the imperial indulgence of the Versailles Suite to the acts of pith-helmeted derring-do, which inspired the Explorer Room. From the disco ball, to the enormous black-and-white photographic mural of Cape Town and from the work of local artists to the Ewok stools (not an official name), MannaBay is a treasure trove of eccentric paraphernalia. There's also a library rippling with African travel literature. Once I'd finished inside, it was on to the vast wooden sun-deck to catch a few rays and to take a dip in the pool which looked all too inviting, with Table Mountain towering overhead and that pure South African sunlight pinging off the water. I was in for a treat staying in the Versailles Suite. Embracing the regal splendour of the Palace of Versailles and the Ancien Régime, this is a suite that would have made Louise XIV cerise with envy (the same colour as the plush sofa). And there's space for his entourage as well. Sumptuous, deep, rich fabrics complement the royal blue-and-silver fleur-de-lis wallpaper. Time to kick back in my massive bed and watch the sun plunge beneath the cityscape into the harbour beyond!

Rooms: 7: 1 suite, 2 luxury rooms & 4 standard rooms.
Price: Standard room: R650 – R1,250 pp sharing.
Luxury rooms & suite: R1,250 – R1,995 pp sharing. Single rates on request. Complimentary airport transfer.
Meals: Full breakfast & high tea included. Wine tastings & private dinners (prior arrangement) take place in wine cellar. Restaurants nearby.
Directions: N2 Cape Town. Take Exit 5, merge onto De Waal Drive/M3 to Cape Town. As rd splits keep L & take lane signed De Waal Drive/Cable Way. Keep L. Turn L to Vredehoek/Cableway. Keep L & take far L slip lane to Gardens Centre marked Mill St. L at 2nd lights onto Buitenkant St. L into Yeoville Rd. MannaBay on 1st corner with Denholm Rd.

Map Number: 3

Entry Number: 20

Bayview Guesthouse

Christine Matti
12 De Hoop Avenue, Tamboerskloof
Tel: 021-424-2033 Fax: 021-424-2705
Email: baychris@iafrica.com Web: www.baychris.com
Cell: 082-414-2052

Christine and her partner Corinne are passionate about their wine and, well, passionate about just about everything. When not buzzing around the house, Swiss-born Christine is usually out cranking up Cape Town kilometres on her racing bike or working on her annoyingly low golf handicap. She arrived in South Africa a wide-eyed whippersnapper some twenty years ago, and has never quite got around to leaving. When I arrived a few renovations were reaching completion. With Christine at the helm, this is a constantly evolving place with new works of modern art from large abstract copper sculptures to paintings of women splashed in colour. But whatever changes take place the fundamental theme of the guest house as an airy haven of healthy living thankfully remains constant. White-washed walls, floor-to-ceiling tinted windows and tiled floors make this a perfect mountain-side retreat from the city centre's summer heat. Breakfasts are an Alpine feast of German breads, selected cheeses and cold meats and guests are encouraged to help themselves to a bottomless bowl of fresh fruit. Take a dip in the pool, head off for a massage at any number of nearby wellness centres, read a book on your decking balcony, and - once you've done all that - lie back on the sofa and gaze at a perfectly-framed Table Mountain through the sitting room skylight. My only disappointment? I didn't have time to stay the night. *Personal computer for guests.*

Rooms: 5: 2 x extra-length king/twins with en-suite shower & bath; 2 x extra-length king/twins with en-suite shower; 1 x s/c unit.
Price: R300 - R750 pp sharing.
Meals: Full and healthy breakfasts included.
Directions: Follow signs from the city centre to the Cableway. From Kloofnek Rd turn R into St. Michael's Rd and then third L into Varsity St. At the T-junction turn R into De Hoop Avenue and Bayview is the second on the right.

Gap Lodge

Linda and Le Roi Steenkamp
13 Newport Street, Tamboerskloof
Tel: 021-424-6564 Fax: 086-6424-674
Email: book@gaplodge.co.za Web: www.gaplodge.co.za
Cell: 082-896-8165

From its foundations to the stylish interior every inch of Gap Lodge has been primped and preened to Linda and Le Roi's exacting standards. With just three double rooms this is a small and ideal pocket of calm in the most vibrant part of the Mother City, 5 minutes' drive from Table Mountain and within walking distance of the restaurants of Kloof and Long Streets. Each bedroom is practical and stylish with an antique hanger here and a vase of fresh lilies there, crisp white linen and towels offset by bold orange or blue bedheads. Linda has artistically decorated the earth-coloured walls with bold and beautiful paintings. After a deep sleep on "the best mattress in Cape Town" – thus spake a previous guest but I had a go too and it is indeed magically giving yet supportive! - Linda conjures up an exceptional full breakfast. Le Roi personally tailors day trips or tours for guests. Having worked as a tour guide since 2002 with his own company (Gap Tours), Le Roi is a fountain of knowledge and will whisk guests away in the house mini-bus. For anyone who has spent a morning queuing, sweating and possibly even swearing in a tourist information office, going on your own personalised tour with Le Roi is like being upgraded from the luggage hold to first class. From 'Flora, Fauna and Vino' day trips to golf tours he will take all the hassle out of holiday-making. 'Beyond the call of duty' is an unfamiliar phrase to this couple: Linda has even been known to raid her own wardrobe on behalf of those guests who forget to pack essential items of clothing!

Rooms: 3 kings with en-suite shower.
Price: R445 pp sharing. Singles R690.
Meals: Full breakfast included.
Directions: From the airport take N2 to City. Follow signs from City Centre to Cableway. Once in Kloofnek Road look out for convenience store 'Kloofnek Superette' on left. Turn left into Newport Street immediately afterwards and Gap Lodge is on the right-hand corner.

Map Number: 3

Entry Number: 22

Southern Comfort Guest Lodge

Michael Thomas & Hans-Juergen Groesz

27 Belmont Avenue, Oranjezicht
Email: contact@scomfort.co.za Web: www.scomfort.co.za
Cell: 076-732-7280

The name has nothing to do with peaches or bourbon. It's a guest lodge that happens to be very comfortable… and in the south. I was met at the gate and given a hearty welcome by Michael who suggested I might like a swim. It was a scorcher of a day in Cape Town and the desire to jump in the alluring turquoise pool almost got the better of me. But I had a house to look at. The rooms along the ground floor all have private patios, much-needed shade and quick access to that oh-so-tempting pool. Inside the interiors are cool, both in temperature and style. Michael and Hans-Juergen have put a lot of thought into transforming this survivor from the 1970s; using light, texture and space they have managed to create a chic, but still informal and very relaxed environment. Upstairs, on the first floor is the open guest lounge and living area; European in layout, but adorned with African art and curios. Coffee was suggested and duly accepted - the sofas looked far too nice to insult them by standing. (Here's a tip: if you're offered coffee in either the New York or the Stuttgart mug go with the latter… it's their home town.) So brownie points in the back pocket and my coffee finished, we climbed the spiral staircase to the roof terrace, unexpectedly covered with a grassy lawn and overlooked by no less a natural monument than Table Mountain. Leaving with a smile on my face I realised I never did manage a swim…. Like leaving my umbrella behind, it's a good enough excuse to come back!

Rooms: 6: 1 self-catering suite; 2 standard rooms; 3 deluxe.
Price: From R790 - R1190 per room.
Meals: Breakfast R100. Restaurants & bars close by.
Directions: See website for details.

Monmouth Cottage

Pru Ruck

24 Monmouth Avenue, Upper Claremont
Email: mylesandpru@thehyde.co.za
Cell: 083-253-0864

While Pru and her husband were renovating their house, they lived in Monmouth Cottage. It was designed to function as a proper home and as a result it feels very warm and… well… homely. Everything has been thought of here, from the louvered shutters that only allow the cool Cape breeze in, to the kitchen stocked with all the basics you never arrive with. It even has two huge televisions so you can watch the cricket if it's on at an 'inconvenient' time (when is it otherwise?!). Although, the chances are it's actually being played just round the corner at Newlands. Taking a seat outside the front of the house, all I could hear was the soft trickle of the fountain, all I could smell were the roses and all I could see was the 'Hen and Chickens'. No, this isn't a working farm. The 'Hen and Chickens' is the name of the profile in the rock formation atop Skeleton Gorge in the Kirstenbosch Mountains (it's also the local nickname for Upper Claremont). I would strongly recommend this as your route to the top of Table Mountain. Monmouth Cottage is 10 minutes' drive to Kirstenbosch Botanical Gardens where one can start the walk up the mountain. It is an exhilarating wild walk (and climb) and simply amazing to consider you are so near the middle of Cape Town (15 minutes by car, 3 minutes if you have wings)! The mountain also provides shelter against the stronger summer winds creating the perfect climate. As I said… everything has been thought of. *Guests are welcome to make use of the pool and tennis court at Pru's house.*

Rooms: 1 king/twin. A fold-out bed can be requested.
Price: R1,400 per night for the cottage.
Meals: Self-catering. Shops and restaurants close by.
Directions: Take M3 towards Muizenburg. Take second Claremont turning, Bowwood Road. First right into Talana Road. Follow to top and bear left into Monmouth Ave.

Hedge House

Judy England
12 Argyle Road, Newlands
Tel: 021-689-6431 Fax: 021-689-1286
Email: hedge@mweb.co.za Web: www.hedgehouse.co.za
Cell: 083-324-0888

Hedge House plays host to many creatures great and small… great and small people too. It has its own tree platform (with prime views of Devil's Peak) and a pirate-boat swing, and Judy, who was once a veterinary nurse, owns two dogs, one cat and an assortment of birds. As I toured the family home, accompanied by the glorious scent of wild jasmine, I arrived at my favourite room, up outdoor spiral stairs to a deck perforated by a camphor tree. On entering, I beheld the setting sun pouring in, making the splendid wardrobe glow an even deeper red. Elsewhere another wardrobe interconnects two rooms, C.S. Lewis-style, which is rather magical for children and adults alike! All the rooms have private entrances - room numbers hand-painted on tiles - so guests can stroll freely to the pool or wander the garden. The pathways, winding their way from the pool deck through tree ferns and indigenous plants, are a mini botanical adventure and all nourished by worm farms. Even a vegetable garden can be found, where a variety of veggies poke out from behind a miniature hand-made fence. As I was presented with freshly-baked cookies, I learnt that "everything here is hand-made"… and Judy isn't the only one to contribute. She is supported by two fabulous ladies, Betty and Sharon, and these delicious treats were made by her youngest. For those who wish to stretch their legs further than the garden walls, Keurboom Park is a stroll away where owls patrol at night. A place of 'Peace, Joy, Love and Grace' indeed!

Rooms: 5: 4 twin/kings & 1 queen with en-suite bath and shower. Families accommodated with single beds on request.
Price: R650 pp sharing. Single supplement R900. R200 for children.
Meals: Full English breakfast included. Dinner & lunch on request.
Directions: From airport travel on N2 towards city. Take Exit 8 – Liesbeek Parkway. At bottom of off-ramp turn L to Rondebosch. Travel 3.5km. When you see lights, one rd before Keurboom Rd, turn L into Argyle Rd. Hedge House is No. 12 on RHS.

Victoria House

Corinne Coste
16 Oak Avenue, Upper Kenilworth
Tel: 021-761-7783/89 Fax: 021-761-9164
Email: vichouse@deunet.co.za Web: www.victoria-house-za.com
Cell: 084-664-0506

Corinne's warm-hearted home is 'a bit of a find', especially for those who want relaxed and comfortable with a touch of elegance. If you take the short drive out to the leafy southern suburbs, not only will you have the absolute pleasure of meeting Corinne, but you'll also be in a superb position to explore the whole Cape. Madame Corinne and her husband (he's a hairdresser in the city) have lived in Cape Town for 13 years and can offer travel advice for your trip in French, German and English. From the hallway original stone-tiled floors and a grand staircase (bathed in a rainbow of light from the stained-glass window) set the tone for the whole house. As does the piano, which is definitely a real instrument not some interior accessory - so if you play, don't be shy! There are five high-ceilinged bedrooms in the main house with big wooden beds and vintage bathrooms. They look out onto an immaculately-tended bush-, flower- and bird-filled garden. Two further suites, dubbed the Twin Cottage, are separate from the main house and thus ideal for those visiting Cape Town with children. The kitchen is never closed and guests are encouraged to help themselves to tea and coffee or something stronger from the honesty bar. The guest book is littered with invites to homes all over the world. I wonder if this has anything to do with the highly-acclaimed breakfast which is served here with deserved pride?

Rooms: 7: 2 kings with en-suite shower and bath, 1 queen with en-suite shower, 2 doubles with en-suite bath/shower and separate shower. 2 twins with en-suite shower.
Price: R990 - R1,250 pp per night. Singles R1300.
Meals: Full cooked breakfast and healthy Continental.
Directions: See website for detailed map

Map Number: 3

Entry Number: 26

Highlands Country House

Carole Armstrong-Hooper

36 Tennant Road, Upper Kenilworth
Tel: 021-797-8810 Fax: 021-761-0017
Email: info@highlands.co.za Web: www.highlands.co.za

Highlands Country House, sitting splendidly on Wynberg Hill beneath Devil's Peak, is one of the Cape's most majestic homes. In front, a formal garden runs along avenues of fig trees down to trim lawns and flowerbeds - picked daily for fresh bouquets - and I went for a wander, ambling past a fountain and various Grecian urns before reaching one of two swimming pools. Here there is a spa where they will pamper you to within an inch of your life. Up at the house, meanwhile, all was efficient bustle, with smartly-dressed maids busily clearing away breakfast, leaving only the faint but delicious smell of bacon and eggs lingering on the terrace. I passed a magnificent, carved foot-throne in the foyer and a dining room all dressed up in starched white linen on my way to meet Carole in the library for a chat… and a delectable strawberry smoothie. She fell in love with the place when she once came here for tea, which is a special time of day at Highlands, honoured with freshly-baked cakes. Meanwhile, gourmet dinners are best served by candlelight in the conservatory. Separate from the house, large European-style rooms are elegant in neutral tones, while England prevails inside a rush-carpeted warren of staircases and wings. Styles vary subtly in traditional rooms from African flourishes, to Cupid-guarded loft rooms, to Brosely-tiled bathrooms, to shades of blue in St Leger silk curtains. Part the shutters or step onto your balcony and look onto woods, sports fields, mountains and sea... and be very content with your choice.

Rooms: 14: 6 twin/king, 3 king, 4 queen and 1 honeymoon suite with king. All are fully en-suite, with the exception of one shower en-suite.
Price: R700 - R1,720 pp sharing. Singles R1,100 - R2,750.
Meals: Full breakfast included. Delicious light lunches and a la carte dinners. Private dinner parties (in the conservatory or pool house) by arrangement.
Directions: Tennant Road is a continuation of Newlands Road, reached either by the Constantia or Rondebosch exits on the M3. See website for more detailed directions.

Dendron

Jill McMahon
21 Ou Wingerd Pad, Constantia
Tel: 021-794-6010
Email: stay@dendron.co.za Web: www.dendron.co.za
Cell: 082-296-0691

(Quite) A few years ago, Jill's late husband Shaun bought a Land Rover in Taunton (UK) and drove it here. Hardly odd when you see the place, now replete with relaxed family atmosphere, collie dogs and verdant lawns. You get all the benefits of living the South African good life by default here. Green-fingered Jill genuinely loves having guests and her enthusiasm for life is evident in everything. The cottages are private in leafy, jasmine-scented gardens and have fully-equipped kitchens stocked with basics, a braai and stunning views to the mountains on the right and False Bay in the distance. They have terracotta or tiled floors and beds with Indian cotton throws - perfect for families. All are fully serviced and have their own braais. Evening pool-side views at sunset and moonrise, helped along by wine from over-the-hedge Groot Constantia vineyard, will make you want to throw away the car keys and stay (which is exactly what Shaun did when he first clapped eyes on the place). When you are hungry, Jill will send you off there through the back gate and across the vineyards to Simon's or Jonkershuis for dinner. Return by torch- and moonlight. Dendron (Greek for tree) is a small slice of heaven.

Rooms: 2: 1 x 2 bedroomed and 1 x 1 bedroomed; 1 with bath & shower, 1 with shower only. Serviced daily Mon - Fri.
Price: R350 - R550 pp sharing. Singles on request.
Meals: Breakfast for first morning provided.
Directions: Fax on request.

Map Number: 3   Entry Number: 28

Klein Bosheuwel Guest House

Tim Scarborough
51a Klaassens Rd, Constantia
Tel: 021-762-2323 Fax: 088-021-762-2323
Email: kleinbosheuwel@iafrica.com Web: www.kleinbosheuwel.co.za
Cell: 083-227-0700

Tim Scarborough, who migrated to Cape Town from Jersey in 1963, and his team continue to offer their unique blend of hospitality, comfort and character, which Tim and his late wife Nicki created when they developed these beautiful properties. Klein Bosheuwel and Southdown enjoy commanding views of Constantiaberg and False Bay from an elevated position and are a couple of minutes' walk from the world-renowned Kirstenbosch Botanical Gardens. There are two acres of well-established gardens and two swimming pools. The bedrooms are uncluttered, while large and elegant sitting rooms, libraries, verandahs and terraces provide refuge during every season. Guests are served delicious breakfasts in a welcoming, relaxed environment and there is knowledgeable advice on hand for guests wanting to seek out restaurants, visit wine estates and enjoy the many attractions which the Cape Peninsula and surrounding areas have to offer. Tim is both owner and manager and this is the bedrock of Klein Bosheuwel. The warmth of welcome leads to happy guests, many repeat visits and lasting friendships. One of Tim's hobbies is vexillology so invariably the flag of your home country will be flying in eager anticipation of your arrival!

Rooms: 8 double rooms all en-suite. Southdown Cottage sleeps 4 (fully serviced).
Price: R710 – R790 per person sharing. Singles R1,050 – R1,180.
Meals: Full breakfast included.
Directions: Fax or website.

Kaapse Draai

Annelie Posthumus

19 Glen Avenue, Constantia
Tel: 021-794-6291 Fax: 021-794-6291
Email: info@kaapsedraaibb.co.za Web: www.kaapsedraaibb.co.za
Cell: 082-923-9869

Annelie has been charming Greenwood Guide travellers since the very first edition and should be in the running for some sort of award for B&B brilliance. Relaxed, simple and beautiful seems to be the rule here. Her daughter is an artist and their talents combine to make the house a peaceful and contemporary temple to uncluttered Cape Cod-style living. Neutral furnishings and white cottons are frisked up with floral bolsters and country checks. Sunny window-seats amid the white-washed walls and light-grey, vintage-pine floorboards make perfect reading spots. Annelie is a prolific gardener and you can walk (perhaps with her dogs) from the tropical greenery of Kaapse Draai, with its mountain stream, monster gunnera manicata leaves, huge ferns and palms, into lovely Bel-Ombre meadow and the forest next door. From there it is a three-hour walk to the Table Mountain cable station. Porcupines come into the garden at night from the mountain (they love arum lilies apparently) and there are many birds too, including the palindromic hadedah. A grand old willow tree is what you'll park your car under. Delicious breakfasts are taken outside in the sunshine whenever possible. All I can say is – go and stay. *Wine estates and Constantia shopping village nearby.*

Rooms: 3: 1 double with en-suit shower; 2 twins one en-suite shower, one with en-suite shower and bath.
Price: R440 pp sharing. Singles R550. There is a supplementary charge of R50 per room for 1-night stays.
Meals: Full breakfast included.
Directions: Ask for fax or email when booking.

Cape Witogie

Rosemary and Bob Child

9 Van Zyl Rd (Van Zyl Way on some GPS), Kreupelbosch (Bergvliet on some GPS), Constantia Tel: 021-712-9935
Email: capewitogie@netactive.co.za Web: www.capestay.co.za/capewitogie
Cell: 082-537-6059 or 082-852-9084

Cape Witogie (requiring a slightly gutteral pronunciation rarely mastered by English visitors) is situated at the foot of the Constantiaberg and is named after the tiny 'Cape White Eye' birds which flitter between the frangipani trees, shrubs, berries and Bob's bonsais - this small bird is as charming as Rosemary and Bob themselves! When I visited, Rosemary was frantically packing for a trip to the UK, but she happily (and patiently) attempted to explain how the Contantiaberg resembles a lateral cross-section of an elephant before showing me round their red-bricked home with two separate guest suites. Both rooms have whitewashed brick walls, terracotta tiled floors and plush white sheets and towels. The larger unit has an airy conservatory/sitting room. Both open on to a braai area and an impeccable garden full of ferns and firs, lavender pots, lemon trees and citrus-smelling verbena. Hot-plates, a small oven and microwaves give ample scope for knocking up your own meals. I'd recommend coming with some pals and taking both rooms as a base from which to explore the Cape Town area. From the City Bowl and beaches to Table Mountain, Kirstenbosch botanical gardens and the nearby winelands there is just so much to do in the Cape that a full week with Bob and Rosemary flies by in the blink of a Witogie! These are great people running a great-value get-away.

Rooms: 2 units, both with 1 double room, twin/king beds (extra bed can be added to each) & en-s showers. Lemon Tree: galley kitchenette & shared DSTV; Apple Tree: separate conservatory with open-plan kitchenette/tv/sitting room, self-controlled DSTV.
Price: R310 - R340 pp sharing. Self-catering. R50 pp supplement for one night booking. Single rate R460.
Meals: Self-catering.
Directions: Directions provided on booking.

Majini

Suzy Digby-Smith
4 Broadacres, Colyn Road, Constantia Hills
Tel: 021-715-0155 Fax: 021-715-0155
Email: suzyds@kingsley.co.za
Cell: 082-439-9490

'Majini' is Swahili for 'by the water' but it wasn't apparent to me why the name was appropriate until I had strolled past vivid flowerbeds to the bottom of the velvety garden. A large wooden deck awaited, laden with huge braais, one side opening to the pool and the other to a small dam and stream with views of the lesser-known Elephants' Eye Peak and Suzy's chickens and ducks squabbling in the foreground. This little farmyard neighbours a flourishing organic veg patch and Suzy's guests are encouraged to help themselves to eggs and any potatoes, passion-fruit or greenery that they like the look of. The garden offerings don't end there either – the lawn to the main house winds its way through beautifully-tended lilies and colourful daisies to a well-stocked herb garden. A self-confessed auction-addict, Kenyan-born Suzy has decorated the Pool House simply, but with great care. Touches like well-thumbed paperbacks and a beautiful kiwinet over the bed make the cottage familiar, while luxuries like a Krupps coffee-machine and computer with wifi ensure that all comfort bases are covered. Suzy easily high-jumps the hospitality bar set by most self-catering owners, happily stocking the fridge for guests, loaning her garden for small parties or braais by the boma fire where the lights in the trees glow magnificently at night. A sign in the loo reads, 'Always Give Thanks'. At Majini this is an unnecessary reminder.

Rooms: 1 double room with dressing room, shower & loo, sitting/dining rm, kitchenette. Unit alarmed, DSTV, DVD, WIFI, private braais & parking.
Price: Pool House R1,200 - R1,400.
Meals: Fully self-catering.
Directions: On the N2 from the airport, take the N3 towards Muizenberg. Exit 16 for Ladies Mile. Turn right at T-junction and take 3rd exit at roundabout. Take second left onto Soetvlei Avenue. After 0.9km left onto Colyn Road and first right into Broadacres.

Map Number: 3

Entry Number: 32

Beluga

Annette White
5 Connor Close, Constantia
Tel: 021-794-4594
Email: info@belugaguesthouse.com Web: www.belugaguesthouse.com
Cell: 082-266-1850

I was encouraged to arrive at Beluga as early as I could to make the most of the sunny day by the beach pool. I took Annette up on this kind offer. And after I'd soaked up enough sun for the day, Annette invited me to join her for an afternoon cup of tea and home-made biscuits. Again, I saw no reason to refuse! Sitting on the wide-open verandah looking out at the lush garden, I had to remind myself that I was only two minutes from the M3 (15 from the V&A Waterfront and 5 from Constantia Hills). Trust me, it's hard to believe. Since her arrival in South Africa (Annette used to run a B&B in the UK), she has been exploring the Cape Peninsula and unearthing its best-kept secrets – farm stalls are her speciality. She will happily share her hard-won knowledge and point guests in the right direction… I took notes as she spoke! Annette loves colour and pattern and the rooms are decorated with a homely, country-cottage feel. As well as her gift for hospitality, Annette is also an expert in nutrition, so I was looking forward to "Annette's Special Healthy Breakfast" (served on the verandah or in the dining room). With a little guidance (I was overwhelmed by the range of choices), I started with a freshly-made fruit smoothie, moved on to natural yoghurt, sprinkled with seeds and nuts and topped with fresh fruit, before finally indulging in a mouth-watering croissant. (Although Annette will happily cook a full breakfast too.) Beluga is a place where the best qualities of a proper B&B are alive and well. *Children welcome 10 years plus.*

Rooms: 3: 1 king with bath + shower, 1 king with shr only; 1 king + single (sleeps up to 3) with shower.
Price: R450 - R600 pp per night sharing. Singles on request. House let as whole on application (3 more bedrooms make for max 11 people). Min let a week in high season and at least 3 days for winter breaks.
Meals: Full breakfast or "Annette's Healthy Breakfast". Gluten- and dairy-free available on request.
Directions: From airport take N2 to Cape Town. Take M3 turn-off to Muizenberg. Go approx 6km. Take Jct 14 signed Constantia Main. At t-jct turn L towards Hout Bay. R at 2nd lights into Brommersvlei Rd. Straight over at stop sign. Connor Close 1st L.

Darling Lodge Guest House

Stephan Moser and Oliver Studer
22 Pastorie Street, Darling
Tel: 022-492-3062 Fax: 022-492-3665
Email: info@darlinglodge.co.za Web: www.darlinglodge.co.za
Cell: 071-154-0243

Business first brought Oliver (Swiss-born) to South Africa, but it's his heart that makes him stay. It didn't take long for his partner Stephan to fall in love too. The main house, whose oak floors were originally laid in 1832, is flooded with life and colour, manifested in the vibrant red wall in the reception hall, mounted with the words: "We create our tomorrow, By what we dream today". All the bedrooms are rich in light and colour too, each with a little touch of the modern and urban to complement the Victorian interior. Each room is named after a different local artist, whose work adorns the walls and is, by the bye, for sale. I would personally opt for Nicolas Maritz with its deep Victorian clawfoot bath. But it was the garden that finally stole the laurels, with its ancient pepper trees, fountain spraying water over blossoming roses and mass of lavender. I could think of nothing better than sitting on the shaded stoep with a good book in one hand, perhaps a glass of wine from one of the five nearby vineyards in the other, intermittently watching the industrious weaver-birds build their nests and taking a dip in the pool between chapters. My stay was rounded off with a delicious breakfast presented with care and thought. "We like to celebrate breakfast... it's important to celebrate the new day", Stephan explains. My thoughts exactly. A darling lodge indeed. *Book early during the Voorkamerfest, Wildflower Show in September and Music Experience in February.*

Rooms: 6: 1 queen, 1 king and 1 twin with en-suite shower only; 1 twin with en-suite bath; 2 queens with en-suite Victorian bath. Tea & coffee facilities, safe for valuables and standing fans in all rooms.
Price: R400 - R490 pp sharing. Singles R550 - R750.
Meals: Full breakfast included. Supper on request.
Directions: From R27, turn off to R315 at Yzerfontein intersection direction Darling. From N7, at Malmesbury turn off to R315 direction Darling. Located in old village next to museum. GPS coordinates: 33 deg. 22'44. 16" S / 18 deg. 22'42. 73" E.

Map Number: 1

Entry Number: 34

Kersefontein

Julian Melck

between Hopefield and Velddrif
Tel: 022-783-0850 Fax: 022-783-0850
Email: info@kersefontein.co.za Web: www.kersefontein.co.za
Cell: 083-454-1025

Nothing has changed at Kersefontein since the first edition. Julian's convivial dinner parties are still a reason to book in on their own. And Julian himself remains a Renaissance man, described on his business card as 'Farmer, Pig-killer, Aviator and Advocate of the High Court of S.A.' He farms cows, sheep and horses on the surrounding fields and wild boar appear deliciously at dinner. He also hires and pilots a six-seater plane and a flight round the Cape or along the coast is a must. He modestly leaves out his virtuosity as a pianist and organist and some of us trooped off one Sunday morning, braving a 40-minute sermon in Afrikaans, to hear him play toccatas by Bach, Giguot and Widor at the local church. When not eating, riding or flying, guests lounge on the pontoon, swim in the river or read books from Kersefontein's many libraries. Or they use the house as a base to visit the coast or the Swartland wineries, which are really taking off. The homestead is seventh generation and the rooms either Victorian or African in temperament, with antiques handed down by previous Melcks. It's certainly worth splashing out on the luxury suite, in a separate barn next to a breakfast room clad in a stunning array of framed, pressed wild flowers from the nearby fields. You are fed like a king, but treated as a friend and I am always recommending people to go here.

Rooms: 6: 2 doubles, 2 twins, 1 separate two-bedroom cottage, 1 new suite with double bed, lounge, en-suite shower & bath.
Price: R520 - R620 pp sharing. Suite: R895 pp sharing. No single supplements. Aircraft hire prices depend on the trip.
Meals: Full breakfast included. Dinners by arrangement: R240 – R260 excluding wine.
Directions: From Cape Town take N7 off N1. Bypass Malmesbury, 5km later turn left towards Hopefield. After 50km bypass Hopefield, turn right signed Velddrif. After 16km farm signed on right just before grain silos. Cross bridge and gates on the left.

Langebaan Beach House

Claire Green

Reception entrance at 5 Jacoba St, Langebaan
Tel: 022-772-2625 Fax: 022-772-1432
Email: lbh@intekom.co.za Web: www.langebaanbeachhouse.com
Cell: 083-461-4408

Langebaan Beach House was once Claire's family's seaside retreat in the days when Langebaan was a small fishing village. It has grown since then, but still has a nice holiday feel. Today the main house is Claire's home, complete with two typically upbeat labradors, Shamus and Kelsey (and one ginger cat), and set right on the lagoon. The garden goes directly to sand and water. The original part is over 100 years old, while the rest has gradually been added as the family expanded and today serves as the guest accommodation. The two self-catering units are situated next to the house, with their own private entrance from the beachfront. I stayed in the Garden Suite and after a walk along Langebaan's Main Beach (did I mention this is on the door step?), I returned to soak up the last of the evening's rays from my sun-lounger on my private patio. My neighbours in the Island View Suite seemed just as content on their verandah. In the early morning I joined the local community on a communal jog along the beach. If time allowed, I would happily re-live this routine for many more nights. The sea is safe and swimmable and all water sports are allowed – motor- and wind-powered vessels, fishing and water-skiing. 250,000 migrating birds, including flamingos, live at the wilderness end of the lagoon. Claire herself is relaxed, warm-spirited and extremely knowledgeable about what's going on in her neck of the woods. Which is a lot.

Rooms: 2: 'Garden Suite': 1 queen, en-s spa bath and shower; 'Island View': 1 twin, en-s shower only. Both with open plan lounge and kitchen.
Price: R700 - R900 per unit. Each sleeps 2.
Meals: Self-catering. Great restaurants in Langebaan within walking distance.
Directions: Enter Langebaan from R27. At 4th stop sign turn right into Bree St. Take 2nd road on L into Jacoba St. House is no. 5 on RHS.

Map Number: 1

Entry Number: 36

Oystercatcher's Haven at Paternoster

Sandy and Wayne Attrill
48 Sonkwasweg, Paternoster
Tel: 022-752-2193 Fax: 086-577-9142
Email: info@oystercatchershaven.com Web: www.oystercatchershaven.com
Cell: 082-414-6705 or 083-267-7051

Sandy and Wayne, ex film and advertising people, do things in style and their guest house is a knock-out! The Cape Dutch house sits on the fringes of the Cape Columbine Nature Reserve, a spectacular, fynbos-covered, hand-shaped headland, bearing its lighthouse aloft like a nine-million-watt jewel. All along the coast and a mere 40 metres in front of the house knobbly fingers of grey and black granite merge into the sea and around the rocks there are secret white sandy coves where the dolphins come throughout the year. It is quite simply beautiful and I can assure you that the Oystercatcher is a haven by anyone's standards. Heave yourself out of that plunge-pool, off the rocks and away from the view (available from your bed) and head inside the house. The interior, with its white walls, untreated timbers and reed-and-pole ceilings, is intentionally blank-yet-rustic to showcase some exquisite pieces, such as a four-foot-high Angolan drum, some Malinese sinaba paintings (you'll have to come and see them if you don't know what they are), Persian rugs, art-deco couches, courtyards…. Just about everything is a hook for an eager eye. Beds and bedrooms too are bliss - trust me, I'm a professional. Although they do not do dinners any more (there is no need with so many good eateries in Paternoster) they do offer fresh-out-of-the-bay crayfish dinners in season on demand.

Rooms: 3: 1 king suite with en-suite shower; 1 queen with en-suite bath and shower; 1 twin with en-suite showers. All rooms have their own private entrances and outdoor areas.
Price: R825 pp sharing for the rooms and R1,100 pp sharing for the Suite. Singles on request.
Meals: Full breakfast included.
Directions: From Cape Town take the N1 and then the R27 north following signs to Vredenburg. Follow signs straight through Vredenburg to Paternoster (15km). At crossroads turn left and travel a full 1km towards the Columbine Reserve. Turn right into Sonkwas Rd. It is No.48.

Paternoster Dunes Boutique Guest House & Spa

Gavin Sproule and Deon Van Rooyen

18 Sonkwas Street, Paternoster
Tel: 022-752-2217 Fax: 022-752-2214
Email: reservations@paternosterdunes.co.za
Web: www.paternosterdunes.co.za Cell: 083-560-5600

Located right on the beach, it's not hard to see why locals referred to Paternoster Dunes as 'lovely'. I was met by Gavin and escorted past the open-air courtyard with its tempting pool and daybed and shown to my room (named Vanilla). Gavin and Deon worked in interior design for ten years before swapping the big smoke for the salt breeze. If Vanilla was anything to go by – open-plan, huge bath with its own sea-facing window, equally huge stone-floored shower and king-size bed with plump pillows and Egyptian cotton - they were surely at the top of their game. But the best treat of all was my verandah, accessed through French doors. The ocean is less than ten yards away between grassy dunes and it was here that I decided to settle down and finish off my book of the moment. Clapping the covers together an hour later, I took my satisfaction up to the communal bar/lounge, with its panoramic ocean views, for a sundowner. The design throughout the house never jars and always excites. The walls are adorned with original artwork, from contemporary pastoral scenes to palette nudes and the leather armchairs in the lounge could have been found in a London gentleman's club. My snoek omelettes at breakfast was clear proof of fine cooking. But by that time you would hardly expect anything less. More 'wow!' than 'lovely'! *Spa on site offers pampering treatments.*

Rooms: 6: king/queen/twins with en-suite shower and/or bath.
Price: R750 - R1000 pp sharing. Singles on request.
Meals: Breakfast included. Light lunch and dinner on request.
Directions: From Cape Town take the N1 and then the R27 north following signs to Vredenburg to Paternoster (15km). At crossroads turn left then travel a full 1km to the Columbine Reserve. Turn right into Sonkwas Street. It is No.18.

Abalone House

Stef Venter and Johan Jansen Van Vuuren

Abalone House, 3 Kriedoring Street, Paternoster
Tel: 022-752-2044 Fax: 086-215-1839
Email: info@abalonehouse.co.za Web: www.abalonehouse.co.za
Cell: 073-844-7722

When owners Stef and Johan returned to Limpopo they kindly left their treasure trove of a home to the Paternoster guest-house scene. I entered Abalone to the tinkling of wind chimes and was immediately welcomed in very friendly fashion by manager Vinohd before being shown past the bonsai-surrounded courtyard pool to my elegant abode for the night. A private patio, high-backed armchairs, elaborate dressing table and hand-carved bedside lamps set the opulent tone for the rest of the guest-house. In the entrance hall rich rugs lie on stone floors and gold scales rest on a grand piano opposite vibrant Tretchikoff prints. Around the corner you'll discover the Africa Bar, where drums are reinvented as coffee tables between wicker thrones and lavish lampshades. The Saffron Restaurant is also an exuberant affair with pieces of silver on antique furniture and jewels draped from candelabras glowing in the orange light. I had entered a veritable Aladdin's cave! And my genies (in the kitchen) conjured up a string of sensational dishes including pea soup with pork belly, fresh crayfish and a devilish chocolate delice with cumin caramel sorbet. The following morning I had time for a peek at the roof terrace where five elegant beach house-style bedrooms surround the sun deck (don't miss the salty-aired Jacuzzi with sea and sky views), before a gourmet breakfast in the Orchid Room. As I spied Christmas and Easter, Abalone's resident ducks, foraging in the colourful garden, I thought to myself: these ducks don't know how lucky they are to live in such swanky surrounds!

Rooms: 10: 8 king/twins; 2 kings. All have en-suite bath & shower.
Price: R1,100 - R1,500 pp sharing for bed, breakfast and high tea. Single supplement.
Meals: Full breakfast and afternoon tea included. Lunch and dinner available in The Saffron Restaurant.
Directions: From Cape Town, take the R27 to Vredenburg. Turn L onto the R45. Follow the road through Vredenburg and continue straight to Paternoster. At the four way stop, turn L and follow Abalone House signs.

Farr Out B&B

Marion Lubitz and Deon van Schalkwyk

17 Seemeeusingel, Paternoster
Tel: 022-752-2222 Fax: 086-560-2275
Email: marion@farrout.co.za Web: www.farrout.co.za
Cell: 083-410-4090

The short drive from Paternoster to Farr Out is not what I would call far. But when you arrive in this sandy bushveld wilderness, you do feel pleasingly remote. Crunching up the glinting shell path came a cheery Marion, who sat me down with tea and chocolate cake fresh from the oven. From the kitchen you can see across their indigenous garden and out to sea. Early risers catch the wildlife that comes by when it thinks no-one's looking – Deon showed me a picture he'd taken at five that morning of a duiker drinking from their koi pond. After 24 years in the air force, he has now qualified as a tour guide and the wild and wonderful West Coast is his playground. I recommend joining him for a tour or a beach buggy excursion (or both!). I only had time for a little loop, but with the wind in my hair I wished I could have packed a coolbox and disappeared over the dunes. Rooms are modern and quirkily decorated with Marion's artworks, while bathrooms contain the snazziest loo seats ever seen. But my three favourite things at Farr Out are in the garden, all housed in a teepee. One: their wonderful, outdoor, wood-fired, hot tub. Two: a full-on braai area complete with *potjie* pot. Three: Wigwam Rising Moon Suite, the twin peaked super-teepee! This bespoke beauty has - along with everything you could possibly need (including WiFi!) - an octagonal bed, perfect for star-gazing and a cosy shelter from the wind. *German, English and Afrikaans spoken.*

Rooms: 4: 3 suites: 1 king/twin, 1 queen and 1 family suite with 1 queen and 1 king/twin room; 1 teepee: 1 octagonal bed (sleeps 2). All with en-suite showers.
Price: R345 - R500 pp sharing. Singles on request.
Meals: Breakfast included. Picnic baskets on request.
Directions: From Cape Town take R27 approx 125km to R45, which passes thro' Vredenburg & continues 15km towards Paternoster. Farr Out at far end of Pelgrimsrust small holdings just before Paternoster on LHS. Latitude: 32°49' 14.50" Longitude: 17°53' 38.28".

Map Number: 1

Entry Number: 40

Oystercatcher Lodge

Luc and Sue Christen
1st Avenue, Shelley Point St, St Helena Bay
Tel: 022-742-1202 Fax: 022-742-1201
Email: info@oystercatcherlodge.co.za Web: www.oystercatcherlodge.co.za
Cell: 082-903-9668

You can't miss Oystercatcher Lodge. If you do, you'll end up in the sea. It's set right on the tip of Shelley Point, overlooking the full curve of Britannia Bay with its flocks of cormorants, pods of passing dolphins and wallowing whales (in season). Luc (smiley and Swiss) and Sue (home-grown, but equally smiley) are both from the hotel trade. After years deep in the Mpumalanga bushveld, they decided they needed a change of air and came here. Quite a change. Here on the West Coast the sea air has a salty freshness unlike anywhere else, the sun shines brilliantly on arcing white beaches and the crunching waves are a bottomless blue. A special spot indeed where the Christens' newly-built guest house juts out towards the ocean like the prow of a ship, a large pointy pool in its bows. Each of the six rooms, painted in calming sandy colours, looks across grassy dunes and beach to the sea. Breakfast feasts are served in the dining room, and if you're lucky Luc might summon some whales for you to view by blowing on his 'kelperoo' (a whale horn made out of seaweed!) as you munch on the Christens' 'special Swiss recipe' bread. A short stroll away is the Christens' latest venture, a set of stunningly modern self-catering apartments, custom-designed so that you gaze out to sea from whichever bed you happen to be lazing in. Simple, uncluttered, each with a full kitchen, lounge with tv and terrace, the rooms share a large pool and are as princely as the original lodge itself. A super spot and super people.

Rooms: 11: 6 rooms in guesthouse: 4 kings, 2 twins, all with en-suite shower and/or bath; 5 self-catering units: 1 studio, 1 honeymoon apartment, 3 x 2-bed apartments. All serviced daily.
Price: Guesthouse: R475 - R725 pp sharing. Self-catering: R900 - R2,300 per unit per night.
Meals: Full breakfast included in guesthouse rate. Full kitchens in self-catering units. Restaurants nearby.
Directions: From Cape Town head north on R27 then turn L into Vredenburg. At lights go R. After 10km, L towards St Helena Bay. Just before Stompneus Bay turn L. After 200m turn R. At the S/Point entrance sign in, then go left past Country Club. Continue until fountain. Half circle fountain, thatched cottages on L, Oystercatcher on R.

Blues Breaker Cottage

Chantal d'Orthez

2 Witbaai Close, Sunset Beach, Britannia Bay
Tel: 076-862-9706
Email: bluesbreaker-sa@hotmail.com
Web: www.bluesbreakercottage.yolasite.com Cell: 076-862-9706

Have you ever flicked through Homes and Gardens Magazine (as I have) and thought, "ooh, I'd like to stay there!"… and then, "I wish I had the design flair to match that"… and then (as I have) contemplated your own shambles of a home and wept silent tears of shame? Well, here is an opportunity. Blues Breaker Cottage featured in February's 2011 edition and you can book in and live the dream for as long as you want! Every flawless inch is as seductive in the flesh, so to speak, as it is to read about. My solitary night amongst the lofty beams, soft-coloured hues, the luxurious linens and shea butter soaps, was beachside bliss. The polished concrete flooring, plumped-up cushions and African portraits among many other details conspire to create a subtle 'beachiness', to coin a word. I for one must have felt most at home here as I slept the sleep of the just for nine hours, intoxicated by the sea air. I would have slept on and on, but I remembered that Chantal had seen whales basking in the morning sun the day before. I strolled along the sandy shores of virtually unknown (and therefore virtually private) Britannia Bay, which was no more than fifty metres from my pillow, before taking a lazy brunch in the sunny white-walled garden. Chantal and husband Jeremy are a relaxed, stylish (did I mention Chantal's career in fashion?) and musical couple (hence the name Blues Breaker) who invite you to experience simple, luxurious beach life the way they like it. It happens to be the way I like it too.

Rooms: 2 doubles with full en-suite bathrooms.
Price: R2,000 - R2,500 for whole unit.
Meals: Self-catering. Choice of local restaurants nearby in Paternoster.
Directions: Emailed upon booking.

Waterfall Farm

Helen & David Untiedt

R303 6km from Citrusdal
Tel: 021-790-0972 Fax: 021-790-0972
Email: stay@perfecthideaways.co.za Web: www.perfecthideaways.co.za
Cell: 082-775-7797

Wow! It's hard to write about Waterfall Farm without eulogising over a certain natural feature. In fact, my first instruction upon arrival was "you cannot leave without seeing the waterfall!" Luckily I didn't. Henry, resident expert on the farm's fauna and flora and a very genial guide, showed me the way. How I longed to shower in the white water cascading over sculpted cliffs, swim in the fresh-water mountain rock pools and picnic on surrounding white sandy beaches. Away from this natural wonder the farm provides fantastic walks, breathtaking views across the Cederberg Mountains with their rich fynbos and spring flowers in season and enough naartjies to keep you in vitamin C for months. For those lucky enough to stay, the main house has a rambling lived-in feel and includes a large pine dining table, well-used sofas around an open fire and table tennis in the games room. Outside, cricket-pitch-sized lawns are bordered by protea beds, oak and gum trees. But it's the thatched boma that really caught my eye. Here bookworms and siesta lovers will occupy the day beds and night-time revelers will light fires, cook and make merry under fairy-lights. For smaller groups the converted stables cottage offers an intimate living area by the country fire and outdoor seating among vines and lavender on the stoep. In both houses fine white linen and fresh-cut roses freshen up the bedrooms. Finally, for convenience, there is a dam pool on the lawn… but whatever you do, don't leave without seeing that waterfall! *The house is a no-smoking zone.*

Rooms: Farmhouse: 4: 3 doubles (2 with en-s sh); 1 room with double & twin beds; 1 extra bathroom. Honey Cottage: 3: 2 doubles & 1 room with 3 singles; bathroom with separate loo & outdoor sh. Weaver's Nest: 2 bedrooms: 1 double & 1 twin with shared bathroom.
Price: Farmhouse: from R2,000 per night; Honey Cottage: from R1,500 per night; Weaver's Nest: R800 - R1,200 per night. Specials available.
Meals: Self-catering.
Directions: Directions provided on booking.

Mount Ceder

Rachelle Marriott-Dodington
Grootrivier Farm, Cederberg, Koue Bokkeveld
Tel: 023-317-0848 Fax: 086-580-9343
Email: mountceder@lando.co.za Web: www.mountceder.co.za

Do not lose confidence as you rumble along the gravel roads that lead through the Koue Bokkeveld Nature Conservancy to this secluded valley - it's always a couple more turns. Finally you will arrive in the southern entrance of the Cederberg, dry sandstone mountains rising all around you in impressive dimensions – aim to get there at sunset for the full effect. You will be given the key to your new home before you drive the final kilometre or so of sandy track to one of three fantastic rustic stone cottages. The river flows past the reeds and rock right by the cottages, clear, deep and wide all year round. You can swim and lie around drying on flat rocks. Birds love it here too. I imagine sitting out on that stoep, on those wooden chairs, looking at that view, beer or wine in hand… a piece of heaven, as they say. You can either self-cater or you can eat at the Old Millhouse restaurant back at the lodge. There are a few other cottages nearer the lodge, which are fine, but you must ask for the stone cottages, which are in a league of their own. A pristine slice of unspoiled nature, cherished by a very knowledgeable Marais family who will help with Bushman rock art, horse-riding and fauna and flora. *Serious hiking is possible from here. Rachelle will happily take you horse-riding.*

Rooms: 3 river cottages with 3 bedrooms each.
Price: R1,990 - R2,995 per cottage per night self-catering (cottage sleeps 6).
Meals: Restaurant with meals on request: breakfast R70, 3-course set menu dinner R150 (not including wine).
Directions: From Ceres follow signs to Prince Alfred's Hamlet/Op-die-Berg, up Gydo Pass past Op-die-Berg. First right signed Cederberge - follow tar for 17km then continue on gravel road for another 34km into a green valley.

Cederberg, Western Cape

Oudrif

Bill and Jeanine Mitchell
PO Box 409, Clanwilliam
Tel: 027-482-2397
Email: oudrif@telkomsa.net Web: www.oudrif.co.za

Fifty kilometres of fabulous sandstone formations, dams and flower-covered passes lead you deep into the Cederberg Mountains and eventually to Oudrif, the perfect hideaway-getaway on the banks of the clear, clean, cool Doring River. I was met by my hosts Bill and Jeanine, who provided me with iced tea, before escorting me to my environmentally-friendly lodge where walls and roofs are straw bales and power is solar and views spectacular. Bill and Jeanine met whilst Jeanine was working as a goatherd (absolutely true) and their shared passion for wildlife is palpable. Together they're a veritable encyclopaedia of life in the wild from eco building to bird rescues to taming their half-Siamese and half-wild pet cat Barry. My room was light-filled, with sofas to snooze on, but it was a hot day, so I donned my trunks and ran to the river for a dip. The main house is the meeting point, library and supper room and I was quickly introduced to the other guests. Oudrif holds ten at full capacity, with a rare atmosphere whereby guests know they are sharing a unique experience, so evenings around the communal table can be very entertaining. After a laughter-filled evening and too much home-made bread (both Bill and Jeanine are master bakers), I headed off to bed. Well, in fact… eschewing the comforts of a lovely king-size double bed, I actually decided to sleep outside under an amazing starlit sky. This is a truly special spot. *Guided excursions also included.*

Rooms: 5: all twin/double with en-suite shower.
Price: R800 pp sharing, including all meals and drinks.
Meals: 3 meals a day and all drinks (wine, beer, soft drinks) included.
Directions: Enquire on booking.

Entry Number: 45

Map Number: 1

Enjo Nature Farm

Andrea and Moritz Conrad
Biedouw Valley, Clanwilliam
Tel: 027-482-2869 Fax: 086-535-1634
Email: rocks@soulcountry.info Web: www.soulcountry.info

Descending into the Biedouw Valley is the New World of South Africa's scenic symphonies: crashing mountains, sandstone cliffs, a vast plain of tawny yellow shot through with a river of green – not to mention spring's blanket of flowers. It's steering-wheel-gripping stuff. Moritz, a pilot (more on that later) and Andrea, a nurse, swooped into the valley from Munich five years ago and have so far conjured up five self-catering cottages, 350 sheep, a few hectares of olives and two happy children. The white-washed thatched cottages are buried down by the river, set privately apart from one another. Inside, find simple beds with Andrea's hand-sewn bedcovers (German-style, two single duvets on a double bed), rough concrete shower rooms, kitchenettes. Older children scamper up hand-built ladders to beds on a mezzanine. And now they have also opened a new totally remote and private Lonely Planet Cottage with 100 percent privacy. Outside... a few wandering horses, the river, stone-built braais. Take note: accommodation is basic. But the setting is supreme and the Conrads are wonderful, generous hosts. If the weather's right Moritz can take you for a flip around the Cederberg in a four-seater plane; or you can wallow in the river, swim in the farm pool, relax in the hot tub, hike up through the valley, view rock art along the Sevilla Trail, even order a pair of hand-made leather shoes in Wuppertal. Bring children, dogs, and meat for the braai. Simple, natural, beautiful and great value - I just loved it.

Rooms: 5: 2 chalets with queen & 2 singles on mezzanine;
1 cabin with double bed & single on mezzanine. Lazy
Leopard sleeps 6, 1 king, 1 queen & 1 twin. Lonely Planet
sleeps 4, 1 king & 1 twin.
Price: Chalets: R295 pp sharing; Cabin: R195 pp sharing
(extra adults R50, kids R25); Lazy Leopard: 690 for unit
(sleeps 4 - 6); Lonely Planet Cottage: R490 for 2 people
(max 4). Extra adult R50, extra child R25.
Meals: Self-catering facilities & braais in all units. Breakfast
(R65) & dinner (R90) on request. Basic supplies avail' to buy.
Directions: From Clanwilliam, take tarred R364 towards
Calvinia. After 40km, turn R, signed Wuppertal Biedouw Valley,
onto gravel rd. Over Hoek se Berg Pass into Biedouw Valley. L
into Biedouw Valley, 11km thro' 2 farm gates.

Map Number: 1

Entry Number: 46

Villa Tarentaal

Graham and Brandi Hunter
Tulbagh
Tel: 023-230-0868
Email: grahamjhb@gmail.com Web: www.villatarentaal.com
Cell: 074-194-8202

Graham, having drunk his fill of life as a highway patrolman in America (abandon any Hollywood stereotypes, Graham is charming!), and his wife Brandi (also charming) returned home to take over the family business - and to start a family of their own... today, a family of four! I was affectionately greeted by Karma and Mufasa, the Villa Tarentaal dogs and as hospitable as their owners. People come for the privacy - each of the three cosy self-contained cottages has its own entrance, a private lounge, kitchenette and sheltered braai patio - but stay, I imagine, to try each and every breakfast option which Graham delivers and presents on your private cottage verandah each morning. The French toast is sinful... but delicious! Peacock Suite is a new addition and serves as the villa's honeymoon suite with double stone basins, a bath for two and double shower-heads. The gardens are as pristine and cared-for as the cottages: wisteria and grapevines spider up the mustard-coloured house; roses provide an orgy of colour; and the lawn is so well-kept it would make the green-keepers of Augusta, well... green with envy. Guests are not the only ones flocking here; you'll witness an abundance of bird life, including the eponymous tarentaal (Afrikaans for guinea fowl), Egyptian geese, fish eagle, peacock and blue crane. The cottages weren't named after these winged beauties for nothing! *Christine, the previous owner alongside husband Mike, still offers therapeutic massages (booking essential).*

Rooms: 4: 1 Peacock Suite, en-s shr & bath; 3 cottages: Blue Crane: 2 singles & 1 king in separate rooms, en-s shr & bath. Fish Eagle: 1 king en-s shr. Egyptian Goose: 1 qu en-s shr. All have a/c, fireplace, ipod docks & full DSTV.
Price: R475 - R550 pp sharing B&B. R425 pp sharing self-catering. Singles on request.
Meals: Full breakfast included served in the privacy of your own cottage or on private verandah. Light meals by request until 1630.
Directions: N1 from Cape Town to exit 47 Wellington/Franschhoek/Klapmuts turn-off, left onto R44 via Wellington. Follow for approx 1 hour to Tulbagh. Straight through town, 1.2km on left.

Bartholomeus Klip Farmhouse

Lesley Gillett
Elandsberg Farm, Hermon
Tel: 022-448-1087 Fax: 086-604-4321
Email: info@bartholomeusklip.com Web: www.bartholomeusklip.com
Cell: 082-829-4131

Heavenly scenery cossets this Victorian homestead in its lush gardens and stands of oak and olive. The wall of the Elandsberg Mountains rises up from the game reserve, reflected in the dammed lake by the house. Guests enjoy a leisurely breakfast in the smart conservatory dining room before heading out for an excursion onto the wheat and sheep farm. You are also taken on late-afternoon game drives to see the zebra, a variety of Cape antelope, buffalo, quaggas (a fascinating experiment to reintroduce an extinct variety of zebra), eagles, flocks of blue crane... and the largest world population of the tiny, endangered geometric tortoises. But just to be out in such nature! The spring flowers are spectacular and there are more than 850 species of plant recorded on the property. Back at the homestead you can cool down in the curious, round, raised reservoir pool, sit in chairs on the stoep, wander down to the boathouse with a drink; or, if you have more energy, bike off into the reserve or go on guided walks in the mountains. Staff are very friendly, food is exceptional and a reason to stay on its own (and all included in the price). I recommend splashing out on at least two nights. A great place indeed and very popular so book ahead of yourself if possible. *Closed July - August and Christmas.*

Rooms: 7: 2 dbls & 3 twins, all with bath & shr. 2 self-catering cottages: Wild Olive House sleeps 8 (3 doubles & bunk beds); Garden Cottage sleeps 2 with double, bathroom & small sitting room.

Price: R1,513 - R2,445 pp sharing. Singles + 20%. Wild Olive House R1,472 - R1,775 pp. Garden Cottage, R1,198 - R1,330 pp for self-catering cottage. Rates include all meals & game drives. 0 - 3 are free, 4 - 15 half price in cottage.

Meals: Coffee & rusks, brunch, high tea, snacks & sundowners & 3-course dinner incl' in room rate.

Directions: From CT take N1 towards Paarl. Exit 47, left at stop. Continue along rd turning L onto R44 signed Ceres. Follow for 30km. Past R46 junction signed Hermon, take next R signed Bo-Hermon. Gravel road for 6km. Bartholomeus Klip signed to L - 5km.

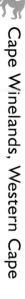

De Langenhof Guest House

Mike & Gail Walters
18 Lang Street, Riebeek West
Tel: 022-461-2188 Fax: 086-575-7070
Email: info@langenhof.co.za Web: www.langenhof.co.za
Cell: 084-255-4109

With a warm sun setting behind the Kasteelberg Mountain, it was with considerable pleasure that I sauntered through the five gardens (Rose, Mediterranean, Aloe, Kirstenbosch and Herb) of De Langenhof ending up by the lap pool. Resisting temptation to dive in, I joined my hosts (and cats Pasha and Minkee) for a glass of the local tipple on the stoep. Mike and Gail relocated all of one hour from Cape Town to enjoy the splendid scenery, food and wine of the Riebeek Valley. Gail is involved in promoting local tourism, which was extremely handy when it came to choosing from a plethora of recommended restaurants for dinner that evening. However, if you don't fancy exploring, Mike is a dab hand in the kitchen as I discovered while savouring my cooked breakfast including grilled brinjals. Both Mike and Gail are well suited to the guesthouse game, possessing an easy manner and a fine collection of furniture. The teak-floored guest lounge, dominated by its chimney and fireplace, is full of prime pieces from grandfather clock to Dutch brass log chest. I stayed in one of two garden rooms, swathed in soft creams and pinks with decadent double shower, Victorian bath and rose-patterned curtains opening onto a honeysuckle-laden verandah and koi pond. The four verandah rooms are equally stylish with their earthy beige and olive walls and 'distressed' country furniture. All rooms offer their guests the highly-acclaimed Allesverloren vintage port and Lindt chocolates. Sound like a treat? Well, it is.

Rooms: 6: 4 verandah rooms: 1 double with en-s sh & bath; 2 double with en-s sh; 1 twin en-s sh; 2 garden rooms: both queen en-sh & bath. All rooms have aircon.
Price: Verandah rooms: R420 - R440 pp sharing. Singles R480. Garden rooms: R520 - R540 pp sh. Singles R580.
Meals: Full breakfast included. Dinners on request R100 - R150 for 2 courses and a glass of wine.
Directions: Take N7 north from Cape Town. Exit 1st Malmesbury off-ramp onto R46 to Riebeek Kasteel & Ceres. Turn L onto R311 & drive thro' RK. De Langenhof signed on L just before leaving Riebeek West. 3rd property on R after turning off R311.

Oude Wellington Estate

Rolf Schumacher
Bainskloof Pass Rd, Wellington
Tel: 021-873-2262 Fax: 088021-873-4639
Email: info@kapwein.com Web: www.kapwein.com

There seems to be so much to catch the eye even as you rumble along the 800-metre paved and cobbled road to Oude Wellington: vineyards on both sides, ostentatious peacocks, geese, hadedas, alpacas (brought over from Australia to be added to the menagerie), pet ostriches peering over a fence... Rolf is clearly the hospitable type (how else could ostriches find a home on a winery?). It took him two years to restore the whole estate to its former glory as a wine-grape farm. Four rustic double rooms are in the original farmhouse (built in 1790) with high, thatched ceilings, low pole beams, whitewashed walls and yet underfloor heating and air-con; the other two are in the more modern main building (well, 1836!), along with the homely farm kitchen with old-fashioned pots, pans and irons, billiard room and bar, and a terrace overlooking the vineyards, where breakfast is served in the summer. There is a partly-shaded pool off to the side of the main house, a brandy still in the barn and handily on the premises is a restaurant popular with the locals (always a good sign). Guests are also invited to watch wine-making taking place at the right time of year. "I farm and dine and love company," says Rolf in his brochure! *Horse-riding lessons available for beginners.*

Rooms: 8: all kings/ twins with en-suite Victorian baths. Self-catering option available.
Price: R480 - R550 pp sharing. Single R600.
Meals: Full breakfast included. Restaurant on premises, open seven days a week.
Directions: From Wellington follow Church Street (Kerkstraat), which becomes Bainskloof Rd (R301/3). 2.5km out of Wellington on right-hand side follow brown signs to Oude Wellington.

Kleinfontein

Tim and Caroline Holdcroft
Wellington
Tel: 021-864-1202 Fax: 021-864-1202
Email: kleinfon@iafrica.com Web: www.kleinfontein.com
Cell: 072-108-5895

An evening leg-stretch with Tim proved the perfect antidote to a long and stressful day on the road. Guided by a German alsatian, an almost-labrador and an incredibly energetic fluffy white thing we strolled past Jersey cows, through a shaded stream and between rows of sunlit vines. Kleinfontein is just an hour from Cape Town at the foot of the Bainskloof Pass and the Holdcrofts are delightful hosts. And this truly is home hosting at its finest; they'll eat and drink with you, show you their farm and even have you out there clipping the vines or feeding the horses if you show willing (and riding them, too, if you're saddle-hardened). In fact there's enough to keep you busy here for days, from hiking in surrounding mountains and cellar tours galore, to the leisurely delights of a good book beneath magnificent oak trees, or a wallow in the pool in Caroline's fabulous garden. She is of Kenyan stock and Tim's British, but they spent years in Africa and over a superb supper we washed down tales of the continent with home-grown cabernet sauvignon. Like me you'll stay in a roomy, restored wing of the thatched Cape Dutch farmhouse with poplar beams and reed ceilings. Like me you'll sleep like a baby. And, like me, you'll wake to breakfast on the verandah with fresh butter and milk, newly-laid eggs and honey straight from the beehive. Sound idyllic? Well, it is.

Rooms: 2 suites, both with sitting room and en-suite bath and shower.
Price: R1,400 - R 1,700 pp sharing. Single supplement + 20%. Includes all meals, all drinks and laundry.
Meals: Breakfast, tea/coffee tray, picnic lunch and 4-course dinner included in price.
Directions: Directions are down dirt roads so map can be emailed or faxed.

Bovlei Valley Retreat

Lee and Abbi Wallis

Bovlei Road, Wellington
Tel: 021-864-1504 Fax: 021-864-1504
Email: info@bvr.co.za Web: www.bvr.co.za

Arriving at Bovlei Valley to the sound of a beautiful aria and the waft of baking lavender cookies drifting in from Abbi's kitchen, I settled onto a squishy sofa near the large fireplace. Abbi did a degree in hospitality and it shows. Her open-plan kitchen is part of the impressive-yet-cosy main room, with high ceilings, sofas and a dining area and she does all her home-cooking there while chatting to guests. Next door is a comfy TV room with DVD library and every board game ever thought up for rainy days. But when the sun shines it will be hard to leave the pool, whose depths are constantly filled with fresh water from the lips of a rather fetching bearded stone head. Panoramic mountain views and a plump, well-stocked honesty fridge under the verandah cater for every poolside whim. The whole place is a working guava, grape and lavender farm, with its own boutique winery, Dunstone, where guest involvement is encouraged. If wine-making is your thing… pick, foot-stomp, bottle and taste to your heart's content! The winery also hosts Abbi's restaurant, The Stone Kitchen, serving delicious local produce with a British twist. The highlight of the recently-renovated stable rooms is the Lavender Suite with a luxurious four-poster and a view over waving fields of lavender. Guava Cottage has its own mini-vineyard and stoep and lies in front of the guava plantation. A granite-topped kitchen with dishwasher and generous range mean you can really self-cater in style. The cottage even has its own solar panel-heated pool, garden and braai area.

Rooms: 6: 5 in converted stables: 2 king/twins, en-s bath & shower; 3 queens, en-s shr over bath; 1 self-catering cottage: 1 dble (en-s bathroom) & 1 twin (shr).
Price: Stable suites: R500 - R850 pp sharing, singles R700 - R1,000; Guava Cottage: R400 - R800 pp. Add breakfast R85 pp. Extra bed in room: R100 - R150.
Meals: Full English breakfast (home-made bread); afternoon tea, fresh-baked cakes & wine-tasting included. Dinner & light lunches by prior booking.
Directions: See website for detailed directions or map can be faxed/emailed.

Ridgeback House

Vanessa and Vernon Cole

Langverwacht Farm, Nr. Paarl
Tel: 021-869-8988 Fax: 021-869-8708
Email: guesthouse@ridgeback.co.za Web: www.ridgebackhouse.co.za
Cell: 072-500-7516

Though the ice-cold Coke that Vanessa – and her team of handsome young ridgebacks – greeted me with was just what the doctor ordered, it really should have been a glass of shiraz. For this is the place to come for the complete wine experience. Guests are encouraged to help in every way in the production of the gods' favourite tipple, whether it be lending a hand with the harvest or just making sure the bottle's not corked. The latter takes place in a smart tasting centre and restaurant in the hub of the farm, with a wooden balcony overlooking the dam – home to twenty-five species of wild fowl. A tour of the cellar is easily and enthusiastically arranged too, although the best place to sample the wine is indisputably on the granite rock at the top of the farm, where Vanessa will lay on a boozy sundowner picnic and retire discreetly, leaving you to contemplate the sky melting to a pinky-purple over the wide, olive- and vine-filled valley. Stroll down through the vines and olive trees to your bedroom in the converted farmhouse, or to the latest addition, a sweet cottage on one side of the house. Meals are served in the cavernous dining room, a short amble from a sitting room lit by wrought-iron chandeliers, and on summer evenings the braai will be fired up out by the pool. Vanessa is a superb hostess and Ridgeback the perfect place to ensure that the 2012-2013 vintage is a fine one. *If arriving after 6pm, arrange for gate to be kept open.*

Rooms: 5 rooms in farmhouse: 1 king, 1 double and 3 king/twins. All en-suite, 4 with baths and showers & 1 with shower.
Price: B&B R510 – R750 pp sharing. Singles R750.
Meals: Full breakfast included in guest-house rate. Lunches available either at tasting centre or at house on request.
Directions: From N1, take exit 47 onto R44 towards Wellington. After 16.5km, turn R after Windmeul Co-op. After 200m, turn R between school and church.

Amberg Guestfarm

Helga Frank and Bernd Schuffenhauer

Du Toitskloof Pass, Klein Drakenstein, Paarl
Tel: 021-862-0982 Fax: 021-862-0564
Email: info@amberg.co.za Web: www.amberg.co.za
Cell: 073-134-9601

From whichever direction you travel, driving along the Du Toitskloof Pass is a must. It is one of those awe-inspiring South African roads and well worth a detour. After gliding down the pass with a satisfied smile on my face, I turned sharply (as commanded by my GPS) at the Amberg sign and meandered my way up the stone drive to find Helga eagerly awaiting my arrival with her own beaming smile. Helga's husband Bernd seems equally happy and equally proud of his South African home. Helga and Bernd first visited South Africa on holiday and some years later... the inevitable happened. Today the couple spend half of the year at Amberg and half back in Germany working in the antiques industry. The rooms are consequently filled with Bernd's collection of art deco furniture – we stood for some time admiring the 1920s wardrobe brought over from France in Berg One Cottage – and Helga's gallery of paintings (Helga once owned an art gallery in Germany). The long hallway in the Poolside apartment even resembles an art gallery with pieces perfectly mounted and lit by wire-hung spotlights. Be reassured that the little things haven't been forgotten either - the kitchen is filled with top-of-the-range kitchenware. Helga and Bernd have not only provided high-class accommodation to fellow fans of South Africa, but have also shared their love for art and design for us all to appreciate. Smiles all round! *Bicycles available.*

Rooms: 5: 4 cottages: Berg One: twin; Berg Two: twin; Mountain View: double; Stone: double. All with en-s shower & loo. Also 1 apartment, Poolside (sleeps 4): king/twin with en-s shower + loo.
Price: Berg 1: R425 pp sharing; Berg 2: R700 pp sharing; Mountain View: R375 pp sharing; Stone: R550 pp sharing; Poolside: R350 pp sharing. Open between Nov 1st - April 30th.
Meals: Self-catering with option to order breakfast from restaurant.
Directions: N1 north towards Worcester. Take Sonstraal offramp at Huguenot Toll Plaza. Turn L at stop. Drive until next stop. R at stop on (R101) Du Toits Kloof Pass to Worcester. 3km from stop on R is Amberg.

Map Number: 4

Eensgevonden Vineyard Cottages

Sally and Douglas McDermott

Near Brandvlei Dam, Rawsonville/Breedekloof
Tel: 023-349-1490 Fax: 023-349-1490
Email: info@eensgevonden.co.za Web: www.eensgevonden.co.za
Cell: 082-829-8923

Often by driving that tiny bit further in South Africa you find something particularly special. Like Eensgevonden. Winding through chardonnay and merlot vineyards, I discovered this beautiful national monument, the oldest Cape Dutch farmhouse in the Breede River Valley and home to Sally and Doug. Under the shady fingers of a giant oak tree, planted nearly three centuries ago under orders of Cape Governor van der Stel, we sampled their unlabelled, excellent wine. The couple (aided by a staff of four) hand-tend and harvest their grapes, honey bees and organic vegetables and will enthusiastically show you around. The farm itself is part vineyard, part natural fynbos, and among 400ha of private nature reserve lies the heavenly, secluded, crystal clear mountain rock pool. If you can wrench yourself away (I couldn't) and up one of the well-marked trails across the rugged reserve, keep one eye peeled: klipspringer, honey-badger and 100 identified birds reside here, as does a recently-photographed leopard! A short hop from the farmstead leads you to three white-washed, spotlessly-clean self-catering cottages, surrounded by pebble-paved indigenous gardens. I adored Sunbird with its white linen, terracotta flooring, wood fire, vases of cut herbs and French windows revealing a wide, cushioned verandah with magnificent views... sundowner nirvana. Eensgevonden is a treasured Greenwood destination, offering a wilder, more genuine wine experience than is on offer in more touristy towns like Franschhoek and Stellenbosch.

Rooms: 3 self-catering cottages: 2 with queen in one room and 2 singles in other, 1 bathroom with bath and shower, and 1 with shower only; 3rd cottage with single with queen, 1 bathroom with shower.
Price: R350 - R550 pp sharing.
Meals: Self-catering. Breakfast in basket with home-made muesli & muffins is available as extra. Braai packs provided on request. Good restaurants nearby.
Directions: Between Rawsonville & Worcester, near the Brandvlei Dam. Full directions given on enquiry.

Fraai Uitzicht 1798

Karl and Sandra Papesch

Historic Wine and Guest Farm with Restaurant, Klaas Voogds East (Oos),
Robertson/Montagu
Tel: 023-626-6156 Fax: 086-662-5265
Email: info@fraaiuitzicht.com Web: www.fraaiuitzicht.com

'Fraai Uitzicht' means 'beautiful view' in Dutch - no idle promise as it turns out. The wine and guest farm, dating from the 1700s, is four kilometres up a gravel road in a cul-de-sac valley ringed by vertiginous mountains. Sitting on the stoep chatting to Karl and Sandra over an excellent espresso, I admired their tumbling water feature, which complements a sculpture-dotted dam buzzing with birdlife and draws your gaze to the blanket of peach, apricot and olive trees and vineyards all around. People come from far and wide for the award-winning a la carte restaurant, and the Wine & Dine Pairing menu option - including such delicacies as warthog carpaccio, perfectly matched with Fraai Uitzicht 1798 wines - is irresistible. Thankfully it's not far to the garden suites, upon which they have let loose their imagination: guests will find huge bathrooms and extra outside showers illuminated by colour-changing lights; one bed has been sunk down to catch views of the highest mountains; another protrudes jauntily from an angled alcove. A few renovated cottages take it easy in the garden, a couple with metre-thick walls and timber interiors; my favourite was the loft bedroom in the eaves. Make sure you take a peek at the wine cellar - guests have first option on the (uniquely) hand-made merlot. I can't count the number of recommendations we had pointing us here. *Restaurant closed to public June to August, but always open for guests.*

Rooms: 9: 4 cottages, 2 with 2 bedrooms (1 queen, 1 twin), 2 with 1 bedroom (king, extra-length); 5 suites, 4 king, 1 queen, all with air-con & en/s shower, some bath, some extra outdoor showers.
Price: Cottages: R850 – R950 pp sharing. Suites: R550 – R750 pp sharing. Singles on request.
Meals: Champagne breakfasts in the Fraai Uitzicht 1798 restaurant which is open for lunch & dinner on Wednesdays to Sundays, but serves dinner every night for residents.
Directions: On R60 between Robertson & Ashton. Approximately 5km from Ashton and 9km from Robertson, Klaas Voogds East turn-off, 4km on gravel road, turn-off to left.

Map Number: 4

Entry Number: 56

Olive Garden Country Lodge

Gina and Fernand Van Wassenhove

Klaasvoogds West, Robertson
Tel: 023-626-2028
Fax: 023-626-2028
Email:
info@olivegardencountrylodge
.com
Web:
www.olivegardencountrylodge
.com
Cell: 082-448-5393

Olive Garden Country Lodge, almost invisibly hidden in a dramatic sea of fynbos, is a destination for those who want to lose themselves in nature... but who don't want to compromise on luxury at the same time. This happy combination is typical of Gina and Fernand, serious back-to-nature, eco-conscious conservationists, passionate about the wild things that crowd round the lodge and especially the award-winning extra-virgin olive oil that they produce on the Estate (IGADI); but also epicurean in their tastes. If my room can be likened to a restaurant it would have a Michelin star - its open fire the oven, its beds a perfect soufflé perhaps. Why all the food analogies? Listen up, I'll only say this one hundred times – they are nothing short of magicians in the kitchen. I just would never have thought that the best sushi I would ever taste would be in a remote olive grove in the South African mountains – and made by a Belgian. Then came the meltingly tender pieces of home-reared mutton; and then more than one slice of fruit tartine. I think a few appreciative expletives may have escaped me at some point. Good job Olive Garden has its own hiking trail, winding its way through olive groves and up the mountain that cradles the lodge. Looking back across the view my mouth made a perfect 'o' – and this time it had nothing to do with food. Gina was right. This place is a slice of heaven. *Newly opened!: a new olive oil & taste room, positioned in the new factory of Igadi Ye-Olive. Olive tasting offered on the IGADI Estate.*

Rooms: 7: 4 queens; 1 family suite with 2 twins/queens & 2 bathrooms; 2 luxury honeymoon suites with king bed, jacuzzi, bath & shower.
Price: Rooms & family suite: R495 - R825 pp sharing. Honeymoon suites: R850 - R1,050 pp.
Meals: Full breakfast included. 3-course dinner R195 - R220 depending on ingredients; 4-course dinner R250 - R270 (not including wine). Wine & Dine Experience R325. Picnics on request.
Directions: From Robertson 9km towards Ashton, then turn L to Klaasvoodgs West (gravel road). At T-jct turn R then immediately L. Olive Garden on R.

Mallowdeen Gardens

Rita and Wim van de Sande
Klaasvoodgs West, Robertson
Tel: 023-626-5788 Fax: 086-509-6764
Email: info@mallowdeen.com Web: www.mallowdeen.com

Driving down a long avenue of olive trees coiled in sunshine, I could have been in the hot heart of southern Spain. Rita and Wim, emerging from their traditional Cape Dutch farmhouse, have the greenest of visions for their little bit of joy caught in the centre of a spectacular panorama of rolling vine-clothed hills and the distant Langeberge mountains. Young olive saplings, nurtured in their greenhouse, fan out from the house, interspersed with spiky cacti and aloes, papaya trees, vivid red canna flowers, an apricot orchard, vegetable gardens... and when the infant Japanese garden matures it will surely embody the peace and privacy you find here. Three square rondavels (yes, that's correct) face each other across a portly figure-of-eight swimming pool. One is a breakfast room where you sit at neat hand-made tables and chairs (if not outside under the lapa) or, more unusually, cupped inside giant, hand-shaped thrones. The other two are thatched, cool, earthy, and rather wonderful, with a full kitchen and a maze-like partition into the bathroom, where you'll find an ingenious sunken bath. Bird-lovers may prefer the more modern flat in the main house, which is close to the dam and its symphonic orchestra of birds. Faithful to their native Holland, Rita and Wim provide bicycles for guests to pedal out to the five wineries, two farm stalls and two good restaurants that lie within an easy 10 km radius. You won't even need the incentive of a discount to stay two nights or more.

Rooms: 3 units: 2 cottages (king/twin with full en-suite bathrooms), 1 flat (twin/king with en-suite shower).
Price: R425 - R580 pp sharing. Highly discounted rates for longer stays.
Meals: Full breakfast included. Full self-catering facilities and braais in each unit. Excellent restaurants nearby (and a free shuttle service provided to and fro if needed).
Directions: 7km from Robertson toward Ashton. Take Klaasvoodgs West turning on the left onto dirt road. Mallowdeen Gardens is 1.5km on the right.

Map Number: 4

Entry Number: 58

Orange Grove Farm

Carlos Araujo
Noree Robertson, Robertson
Tel: 023–626-6442 Fax: 023-626-5387
Email: carlos@ogf1812.co.za Web: www.orangegrovefarm.co.za
Cell: 076-718-0760

You're probably going to say "Wow!" a lot during your stay at Orange Grove. I know I did. I would recommend one thing on the drive up to the farm: if you can wangle it, try not to be the driver. As I sat behind the steering wheel, sun beating down, right arm hanging loosely out of the wound-down window, I felt my heart begin to race and my eyes widen to fit in the immense mountain-olive-river-vine panorama that surrounded me. It was clear I had struck gold. Greenwood Guides gold that is. Abundant tortoises roam free and wild amongst the vines here, so don't forget to keep an eye on the road. I saw no fewer than six on my approach. There's a choice of four delightful thatched cottages of varying sizes, all tucked into the mountainside and offering luxury, comfort and mod cons, including your very own pool. And there are thoughtful touches everywhere. Olive oil, vinegar, wine and toiletries (all farm produce) are provided as well as freshly-picked proteas (in season) and other flowers, which perfume the cottages outside and in. Carlos, a Portuguese diamond prospector - and a bit of a diamond himself - will bend over backwards to ensure that you have everything you need during your stay from guided mountain hikes, farm tours, delicious picnic or breakfast hampers, candlelit dinners under the southern stars… and, if you're lucky, stories so fascinating that Hollywood couldn't dream 'em up. "Are you afraid of heights?" asked Carlos, as we off-roaded 90 degrees vertically up and then down the mountains in his 4x4. My heart is still racing!

Rooms: 4 self-catering cottages: Wouterspan sleeps 6, 1 dble, 1 king, 1 qu; Mosesberg sleeps 2, 1 king; Longlands sleeps 4, 1 dble, 1 twin/king; Delportshoop sleeps 2, king/twin. All en-s, private pool & parking. (Delportshoop has access to a pool tho it's attached to a cottage).
Price: R780 - R3,000 per unit per night.
Meals: Breakfast/lunch baskets on request. Personal chef can be arranged in cottage or in mountains.
Directions: Take N1 Cape Town to Worcester, then R60 Worcester to Robertson approx 30km. L at Rooiberg Kelder. Over railway on tar rd to Noree sign to R. Turn R on tar rd, cross stop sign, Vink Rivier Primary on L. Rd will become gravel. Go straight until Orange Grove Farm.

Tierhoek Cottages

Bruce and Alison Gilson

Tierhoek Farm, Noree, Robertson
Tel: 023-626-1191 Fax: 023-626-1191
Email: gilson@barvallei.co.za Web: tierhoekcottages.co.za
Cell: 082-789-9205

Despite its name (tiger corner) the only big cats round here are the Cape mountain leopards. Bruce is sanguine: 'losing a few sheep is a small price to pay for keeping the baboons off my peaches." However, the Gilson family has yet to sight such a predator since relinquishing Boschendal Wine Estate for their organic fruit farm fourteen years ago. Standing on the stoep of Quince Cottage I admired the blossoming Noree Valley and McGregor/Greyton Mountains beyond. A plum spot indeed! Come nightfall, I was equally mesmerised by the silence and the stars. Accommodation is in one of four farm cottages, which nicely combine rusticity with modernity: an old wood-burning stove with potjie and kettle sits alongside the gas cooker for example. While braai enthusiasts face a tough choice between a Neanderthal fire pit and a 21st-century Weber! At first light, tucking into Alison's scrumptious quince jam and dried-fruit selection (help yourself and leave your money in the honesty bread bin), I observed the malachite sunbird performing a merry song and dance among agapanthus and surrounding fynbos. I contemplated the day ahead: whether to plunge into the private pool or dam, hike up the mountain or pick fresh fruit and veg (all you can eat in season). Or, back along the track, past resident donkeys Milly, Tilly and Violet, to sample the produce at Rooiberg Winery and their acclaimed Bodega de Vinho restaurant and bakery. Although, that would mean forsaking this heavenly hideaway… and I'd rather not.

Rooms: 5 cottages: 1 queen (en-s bath only); 1 queen & 1 twin (+ bunk-beds) with 2 bath & sh; 1 king (en-s bath & sh);1 queen & 1 twin (+ sofa bed) with shared bath & shower; 2 queens, both en-suite bath & sh, 1 twin with separate bath & sh.
Price: R650 per cottage (2 pax) - R 2,500 (10 pax).
Meals: Breakfast basket (self-cook) R65 pp; Dinner on request (self-cook) R100 pp.
Directions: On R60 betw' Robertson & Worcester take road to Noree. Follow tar rd for 6km. At stop by school continue straight onto dirt road. Go thro Orange Grove Farm and take L turn to Tierhoek.

Map Number: 4

Excelsior Manor Guesthouse

Freddie De Wet, Carin Visser
Excelsior Estate, Ashton
Tel: 023-615-2050
Email: guesthouse@excelsior.co.za Web: www.excelsior.co.za
Cell: 082-823-6703

Excelsior is a wine farm, so the grazing alpacas came as a bit of a surprise. After an exchange of confused staring, I double-checked my passport (to make sure I was in South Africa) and drove on past the winery and tasting rooms to the single-story Victorian farmhouse at the heart of the estate. In 1859 the De Wet family started clearing the land for pasturage and they're still here… obviously they finished clearing the land quite a while ago now and the views from the deck are long and soothing. In fact five generations of De Wet have successfully bred ostrich, race-winning horses and now Freddie and family produce citrus and delicious wine. Entering this feather palace is like stepping back to a more decadent era, with its original wooden floors, grand fireplaces, immaculate antiques and family portraits adorning the walls of the drawing and dining rooms. The bedrooms, all named after famous Excelsior-bred horses, come equipped with all you need, including incredibly comfortable beds and complimentary muscat. After a good cup of coffee with Carin, I was encouraged to stroll through the vineyards, sample the produce and even blend, bottle and cork my very own wine. Unfortunately there was no time for the cellar tour, a hike in the surrounding mountains or a swim in the pool. There was, however, plenty of time to pull up an armchair in front of the fire, pour myself a large glass of Excelsior merlot and put my feet up before three delicious courses of Carin's signature 'gourmet farmhouse'.

Rooms: 9: 1 super-king, 2 queens, 6 king/twins. All en-suite.
Price: R565 smaller room, R720 for a luxury room and R825 for a luxury suite.
Meals: Packed lunches can be organised. Three-course evening meal including wine R250 pp.
Directions: From the R60 Robertson to Ashton, take Bonnivale R317. Excelsior Estate is signed on the left.

Tanagra Wine and Guest Farm

Robert and Anette Rosenbach
Robertson Road, McGregor
Tel: 023-625-1780 Fax: 023-625-1847
Email: tanagra@tanagra-wines.co.za Web: www.tanagra-wines.co.za
Cell: 076-112-5490

On arrival at Tanagra I was met by Robert and Anette… and Jupp, their charismatic dog, who is bound to steal your heart. The first thing that caught my eye is the giant wild fig tree. Not only is it a natural air-conditioner, creating shade and a cool breeze in the burning summer months, but it also provides the name of the farm. Tanagra echoes the Khoisan word for 'shady place'. Robert and Anette have done an incredible job since moving here from Germany in 2009. Not only are they producing their own wine (the Heavenly Chaos is a must… and I don't mean unfermented grape juice!), but Robert also brought with him a German potstill resembling something of a spaceship. I couldn't wait to try his selection of grappas or the delicious lemon eau de vie, which is infused with the fruits from a tree in their garden. The surroundings are magnificent and since the property adjoins Vrolijkheid Nature Reserve (direct access from the farm) and is 'cushioned' between the Riviersonderend and the Langeberge mountain ranges, guests are spoilt for choice with walks, bird-watching or, in my case, a great view for sundowners. There are four country cottages dotted about for guaranteed privacy. But if you really want to get away from it all, stay in Hill Cottage. Just a short drive away through the vineyards, it boasts spectacular views of Tanagra and the McGregor Valley and even has its own plunge pool. *Stop Press! Ask about the brand-new, eco-friendly, rather spectacular architect's house, Faraway, which has just been created at the most solitary spot of the farm.*

Rooms: 5: 1 queen en-s bath & shower; 2 king en-s shower; 1 king en-s bath & sh'r; 1 king/twin sh'r only. All cottages have fully-equipped kitchenettes & are let on either self-catering or B&B basis.
Price: R300 - R375 pp self-catering; R450 - R475 B&B.
Meals: Full breakfast included for B&B guests. 5 mins' drive to McGregor with good restaurants; 1 country restaurant in walking distance.
Directions: Follow R60 to Robertson. When in Robertson turn R at main junction (La Verne Wine Boutique on R corner), direction McGregor. Continue for 14km. Tanagra is on R. No gravel rd driving required.

Map Number: 4

Natte Valleij

Charlene and Charles Milner

R44 between Stellenbosch and Paarl, Klapmuts
Tel: 021-875-5171
Email: milner@intekom.co.za Web: www.nattevalleij.co.za
Cell: 079-037-4860

Come and lose yourself in the depths of this wild and fecund garden - or do I mean jungle? Ancient trees such as the rare gingco (the oldest in South Africa, once thought extinct), several 200-year-old oaks and a wealth of growth besides keep the pool, 'moon gate' and handful of retired ponies secreted in their midst. Guests stay in the simple B&B room next to the main house, its verandah festooned with grandiflora, and eat breakfast in this most lovely of Cape Dutch homesteads (pictured above), built in 1775. If the weather's fine then you eat out on the patio under its cooling roof of vine. Or you can take one of the cottages lost down garden paths. Vineyard Cottage (pictured below), with direct access to the swimming pool, is the oldest building on the property, its original 1714 reed ceilings still intact, while Cellar Cottage is small, cute, rustic and perfect for couples. Charles and Charlene are charm personified, with the latest excitement in the shape of their son Alexander, a bright young thing whose wines are already topping the charts and who offers tours of the cellar and tastings in the new tasting room. Walks are in all directions up mountains and into surrounding vineyards. Or guests are welcome to enter next door's park, where wildebeest, eland, springbok, bontebok, kudu, oryx and zebra (among others) can be seen. Local bird-watching tours with Charles are a speciality. Well-positioned on the Stellenbosch and Paarl wine routes. *Self-catering available in the cottages.*

Rooms: 3: 1 B&B room, double with en/s bath; 2 cottages (self-catering): Cellar Cottage sleeps 2 (plus 2 kids' beds); Vineyard Cottage sleeps 6 (3 bedrooms and 2 bathrooms).
Price: B&B R340 - R380 pp sharing. Cellar Cottage: R560 - R650 per night/whole cottage; Vineyard: R600 - R1,400 per night/whole cottage.
Meals: Full breakfast included in B&B and an optional extra in cottages.
Directions: From Cape Town take N1 Exit 47. Turn right onto R44. Farm 4km on left.

Lekkerwijn

Simon Pickstone-Taylor and Ross Hutchison-Taylor

Groot Drakenstein, Franschhoek Road, Franschhoek/Groot Drakenstein
Tel: 021-874-1122 Fax: 021-874-1465
Email: lekkerwijn@new.co.za Web: www.lekkerwijn.com

Lekkerwijn (pronounced Lekkervain) is a 1790s Cape Dutch homestead with a grand Edwardian extension designed by Sir Herbert Baker, complete with curling chimneys and original coal fireplaces imported from England. Simon's family have lived here since the late 19th century when his great grand-father Harry Pickstone, pioneer of the fruit farming industry, bought the farm. You would probably have to pay to look round if Simon and his partner Ross didn't live in the grounds. You can tell when one family have lived in a grand house for generations - all the furniture, fittings and decoration look so at home. It positively creaks with family history. The house is now fully child-friendly, while large parts of the house have been kept completely quiet and free of them! There's a new play room and children's courtyard and rabbits, miniature goats and Transkei pigs happy to be petted and there are two family suites now. Susan has done a 'super-nanny course' and is now certified to look after people's kids, so babysitting is available in-house. My strongest impressions at Lekkerwijn are of the central courtyard with its orchid-lined gallery and cloister around an ancient pomegranate, the wood floors and yellowwood beams and the towering palms planted by Simon's great-grandfather, the informal taste of the nursery bedroom, a wonderful breakfast... and Simon and Ross who, together with their team, are so caring of their guests. *Simon's mother Wendy visits Lekkerwijn for returning guests.*

Rooms: 6: 5 double rooms (en-suite) plus a self-catering cottage.
Price: R290 - R780 pp sharing depending on season and room. Quotes for singles on request. Minimum stays of 2 nights at weekends (Fri-Sat or Sat-Sun). Offers on occasion.
Meals: Full breakfast incl' for B&B. Breakfast can be served in courtyard rather than dining room. Other meals by prior arrangement.
Directions: On R45 at intersection with R310 from Stellenbosch (after passing Boschendal), alongside the Allée Bleue entrance walls.

Map Number: 4

Entry Number: 64

Angala Boutique Hotel

Peter & Tisha Cunliffe

Klapmuts/Simondium Road (Off R45), entrance on "Vrede en Lust" Wine
Estate, Simondium, Franschhoek
Tel: 021–874-1366 Fax: 021-874-3918
Email: info@cathbert.co.za Web: www.cathbert.co.za

If warm hosting, gourmet food and eye-watering natural beauty in the heart of the winelands doesn't sound like your sort of thing then turn away now, because Angala Boutique Hotel is all of these things. Aubrey, ever the attentive host (and a connoisseur on local wineries), came out to greet me with great warmth. Now you don't have to so much as turn your head to see fabulous views over the vineyards, farmland and the dam that so immaculately mirrors the high Simonsberg Mountains. Local wooden carvings and Tisha's words of inspiration hide amongst the indigenous garden where you will also find the eco-pool that uses aquatic plants to filter the water. Peter and Tisha Cunliffe, the owners, have recently completely redesigned Angala in modern sophisticated French country style: restored French oak, natural fabrics, scatter cushions placed just so and delicate shades of grey. Much is new including the huge covered terraces outside the restaurant and the enlarged and upgraded luxury suites with their outdoor showers. Half an hour later the in-house chef was conjuring up the gourmet creations that are one of Angala's major draw cards – in fact, guests generally eschew Franschhoek's offerings in favour of their local, often organic, always home-made culinary compositions with fresh ingredients either home-grown or locally sourced. The best thing? You can spend the day hiking, touring, wine-tasting, or perhaps just drinking up the peace and a local vintage by the eco-pool... and not have to get in the car to find a great meal at the end of it all.

Rooms: 9: 2 Deluxe rooms, 4 luxury suites with outdoor sh'r, 1 executive suite, 1 x 2-bed luxury suite, all king-size/twin beds, en-s bath & shower, air-con.
Price: R2,200 - R3,700 per room/unit (sleeping 2 – 4 people). Rates for singles & special offers on request.
Meals: Full breakfast included in all room rates. Set menu 3-course dinner, R300 pp (Mon to Sat).
Directions: From CT take N1, take exit 47, R at end of ramp, over 1st set of lights, L at 2nd set of lights towards Franschhoek. Pass Backsberg Wine Estate. Just before T-jct R into gates of Vrede en Lust Wine Estate, & follow tar rd, following Cathbert signs for 2.5km.

Clementine Cottage

Malcolm and Jackie Buchanan

L'Avenir Farm, Green Valley Rd, Franschhoek
Tel: 021-876-3690 Fax: 021-876-3528
Email: lavenir@iafrica.com Web: www.clementinecottage.co.za

Running late with my mobile battery dead, I was touched to find Jef waiting expectantly for me just beyond the low-lying bridge that marks the entrance to L'Avenir Farm. He kindly guided me through the orchards of plums (no, not clementines) to meet Malcolm, who runs this 21-hectare, family-owned, working fruit farm. Jef, by the way, is a boerboel, as loyal to the Buchanans as Robin is to Batman – although after the birth of their daughter Sarah, Jef now has a rival for Malcolm and Jackie's affections. In retrospect, my timing was perfect: the sun was setting behind the mountains that frame the Franschhoek Valley and from the stoep of Clementine Cottage, looking out over the pool and the vineyard beyond, the sky was stained a deep red. The only sounds I could hear, as I enjoyed a most welcome cold beer with Malcolm and Jackie, were the frogs croaking contentedly in the dam that forms the centrepiece of the farm. If you find the pool too confining, a few lengths of this dam should satisfy any Tarzanesque impulses you may harbour. Being only a five-minute drive from the village (longer if the geese are crossing the road) I was able to enjoy a fine meal before returning to the biggest bed I've ever had the pleasure of sleeping in. Nicely done up in the original farm cottage style, Clementine Cottage has everything you could desire for a lazy break, from pool, braaing area and satellite TV to large, stylish en-suite bedrooms.

Rooms: 1 cottage: 1 double with en-suite bath and shower and 1 twin with en-suite bath and shower.
Price: 2 people sharing R650 pp per night, 3 people R600 pp, 4 people R550 pp. Minimum stay 2 nights. With regret no children 2-10 or pets.
Meals: Self-catering, but numerous restaurants nearby.
Directions: From Franschhoek Main Rd driving towards Franschhoek Monument turn R. Drive for 2km. Turn L up Green Valley Rd (Clementine Cottage signed). Turn L up 1st gravel rd (signed again). Drive over bdge onto L'Avenir, thro' orchards, pass shed on L, Cottage 150m further on R.

Map Number: 4

Entry Number: 66

Akademie Street Boutique Hotel and Guesthouses

Katherine and Arthur McWilliam Smith
5 Akademie Street, Franschhoek
Tel: 082-517-0405 Fax: 021-876-3293
Email: info@aka.co.za Web: www.aka.co.za
Cell: 082-517-0405

From the moment I arrived until my too-soon departure from this glorious patch of Franschhoek it felt like Katherine and I had met before, so easy and harmonious was my visit. Katherine's interest in life, literature and art is displayed throughout the house in every delicate and refined detail. There are two suites in the manor house, Twyfeling A and B. They are large and luxurious suites with paintings, gleaming bathrooms and underfloor heating. The parade of flowers and stepping-stones through citrus trees, fig trees and rose bushes lead to the garden cottages, which sit detached within the flower arrangements, opening out onto private stoeps, gardens and even swimming pools. Vreugde is a garden suite for two that has an alcove kitchenette and a sofa on the terrace. Oortuiging is a restored 1860s cottage that retains the old Cape style with antiques throughout. Uitsig is a stylish addition to the guesthouse, with a private balcony that looks out over the mountains. And Gelatenheid is a luxurious villa with, again, a private swimming pool and balcony. At the end of the balcony, suitably screened by treetops, is an outdoor, repro Victorian bathtub in which you can soak while gazing out at the mountain views. Inside, an expansive, open-plan studio is home for just two people (although there's space enough for a four-bed house), with high wooden ceilings and Venetian blinds… a decadent holiday home. As full as a full breakfast can be (including boerewors) is served under the vines at the homestead. Katherine and Arthur are two more reasons why you will love staying here.

Rooms: 6: 4 cottages & 2 bedroom suites: Oortuiging: 1 king/twin & 1 single, both en/s bath & sh'r; Vreugde, Gelatenheid and Uitsig: 1 king/twin, en/s bath & shower. Main House: Twyfeling A and B: 1 king en/s bath & sh'r.
Price: R2,100 – R4,600 per cottage.
Meals: Full breakfast included.
Directions: From Cape Town take N1 then R45. Akademie St is parallel to main road in Franschhoek, two streets up the hill.

The Explorers Club, The Library & The Map Room

Jo Sinfield

18 Wilhelmina Street (Explorers), Cabrière Street (Map Room), 16a
Wilhelmina Street (Library), Franschhoek
Tel: 021-876-4356 Email: bandoola@mweb.co.za
Web: www.explorersclub.co.za Cell: 072-464-1240

Jo sailed solo down Burma's Irrawaddy River and across the Andaman Sea before settling on a quiet mountain-ringed corner of Franschhoek and working magic with these three large and immensely stylish houses. Every piece of furniture is eye-arrestingly innovative. Check out The Explorers Club's dining table perched on wagon wheels and its contemporary-rustic rooms dotted with safari chairs and artefacts from far-off lands; or the Map Room's spiralling staircase and lampshades created from milk pails. The journey through either house is one of discovery. I say 'journey' because this really is a traveller's paradise: tales of exploration, ancient and modern, are illustrated by Jo's extensive map collection and in expressive African scenes by celebrated photographer Horst Klemm. The hub of The Explorers Club is the open-plan living area, with state-of-the-art kitchen, indoor braai, fireplace, air-con, DVD library, mod-cons *ad infinitum*, opening out to a stunning deck-bound lap pool. So simple, so clever, so very, very comfortable. The Library, with its ingenious use of space (rooms downstairs opening out on the pools, living area upstairs with those spectacular views) showcases yet more of Jo's creativity and panache and is perfect for the more sophisticated explorer. The Map Room's highlight is the upper terrace, which wraps its arms around the sociable kitchen and lounge, the perfect place to drink in mountain views along with a glass of wine or two. The only exploring I did when I stayed was a short walk to one of Franschhoek's many great restaurants. Otherwise I stayed right where I was….

Rooms: 3 houses. Explorers Club: 4 rooms (king, queen, twin, bunk + cot), all en-s except twin. Map Room: 2 rooms (king, tw), both en-s. Library: 3 rooms (all king/tw), all en-s. S/C facilities in all.
Price: R550 - R800 pp sharing (min rate per cottage applies). Laundry & cleaning service on request.
Meals: Full kitchen in each house. Meals, groceries, braai packs delivered on prior request. Many restaurants nearby.
Directions: From CT take Franschhoek Main Rd, after Post Office 1st R into Reservoir St, then 1st R into Wilhelmina, Library & Explorers on L. To Map Room turn L past Explorers into Daniel Hugo, then next L into Cabriere. Map Rm on LHS.

Map Number: 4   Entry Number: 68

Nooks Pied-à-terre

Lesley and Kevin Dennis
6 Haumann Street, Franschhoek
Tel: 021-876-3322 (Tom who is the local manager)
Email: nookspied-a-terre@hotmail.com Web: www.nookspied-a-terre.co.za
Cell: 079-955-3114

After years of work, Lesley and Kevin finished their perfect home only to be called away to America. Well, their loss is our gain... and boy is it a gain! To describe this as self-catering would not do it justice – this is a personal palace. The second I entered the double-height doors I could see that there were no design compromises: from the turquoise glow of the chef's fridge to the cobalt blue of the mosaicked pool, it is sensational throughout. The back wall of the main room slides away to create a fully open-plan route to your garden, complete with lemon trees, brightly-coloured walls, a delicious pool and an enticing-looking outdoor shower. But it was one of the mezzanine floors that caught my eye: an entertainment area with leather armchairs and every shiny bit of machinery a gadget magpie could ask for. The master bedroom, with its air-con/heating unit, electric-blue bed-head, en-suite underfloor-heated bathroom with free-standing bath and open-plan shower is truly, well... masterful. And that's not to say that the second bedroom is plain. With Chinese black-lacquered fitted wardrobes and opulent fur bedspread they're both idyllic spots to end a wine-soaked evening in SA's gourmet capital.

Rooms: 2: 1 king with en-suite full bathroom; 1 king with own adjacent bathroom & large shower.
Price: Winter (May to October 2013) from R1,450 per night (for 2 sharing) to R1,850 per night (for 4 sharing) for the villa. Summer (Nov 2012 to April 2013) from R1,850 per night (for 2 sharing) to R2,500 per night (for 4 sharing) for the villa.
Meals: Self-catering only.
Directions: From Paarl/Stellenbosch, as you enter Franschhoek, take second turn on left into Uitkyk St (signed to Chamonix). Nooks Pied-à-terre is on the left on the corner of Haumann St & Uitkyk.

Riverside Cottages at La Bourgogne Farm

George Mayer
La Bourgogne Farm, Franschhoek
Tel: 021 876 3245 Fax: 086 542 3615
Email: info@labourgogne.co.za Web: www.labourgogne.co.za
Cell: 083 441 8272

Loesje (the manager) caught me struggling to align my car within reaching distance of the bell (I suppose I could have got out!). "Follow me, I'll take you straight to the guest entrance", so along the gravel drive and through the blossoming pear orchard we went. I was in a fairy-tale. The six very comfortable self-catering cottages are converted labourers' houses on La Bourgogne farm and date back to 1952. The farm is one of the oldest fruit farms in the valley, producing a farm stall of fruit, olives and grapes from the twenty-five-year-old vines from which Progeny Wines are made. "Come over for a wine-tasting when you're ready". I had never unpacked so quickly. Over the wooden suspension bridge, crossing the stream (a tributary of the Franschhoek River), signs guided me in to the wine cellar at the back of the original farmhouse. After browsing the wine list and admiring the hand-stacked wine bottles that cover the cellar walls, I was led to the stoep, joined by Joey and Sasha, the farm's affectionate St Bernard and border collie respectively. Soaking up the warmth of the evening sun, my thoughts wandered down the undulating lawn, lined with 150-year-old oaks, my eyes peeled for the resident spotted eagle owl. Progeny Wines are so-called in deference to George's children and 'Blossom', named after his youngest daughter, was my personal favourite, served with fresh bread and La Bourgogne's olive oil. I skipped (merrily) back to Plum Cottage with my bottle of choice, pausing en route to absorb the spectacular view of the Middagkrans Mountains. My fairy-tale on La Bourgogne only ended when I left.

Rooms: 6 cottages: 4 with 1 bedroom (sleeps two); 2 with 2 bedrooms (sleeps 4). All with en-suite showers.
Price: One-bedroom cottage: R650 - R850 per night. 2-bedroom cottage: R1,100 - R1,300 pn.
Meals: Self-catering.
Directions: From Cape town (on the R45) thro Franschhoek. Turn R at T-Jct (Huguenot Monument in front). Carry on 1.5km (Excelsior road) to La Bourgogne Farm 100m after gate, see Riverside Cottages gate on RHS. Buzz 1/2/3 at gate.

Map Number: 4

Entry Number: 70

The Beautiful South Guest House

Katarina and Peter Stigsson
4 Hospital St, Stellenbosch
Tel: 021-883-8171
Email: enjoy@thebeautifulsouthguesthouse.com
Web: www.thebeautifulsouthguesthouse.com

Katarina and Peter never do anything in half, or even three-quarter, measure. Hearing them chat about their hobbies was enough to make me want to lie down… or was it the sight of the sun-beds by the pool? Since flying in from Sweden they have poured endless energy and enthusiasm into making The Beautiful South the bright, modern, luxurious guesthouse that it is. On the outside, it is quaintly thatched and whitewashed, with Cape-Dutch-style gables and wooden windows. The surrounding garden with its mature trees and large pool is directly accessible from each of the bedrooms. On the inside, however, it's far from traditional. Katarina's inventive ideas in the bedrooms work a treat, such as the smooth pebbles in the bathroom and the old window-frame reborn as a table. The colours in the 'Austin Powers' room, complete with framed retro shirt and gigantic green leaf over the bed, hit you like a sensory bomb; 'Desert Rose' is full of romance, with a deep egg bath in the room; 'Sunrise' gulps in views of the Stellenbosch mountains; 'Sunset' has a terrace for… well, watching the sun set. They're up to their ears in community projects, supporting a crèche and football team in the local township, yet they still find time to seek out (and tell you about) the best spots in the area. 'Catch of the Day' appears at breakfast, the coffee is great and the staff are delightful. Hosting comes only too naturally to Katarina and Peter, which is presumably why they also run the Beautiful West guesthouse in Somerset West.

Rooms: 9: 7 doubles, 6 with en-suite bath or shower, 1 with private shower room opposite; 2 family suites with en-suite bath or shower.
Price: R320 - R650 pp sharing.
Meals: Breakfast included in rate with new 'special' every morning.
Directions: From N1 or N2 take turn-off to Stellenbosch. Entering Stellenbosch turn into Merriman St. After white pedestrian bridge 2nd L into Bosman, 1st R into Soete Weide, L into Hospital St. GPS: Longitude 18. 870177 Latitude 34. 929296

Mitre's Edge

Bernard and Lola Nicholls

R44 between Stellenbosch and Paarl, Klapmuts
Tel: 021-875-5960 Fax: 021-875-5965
Email: info@mitres-edge.co.za Web: www.mitres-edge.co.za
Cell: 082-400-1092 or 072-266-2990

The sea of welcoming dogs that flowed around my feet as I got out of the car made progress slow, but I managed to wade to the fine front door of Mitre's Edge, HQ for a small but busy vineyard. Bernard and Lola were in the middle of shipping some of their rosé to a thirsty recipient in Europe. "We're a hands-on and hand-crafted set-up here," Bernard reassured me, as he showed me the atmospheric little cellar and gleaming drawing room where they sometimes hold intimate meals and tastings. Well, the same can be said for the small self-catering cottage (breakfast included) at the top of the garden just opposite a home gym. The sunshine followed us in through the generous windows and glass door, lighting up an open-plan kitchen and living room. The main feature – a dark, wooden dining table – doubles as a pool table. Bookshelves are packed with books, art and board games and a flash of tropical colour emanates from the fish tank. The bedroom (beyond the sauna, obviously) is unfussy and comfortable, with proud mahogany furniture on a sisal carpet. Outside, the stoep (with a pizza oven the size of Naples, a braai, large table and Jacuzzi – you're welcome to invite friends round, whether it's you or Lola in charge of the food) leads on to the swimming pool, which in turn leads on to the mountains, with resilient snow glinting on their summits. I can see why Angela the Vietnamese pot-bellied pig seems so content to call this place home – I only wish I could. *Wine tours and tastings are available.*

Rooms: 1 self-catering cottage with one bedroom. 1 queen-size bed and separate bathroom.
Price: R1,250 - R1,450 for the whole unit. R250 for the sleeper-couch.
Meals: Full breakfast included. Other/special meals by arrangement.
Directions: See website. Detailed directions can be emailed upon request.

Plumbago Cottage

Nathalie Ammann

Auberge Rozendal Winefarm, Omega Street, Stellenbosch
Tel: 021-887-5612 Fax: 086-612-90-46
Email: info@plumbagocottage.co.za Web: www.plumbagocottage.co.za
Cell: 083-261-9119

If cottages attended parties (and Stellenbosch was the venue), Plumbago would be the beautiful wallflower that stands on the periphery, calm and serene, unaffected by the attention-seeking masses and uninterested in following the crowd. The cottage itself sits on a small farm, Rozendal, which is found on the outer Stellenbosch boundary. It is farmed on organic and bio-dynamic principles and produces award-winning vinegar (delicious on freshly-picked salad and asparagus from the farm veggie patch). Steps, lined with blooming plant pots, lead up to the front door which opens straight into the fully-equipped, slate-tiled kitchen… wine and vinegar included in the price. The large sitting room is blessed with unthinkably lofty ceilings and I wondered how those three oriental lanterns ever got up there. There's a well-stocked open fire, fragrant flowers in abundance throughout the cottage and Natalie's insect thesis (from her natural sciences degree) hangs proudly on the west wall. Beyond the double doors there's a secluded garden, rural pastures and the neighbouring Simonsberg Mountains, which can also be seen from the double bed in the master bedroom… as can the sunrise if you wake that early. Rozendal Farm - and therefore Plumbago Cottage – is ideally positioned. Turn right out of Omega Drive and within moments the delights of Stellenbosch can be explored: bookshops, craft markets, restaurants, pubs, cafés and delis. If you turn left you'll soon be winding your way through the wooded ravines of the Jonkershoek Valley. After a day out and about you can head home to farmyard tweets and snorts, some meditation, a distant view of Table Mountain… perhaps a sauna?

Rooms: 2: 1 double & 1 twin. Separate dble sh'r & sep' toilet. With kitchen, lounge, sauna & private gardens.
Price: 2 people sharing R450 pp per night; 3 people R350 pp pn; 4 people R300 pp pn. Singles on request.
Meals: Breakfast at lodge optional.
Directions: From CT airport, take N2 for Somerset-West. Exit 33 to Stellenbosch. At junction turn R. After train station L slide into Adam Tas Rd, then 2nd lights R into Merriman Ave. Thro 3 sets of lights, over roundabout, 2km L into Omega St, Rozendal at end.

WedgeView Country House & Spa

Dave & Anouk Bakker
Bonniemile, Vlottenburg, Stellenbosch
Tel: 021-881-3525 Fax: 021-881-3539
Email: info@wedgeview.co.za Web: www.wedgeview.co.za
Cell: 079-526-8093

I was sitting on a rose-wrapped, vineyard-facing stoep, inhaling the Stellenbosch dusk and generally savouring a purple moment with a glass of Zonneweelde chardonnay, when I received a welcome visit from Anouk and three tiny barefoot children intent on handing me a wriggling brown ball of hair. After much cooing over the ridgeback pup, Anouk wheeled her sprites away through multi-coloured gardens to bed next door, leaving me with Dave, a former fine food importer and Holland cricket captain, now a family man and luxury Winelands guest-house proprietor. We were joined at the al fresco dining table by other WedgeView guests (as is the friendly tradition here) and we all tucked into some expertly-crafted menu of squid ink risotto, gemsbok fillet and delicate strawberry blancmange. Dave - who brought his clan here in 2007 - told me things weren't always so decadent and chilled out. Life heated up when a fire devastated WedgeView in 2010, but Dave, the eternal optimist, took this as a sign to do some renovating. So, aromatic thatched roofs were re-twigged; bathrooms received deep tubs and showers big enough to do cartwheels in; a brand new spa cottage was born. At the head of the pool sits the latest addition, the WedgeView lapa, which on this occasion is a raised deck with a thatched roof, bar, pool table and huge sofas, perfect for watching the sun go down over the neighbouring vineyard.

Rooms: 13: 5 Deluxe & 5 Superior Rooms; 1 Honeymoon Suite with adjoining door to Deluxe Rm to form Family Suite (sleeps 4 adults, or 2 adults & max 3 kids); Exec' Honeymoon Suite; Garden Family Suite (sleeps 4).
Price: R550 - R1,095 pp sharing. Exec' Honeymoon Suite: R2,195 – R2,995; Garden Family Suite (sleeps 4): R2,195 – R3,295; Family unit R2,750 - R4,195 for whole unit.
Meals: Full breakfast included. Lunch, picnic baskets and 3-course gourmet dinners available on request.
Directions: On N2 towards Somerset West take R300 towards Kuilsriver. R onto M12 (Polkadraai Rd) towards Stellenbosch. Thro' 5 lights, take WedgeView & Nassau turning L onto Bonniemile. L into WedgeView Dr.

Longfield

Pieter and Nini Bairnsfather Cloete

Eikendal Rd, off R44, Somerset West/Stellenbosch
Tel: 021-855-4224
Email: ninicloete@iafrica.com Web: www.longfield.co.za
Cell: 082-365-7554

Perched on the foothills of the dramatic Helderberg mountains, Longfield occupies a truly sensational vantage that drifts across the Winelands and over to the very tip of False Bay at Cape Point. Dreamy by day and by night (when Cape Town's lights put on their glitzy show), there are three cottages from which to enjoy the view. All are fresh, breezy and decorated in a relaxed country-house style and many of the furnishings are rare, early-Cape family heirlooms. This is luxury self-catering. Comfy beds are made up with the highest-quality, hand-embroidered linen and there are spoiling lotions in the pretty bathrooms and coffee-table books on SA wine, flora and fauna etc and African *objets d'art* in the cosy living areas with a wood-burner for good measure. Each has its private patio or lawn and fridges and cupboards are re-stocked each day with breakfast materials to help yourself to. You'll probably want to disappear into your own world here, but Nini and Pieter, who live on the mountain with you, are the nicest people you could wish to meet. Formerly wine-farmers themselves, they will happily point you in the right direction for good wineries, as well as gardens, restaurants and golf courses, all invariably within easy striking distance. But it's quite possible you won't want to go anywhere, what with the almond and olive trees (they also bottle their own olives and press their own oil) and the immense pool in the rolling hills of their garden. This is a wonderfully secluded spot, serene and calm and ideally placed for many of the Cape's attractions.

Rooms: 3 cottages: 2 with twin beds, 1 with king-size bed, all with bath and separate shower.
Price: R600 to R800 per person per day sharing. Single supplement by arrangement.
Meals: Continental breakfast on request.
Directions: From CT take N2 past the airport, take exit 43 Broadway Bvd. Left at lights. From the next lights 6.3km exactly, turn right into Eikendal Rd. Follow up road, jink left onto tarmac strip and follow to top and Longfield House.

Blaauwheim Guest House

Johan and Jo-Anne Blaauw

22 Bakkerskloof Road, Jonkershoogte, Somerset West
Tel: 021-855-0243 Fax: 021-855-0243
Email: blaauwheim@telkomsa.net Web: www.blaauwheim.co.za

Make no mistake: *this* is the place to experience genuine Afrikaans hospitality. After a military career and time in Kenya as defence attaché, Johan retired with Jo-Anne to the tranquillity of Somerset West having gained much experience in entertaining, a reputation for home-made boerewors and an African Grey parrot. Over a glass of Muscatel, with the indoor braai emanating delicious aromas behind me, I surveyed the place at leisure... and found it refined, generous and thoroughly magnificent. Every single artwork is original South African. Furniture is custom-made from blackwood and beautifully upholstered. The garden is an anthology of yellowwood trees, clivias, cycads so rare they're micro-chipped, with railway sleepers leading to dreamy hidden corners. Behind the house, a solar-heated plunge pool, huge braai and breakfast table. Did I say breakfast? Expect a Boer breakfast, not a puny full English version. The same goes for dinner if you request it – perhaps eland fillet or apricot-basted snoek with grape jam. Sunlight streams into the two large suites, Chardonnay and Pinotage, the latter swathed in blood-red furnishings, the former in softer blue and gold. Both are utterly luxurious with bespoke velvet couches, the best crystal glasses, gas and electric oven, a dishwasher behind smart mahogany cupboards, gleaming bathrooms with slinky sinks, vast beds and silk duvets. Shiraz, a double/twin room, is for those who require a little less space than the suites - although if you include the private patio and braai there's not actually much difference!

Rooms: 3: 2 luxury suites, super-king, extra-length or twins, en-s bath & shr, lounge with guest loo, fully-equipped kitchen; 1 dble/twin en-s bath & shr, private patio & braai.
Price: Suites, R750 - R850 pp for 2 sharing. Singles R1,050 - R1,200. Shiraz, R650 - R750 pp for 2 sharing. Singles R950 - R1,050.
Meals: Full breakfast incl'. Other meals & braais by arrangement (SA cooking). Self-catering in suites available.
Directions: From CT, N2 to Somerset West, exit 43 onto R44 towds Stellenbosch. Pass Lord Charles Hotel, R44 up hill. 500m past bdge, L to Helderberg Village. At T-jct, L into Bakkerskloof Rd. 3rd hse on L. GPS: S 34,03,05, E 18,49,35

Seringa House

Peter and Lydia Hauspie
8 Leylands Lane, Somerset West
Tel: 021-855-2394 Fax: 021-855-2394
Email: seringahouse@gmail.com
Cell: 083-409-2722

The fact that Seringa House is perched on the slopes of Helderberg mountain overlooking Gordon's Bay and the Hottentots Holland would usually be enough on its own to attract a steady flow of guests. But the picturesque setting plays second fiddle to Seringa's most valuable asset... its hosts. Peter (an accomplished architect) and Lydia (a geologist recently returned from a Congo gold exploration adventure!) came on holiday to South Africa and within weeks they were building a home here. Drawing inspiration from their extensive travels in Africa's remotest corners and from their passion for sustainable building techniques, first they built a home, then a family (twin girls) and finally, 15 years later, on their adjoining plot, Seringa House. No two rooms are the same and the twins have given them names like Tinga Tinga, Tulip, Sunset or Sahara reflecting their individual feel. Each bathroom is a unique discovery of mosaics, pebbles or recycled tiles. Speaking of recycled, your bath and shower water is processed through a grey-water system and used to irrigate the gardens. Peter's ability to incorporate sustainable design sees skylights, solar geysers, airflow showers and many other initiatives included to reduce their/your impact on the environment. Whether you book the downstairs apartment or the more conventional double en-suite options, flexibility is key as you can self-cater using the entertainer's dream kitchen full of mod-cons; or request a B&B arrangement; or even go DBB and allow Peter to wave his magic spatula and prove he is as much a maestro in the kitchen as he is behind his drawing board.

Rooms: 6: 1 apartment with 1 double with en-suite shower and 1 queen and single with en-suite shower; 1 king; 2 queens, 1 double; 2 twins, all with en-suite bath and shower.
Price: R450 - R650 pp sharing.
Meals: Self-catering. Meals on request.
Directions: From Cape Town take Broadway R44 exit off N2, head towards Stellenbosch & turn R at 1st lights, L at next lights into Helderberg College Rd, cross 3 stop streets, after 3rd stop take 2nd R, then 1st L, then 1st R into Leylands Lane.

Entry Number: 77   Map Number: 4

The Vintner's Loft

André and Rhona Liebenberg
Romond Vineyards, Klein Helderberg Road, Somerset West
Tel: 021-855-4566 Fax: 012-855-0428
Email: accommodation@romond.co.za Web: www.romondvineyards.co.za
Cell: 082-445-8838

Gargoyles are watching me. Crouched on reddening wine barrels, they follow as André leads me through his rustic wine cellar, under gothic chandeliers, into a theatrical tasting-room resembling the Crystal Maze's Medieval Zone. Faint orchestral melodies mingle with crackling fire, the aural mélange completed by the de-corking of Romond's Cabernet Franc Rebus. Phew, a screw-top would really have spoiled the effect. "Those," says André, indicating the goblin props in his soothing, witty timbre, "are my other hat." Where primary headgear (wine-maker, film director) collide, André's third hat (guesthouse proprietor) is born. Above the warehouse, up terracotta steps, is the loft, a wide, open, exposed-brick apartment brimming with tokens, trinkets and treasures narrating André and his wife Rhona's traveller days. Nepalese bedspreads adorn a robust, elbow-high master bed, itself constructed from old cellar doors; red silk Indian curtains hang to blackwood floors partially hidden by colourful chunky rugs; heavy antique trunks brim with games to keep little people happy in the absence of telly. I long to lie among the rubber ducks in the claw-footed bedroom bath, to explore Romond's bookshelves in the open-plan living space, to rustle up a rustic feast in the industrial kitchen before a game of pétanque on the court outside. Truthfully? I want to dangle a hosepipe through the internal window into a barrel, bagsy the inviting rocking chair and watch the vines dancing outside my door.

Rooms: 1 loft apartment: 1 king with full en-suite, 1 double with separate bathroom.
Price: R1,800 for entire loft, max 4 pax.
Meals: Self-catering, but if you're lucky you may find a few "yummy things" in the fridge when you arrive...
Directions: From Cape Town take N2 towards Somerset West. Turn off at exit 43 and left onto R44 at lights. Look for Romond sign, 4km from Lord Charles Hotel. Turn into Klein Helderberg Road and follow signs through vineyards.

Map Number: 4

Entry Number: 78

Fig Tree Cottage

Jillian Paynter and Alan Paine
40 Vigne Lane, Greyton
Tel: 028-254-9353 Fax: 028-254-9353
Email: jgpaynter@icon.co.za
Cell: 072-341-8061

Vigne Lane is surely the prettiest and leafiest street in the historic village of Greyton. I admired all the cottages with their proud blossoming gardens standing behind whitewashed walls, before finally arriving at my destination, Fig Tree Cottage. Grapevines and wisteria were wrapped around the front stoep, roses below jostling for sunlight... a perfect picture. I was warmly greeted by Jillian, South African born, and Alan, a fellow Englishman. Over a cup of tea and a cookie or two, I heard the tale of Fig Tree Cottage. In the mid-19th century the cottage was inhabited by farm labourers as the village began its life as a collection of farms. The tranquillity and charm of the town attracted the owners to Greyton and for many years the cottage served as their weekend home. Recently, with Alan's architectural eye and Jillian's artistry as an interior designer, the couple have combined their talents and breathed new life and warmth into the cottage, which is filled with original paintings and masses of books and artifacts. After a stroll around the exuberant garden, with its spectacular mountain views, - this is where Jill and Alan had their wedding reception - I continued to one of the many local restaurants for an early supper, returning by moonlight to enjoy the fire, kindly lit on my arrival, and to admire the work of art that is Fig Tree Cottage. *Greyton is just an hour and a half from Cape Town.*

Rooms: 1 cottage: 1 king/twin with en-suite shower over bath + outdoor hot & cold shower; 1 queen with en-suite shower.
Price: R1,200 per night for whole cottage for 2 people; R1,500 per night for up to 4 people. Min 2 nights. Midweek (Mon-Thurs) special: R1,000 per night. EFT payments accepted. No credit cards.
Meals: Self-catering. Fully-equipped kitchen and braai.
Directions: From Cape Town: Take N2 towards Caledon. Just before Caledon turn L onto Greyton Road (R406). After approx 30km, you will reach Greyton. Turn R at 2nd stop street into Botha St. Turn immediately R into Vigne Lane. FTC is no. 40 on LHS.

Rouxwil Country House

Thys and O'nel Roux
Caledon
Tel: 028-215-8922 Fax: 0866-153-230
Email: rouxwil@intekom.co.za Web: www.rouxwil.co.za
Cell: 082-575-6612

Rouxwil is perfectly positioned in the middle of nowhere. I say 'perfectly' because nowhere happens to be in the middle of everywhere. You couldn't wish for a better base from which to explore the region, with Hermanus, the Winelands, Greyton and Cape Agulhas all less than an hour away. The farmhouse is always buzzing with its farm kitchen, lounge with open fireplace and outside braai area. This is where Thys holds sway, whether grilling oryx sirloins over open coals or dispensing encyclopaedic advice on the surrounding towns' best-kept secrets (his is a brain worth picking). Since the closest restaurant is thirty kilometres away, it is an added blessing that food is one of O'nel's great talents. She likes her guests to taste traditional recipes, but regularly throws a wild-card onto her menu… springbok shanks, for example. And, having voted Rouxwil 'South Africa's best farm accommodation in 2010, 2011 and 2012' her guests seem to approve. The rooms are certainly not what you would expect on a wheat and sheep farm. No rusted old plumbing or creaking termite-eaten floorboards here. Rather slate tiles, stainless-steel power-showers and plenty of king-size comfort. Sliding doors open onto gardens of cycads, roses and lavender, zebras, antelope and blue cranes. Come to think of it, with a pool to cool off in, farm tours and a river raft for sundowners, why would you want to leave Rouxwil at all? But apart from the views, food, river and wildlife, what makes this place an essential GG entry are the two charming people at the helm.

Rooms: 4: all doubles with en-suite bath and shower.
Price: R550 - R695 pp sharing. Free farm tour for those staying 2 nights or more.
Meals: Full breakfast included. Dinner R215.
Directions: From Cape Town take N2, and 8km beyond Botriver on N2, take left turn on to the Villiersdorp R43. After 14km turn right off to Greyton and Helderstroom. Follow road for 1km, Rouxwil Country House signposted.

Map Number: 4

Entry Number: 80

Beaumont Wine Estate

Jayne and Ariane Beaumont
Compagnes Drift Farm, Bot River
Tel: 028-284-9194 (office), 028-284-9370 (home) Fax: 028-284-9733
Email: info@beaumont.co.za Web: www.beaumont.co.za
Cell: 082-982-2300

Jayne's guests stay in the charming buildings of an 18th-century former mill house and wagon shed, today snug with wood-burning heaters, but left as far as comfortably possible as they were, with original fireplaces in kitchens and hand-hewn, yellowwood beamed ceilings. Outside, you can sit around an old mill stone and admire the antediluvian water wheel, which after restoration works as it once used to and serves as a living museum. It's also worthy of appreciation from the inside. The willow-shaded jetty on the farm lake offers one of the Western Cape's prettiest settings for sundowners and wheatland views. While Jayne and her family busy themselves producing their annual 150,000-odd bottles of wine, you can swim in the informal swimming pool (the lake) under the weeping willows where the weaver-birds make their nests; or you can meander through the flower-filled garden and roam about on their land – they own half a mountain! To find horses and horse-riding you only have to trot down the road. You can even put the idea of cooking on the backburner and instead arrange to have home-cooked meals delivered to you and wine-taste in the cellar flanked by an old wine press. The estate is a proud member of an exciting bio-diversity wine route which includes tours, tastings, hiking and mountain-bike trails (www.greenmountain.co.za & www.greenmountaintrails.co.za). Well worth spending several nights here. *There are a number of venues within the grounds ideal for weddings and small functions.*

Rooms: 2 self-catering cottages. Mill House has 2 bedrooms (plus 2 extra can sleep in living room); Pepper Tree has 1 double (again 2 extras possible).
Price: Low season: R300 - R450 pp sharing for 2, extra people R150 - R250 pp. High season: flat rate R900 - R1,400 per cottage.
Meals: Self-catering. Breakfast and home-cooked meals by arrangement. All meals are self-served.
Directions: From N2 take exit 92, sign-posted to Bot River. Follow signs to Bot River. Beaumont Wine Estate is signed off to R-hand side. Map can be faxed.

Barton Villas

Peter Neill

R43 Hermanus Rd, Botriver
Tel: UK +44 (0) 1489-878-673; SA +27 (0) 28-284-9283
Fax: UK +44 (0) 1489-878-715; SA +27 (0) 28-284-9776
Email: info@bartonvineyards.co.za Web: www.bartonvineyards.co.za
Cell: 083-327-3887

In the middle of the Kogel National Park, up a winding avenue of pine trees, I finally found three beautifully-designed, Tuscan-style villas scattered across the raised valley of a working farm. As we climbed the track and stood under the arches the beam of my gaze shot straight out of the window and spread across the vineyards and over the sprawling mountains beyond. The views are spectacular, a rolling canvas of working fields, rows of lavender and fynbos-clad mountains which wraps right around you. Built into and around the rocks the villas all have wide verandahs on which to conduct your feasts and to soak up the views. It's no secret Peter built them to stay in himself and consequently no expense has been spared. Notably the bedding, shipped straight in from The White Company because no other duvets would do! With huge sweeping lounges, open-plan kitchens, long tables, big fireplaces and an emphasis on natural materials, the villas are immaculately finished throughout. Peter has a soft spot for Persian carpets bringing colour and warmth to the airy rooms and I'm told a new one sneaks in on his every visit. With spa baths and swimming pools built into the rocks it's easy to forget this is a working farm abundant with wildlife. Don't miss the opportunity to get involved, especially with the wine grown on the farm. I imagined inviting everyone I knew to come for a week of long sunset dinners, lazy days of swimming, riding, tennis, golf, hiking and landscape painting….

Rooms: 3 villas: Heron, 3 doubles and 1 twin, indoor swimming pool; Blue Crane, 2 doubles, 1 twin; Plover, 3 doubles; all have en-suite bathrooms, outdoor pools, outdoor spa baths, DSTV & wifi.
Price: 15th Dec-15th Jan R4,500 per villa per night; Nov, Dec, Jan, Feb, March, April R3,250; May, Sept & Oct R2,250; June, July & Aug R1,900.
Meals: Self-catering.
Directions: From Cape Town take N2 to Somerset West & Caledon. Follow exit 90 for Hermanus, Barton Vineyards on R43 Botriver to Hermanus Rd, 100m after & on same side as Shell petrol station.

Map Number: 4

Porcupine Hills Guest Farm

Tony & Cha Davenport
Van der Stel Pass, Botriver/Viliersdorp
Tel: 028-284-9066
Email: info@porcupinehills.co.za Web: www.porcupinehills.co.za
Cell: 074-106-7972

The closer you get to Porcupine Hills the quicker your worries dissolve. In fact, by the time I arrived I had barely a care in the world. Tony, Cha and family have injected life and energy into the farm that's hard to miss: the olive grove has been nurtured, the renosterbos is strong and the birdlife abundant. On the action side of the farm – wifi, phone signal – there are two fabulous homes, the Farm House and the Hill House. On the nature side – no signal! – is idyllic River Cottage. We were staying in the sumptuous Hill House, where the view from the deck is quite simply awe-inspiring. The house has a large lounge-cum-dining room, farmhouse kitchen, pool and three en-suite bathrooms, two with outdoor showers. There's also a quaint little cottage attached that you can use as an extra bedroom. Sitting out on the shaded deck we chatted over drinks and olives – grown on the farm – about ways of utilizing the two rivers running through the farm, how to eat the artichokes we'd just picked, and what meaning Balthazar – a fila Braziliero (which is a dog!) - was trying to convey with his grooving in the bamboo. Tony pointed skyward in the direction of the mountains on the other side of the valley. The two resident black eagles with their soon-to-depart juvenile were circling above. No doubt the young eagle didn't want to leave this magical place… and neither did I.

Rooms: 3: Hill House, 3 en-suite rooms + Cottage (sleeps 2); Farmhouse, sleeps 6; Riverside Cottage, sleeps 6.
Price: R400 - R600.
Meals: Self-catering. Breakfast baskets available with prior arrangement.
Directions: From N2 take Grabouw turn-off. Go through Grabouw & take R321 towards Villiersdorp/Franschoek. After 22.5km turn R onto (tar/gravel) road towards Botriver. Farm 11km on Left. See website for alternative routes.

The Barnacle

Jenny Berrisford

573 Anne Rd, Pringle Bay
Tel: 028-273-8343
Email: barnacle@maxitec.co.za Web: www.barnacle.co.za
Cell: 082-925-7500

Come and explore Jenny's seaside idyll. Several natural environments collide right outside the cottage. From the private viewing deck – with views all the way to Cape Point – you walk down to a private lawny enclave in the marsh reeds where narrow paths lead you to the river and beach. The sea is a hundred yards of the whitest, finest sand to your left; beyond the river, fynbos and milkwood 'forest' climb the mountain, a nature reserve. Situated on the lagoon, Barnacle is perfect for families with young children… but you don't have to be a kid to love this. The small, enclosed area of the garden around the cottage has two gates. The main one is 3 metres wide and when open the cottage garden flows into the rest of the garden and then on down the path to the lagoon through the marsh reeds. Guests can make use of tables and chairs dotted about the main garden and under the trees. There are whales in the ocean (during season), otters in the river, baboons on the mountain, estuarine and fynbos birds aplenty… and Jenny is a horticultural expert in one of the world's most amazing natural gardens. The open-plan cottage is simple, rustic and country-cosy, with an elegant solid brass bed and a separate sleeping alcove ideal for accommodating smaller members of the family; the kitchenette is equipped with all you need and the sitting area, with its own fireplace, opens out to the paved braai courtyard, the garden and the lagoon beyond. The whole place is super-relaxed… a hidden gem. *Jenny has a canoe to take out on the river. This area has been proclaimed a world biosphere reserve.*

Rooms: 1 cottage: sleeping 4 with 1 double, en-suite shower, kitchen/dining area and 2 singles.
Price: R450 - R550 pp sharing. Single and family rates negotiable. Discounts for longer stays.
Meals: Breakfast basket on request. Restaurants in Pringle Bay.
Directions: From Cape Town along N2 turn towards Gordon's Bay before Sir Lowry's Pass - follow coast road for 30km to Pringle Bay turn - follow signs down dirt roads.

Map Number: 4

Entry Number: 84

Wild Olive Guest House

Gloria and Peter Langer

227 Hangklip and Bell Rds, Pringle Bay
Tel: 028-273-8750 Fax: 028-273-8752
Email: g-langer@mweb.co.za Web: www.wild-olive.co.za
Cell: 082-442-5544

"How do you like your ostrich?" probed Peter, poking a chef's hat into the open-plan dining room where Gloria was refilling glasses and bending us double with tales of her culinary husband's aerophobia and the obvious palavers which ensue when they visit his Viennese home town. Peter swapped land-locked for coastal-mountain-backdropped upon meeting South African Gloria and they opened Beachcomber restaurant in Camps Bay; he chef-ing, she front of house. In 1980 they bought one of Pringle Bay's first five homes, a tiny cabin, transforming it into a spacious, elegantly-yet-homely guest house. But Wild Olive is no ordinary B&B. It's B&B&D for a start… dinners here are an Overberg talking point. Peter's cooking awards dangle beside pots and pans, but trophiescan't convey quite how tickled my taste-buds were by his red-wine-poached pear, a sublime follow-up to salmon teriyaki and rare ostrich fillet. Tummy happy, it was a woozy delight to slip downstairs through the shell-coloured guest lounge, past french doors leading onto the tree-lined pool (signposted 'Cuddle Puddle'), into my bright, lavender-scented, beach-blue room and wrap myself in goose-down. Waking to both sea and mountain was a breathtaking treat. I cooled myself with an al fresco shower on my secluded wooden terrace before breakfast, taken privately ("not everyone is a morning person") on the upstairs sun-deck. I hear Peter took early-bird guests out in the boat and it's Cape Malay prawns tonight - I wonder if there's room for one more?

Rooms: 3: 1 queen with en suite shower & 'al-fresco' shower, 1 with en-s shower & 'al-fresco' shr & separate loo; 1 twin/king with optional single loft bed, en-suite shower and 'al-fresco' shower.
Price: R550 - R650 pp sharing. Singles available on request.
Meals: Full breakfast included. 3-course evening dinner prepared by Peter.
Directions: From Cape Town on N2, turn towards Gordon's Bay, follow coast road for 30km to Pringle Bay turn – follow signs to Wild Olive.

96 Beach Road

Annelie and Johan Posthumus
Kleinmond
Tel: 021-794-6291 Fax: 021-794-6291
Email: info@kaapsedraaibb.co.za Web: www.kaapsedraaibb.co.za
Cell: 082-923-9869

When the family bought "the beach house" in 1954, the milk was delivered by bike. Kleinmond still feels like a sleepy little town, but it's hardly surprising that more have fled here since. The house is but a kite-tail's length from the sea, the blue Atlantic stretching forth beyond a strip of fynbos. You can choose to watch the whales (from August to December) from two spots, the sea-side verandah or the upstairs bedroom. The latter runs from one side of the house to the other under a vaulted ceiling and ocean-side the walls stop and the glass starts, forming a small square sitting room jutting out towards the blue. Here there is a soft couch and cushioned chairs, perfect for siestas, sunsets (and, of course, whale-watching). Downstairs is equally adorable. It feels a bit like a Nantucket Island house: white, light, airy and adorned with simple understated beach furnishings. It is totally self-catering here, but walk a kilometre west and you'll find some untouristy cafés in the old harbour; a short drive away are white, sandy, blue-flag beaches, perfect for kids, flying kites, swimming and walking. There is a rock pool about 50 yards from the house, and apart from that all the swimming takes place at the beach and lagoon which is a 15-minute walk away. Kleinmond is near the Arabella Golf Estate, the Kogelberg Biosphere with its myriad fynbos species, the wild horses of the Bot River Estuary and Hermanus, but avoids its touristyness. *Closed 10th December – 10th January.*

Rooms: 1 unit with 2 rooms: 1 double with en-s shower, 1 twin with bath. Open-plan kitchen/dining/living area. Heating. Kitchen fully equipped with dishwasher & washing-machine. Serviced once a week... more frequently on request.
Price: R800 per day for 2; R200 per day for each additional person staying. Maximum 4 people.
Meals: Self-catering.
Directions: From the main road, turn down 9th Street and travel right down to Beach Road. Turn left into Beach Road. Cross 8th Street. No. 96 is the second from the corner of Beach and 7th Sts.

Map Number: 4

Entry Number: 86

Schulphoek Seafront Guesthouse

Petro and Mannes van Zyl
181 Piet Retief Crescent, Sandbaai, Hermanus
Tel: 028-316-2626 Fax: 028-316-2627
Email: schulphoek@hermanus.co.za Web: www.schulphoek.co.za
Cell: 083-346-0695

Wandering through Schulphoek I couldn't wipe the smile from my face; verdant vegetable gardens, daily home-made cakes for peckish guests, a sunny salt-water pool, sumptuous mahogany bedrooms and deep-set squidgy sofas in the luxurious, gold-tinted guest lounge (all of which offer front-row whale-spotting). After a sunset stroll over the rocks it was time for supper, an event unto itself. House guests sit at a long, oak dining table and as an amouse-bouche, we're led into a vast wine cellar, home to some 12,000 bottles, to pick our accompanying wine. Which grape complements spicy tomato soup and succulent beef fillet, I wonder? Petro nudged me towards a hearty pinotage and ensured my glass was never empty as we discussed Stony Point's penguins, life in Namibia and September's Whale Festival. With regards to the outstanding food, Mannes, the resident chef insists that food melts in the mouth. And so it does! Feeling rather content I retired to my elegantly-decorated garden suite, resisted the temptation to open another bottle of wine or enjoy a few hours in the enticing two-person spa bath and opted instead for the comfort of my gargantuan bed. My heart sank as I woke and realised it was time to leave. Petro and Mannes have been providing their own special brand of wonderful hosting at Schulphoek for 12 years and counting. Long may it continue! *Massages and treatments on request.*

Rooms: 7 suites: superior, luxury and standard, all with luxurious en-suite bathrooms. 1 family suite.
Price: R800 to R2,100 pppn, incl' breakfast. Complimentary fine-dining dinner on 1st night. Single supp' +50%. Discounts for longer stays & winter specials.
Meals: Professional kitchen with chef. Dinner every night: menu du jour. Lunch: on request. Cellar with 12,000 SA wines. Full breakfast included.
Directions: Take R43 towards Hermanus. At Engen petrol station before Hermanus by lights (signed Sandbaai) turn R. At 2nd 'stop' turn L into 3rd St. Continue to next stop & Lt. Marked by flags – entrance off Piet Retief Cresc.

Hermanus Lodge on the Green

Nobby and Wendy Clark

8 Fernkloof Drive, Hermanus
Tel: 028-313-2517 Fax: 028-313-1618
Email: info@hermanuslodge.co.za Web: www.hermanuslodge.co.za
Cell: 082-900-7290

Golfing enthusiasts may take one look at Hermanus Lodge on the Green and assume all their Christmases have come at once! As the name suggests, it's situated on the 25th green of South Africa's 4th most popular golf course. It's no surprise that so many contented guests, golfers and non-golfers alike, congregate for evening drinks on the lodge's colonial-style, wrap-around balcony to contemplate remarkable views down the tree-lined fairway. These can be enjoyably achieved with equal smugness on colder days in the Rocky Lounge where you can absorb the warmth of a roaring fire. A lazy breakfast can be enjoyed in the downstairs dining room, which spills out onto a patio just metres from the course. Others may enjoy the sun-trapped swimming-pool surrounded by olive trees and watch para-gliders catching thermals over the mountainous Fernkloof Nature Reserve. The house, with its Zimbabwean wall hangings and sunset-slate flooring, has a subtle African flavour and is restful on both eye and spirit. The only sounds that will interrupt your peace will be the tree frogs and if you're lucky the Cape eagle owl (apart, of course, from the satisfying clunk of a golf ball being middled). What clinched it for me? It's close enough to the whale-watching frenzy down at the village that you can join in if you want... and just far enough away that you can savour the blissful quiet if you don't.

Rooms: 6: 2 kings, 4 king/twins, 1 sofa-bed for children under 12 in family room; 4 with en-s bath and shower, 2 with en-suite shower.
Price: Standard: R390 - R520 pp sharing. Deluxe: R520 - R690 pp sharing. Single supp' on request. No charge for kids under 12 sharing with parents.
Meals: Full breakfast included. Nobby & Wendy can recommend & book restaurants & call local 'tuk-tuk' service for those that don't wish to drive.
Directions: From N2 take R43 to Hermanus. Go thro' the village and turn left at the Shell garage onto Fairview Ave. Hug the golf course and turn first right before the school. House is second after the bend.

Hartford Cottage

Gys and Wendy Hofmeyr

3, 3rd Ave, Voelklip, Hermanus
Tel: 028-314-0102
Email: gyswendyhof@telkomsa.net
Cell: 082-897-1773

If you were asked to paint a picture of your perfect country cottage, I suggest it might look a bit like Hartford; white walls, soaring chimney and a perfectly-pitched thatched roof, all enveloped by a large, tranquil, lawned garden where I challenge you to find anything out of place. As I sat under the welcoming shade of the umbrella sipping tea and thinking how delicious it would be to live here, Wendy told me - and I didn't register much surprise - that complete strangers have knocked on the door begging to stay, even though originally they only built the cottage for the family. Hiding away from the hurlyburly of Hermanus in a seaside suburb, Hartford is enviably positioned, with mountain walks five minutes in one direction, beach, sea and whales a minute or two in the opposite. Gys is a stickler for detail and a lover of wood and thatch. Door surrounds and light switches were rescued and resurrected from a condemned house in town, while an original yellowwood door hanging on huge hinges is his pride and joy. Don't think Wendy hasn't been busy too. Her eye for interior designs led to the stunning black slate fire hearth, bathroom sink surrounds and kitchen worktops. The open-plan A-frame roof makes it cool and spacious, while the whitewashed walls and an abundance of Cape antique furniture, means it retains all of its delightfully cosy cottage charm.

Rooms: 1 cottage with 1 dble room with full en-s & 1 twin bedroom with separate bathroom. Also large attic bed/sitter with 3 beds for kids. Cottage not available 20th Dec - 15th Jan.
Price: 2 people sharing whole cottage: R1,000 plus R100 an extra head (May - Aug inclusive). R1,500 plus R200 a head per extra person (Sept - April inc'). Min 2-night stay. Children under 12 free.
Meals: Self-catering. Kitchen fully provisioned. Breakfast essentials included for 1st morning.
Directions: 4km from Hermanus, direction Stanford, take 3rd exit off roundabout into 10th St (Seafront Rd), past CEM Motors & on for 300m. 3rd Ave on R, then thatched house on R.

Selkirk House

Ina Schirmeisen

29 Selkirk Street, Hermanus
Tel: 028-312-4892 Fax: 028-312-4387
Email: info@selkirkhouse.co.za Web: www.selkirkhouse.co.za
Cell: 076-587-4753

When William Selkirk landed 'that' 967kg shark onto the rocks of Hermanus in 1922, I doubt he ever dreamt his name would appear in lights that shine quite as brightly as they do at this multi-levelled mountain-side retreat. The exceptional use of space and natural surroundings through levels, landings, terraces and quiet mountain recesses is visionary, not only aesthetically but also functionally. Everything is slick, chic, minimalistic and clean, accentuated by bursts of bright fynbos flower paintings. Stainless steel balustrades lead you up wooden stairs to your next indulgence, whether it's your room, the pool and first living space, complete with temperature-controlled wine cellar and vent-free fireplace, or the contemporary bar room with outside deck and fireplace, or the roof-top viewing deck which provides 360° views of mountains and ocean. All suites are a spacious dream and completely automated, allowing you to control your immediate environment whether through music, climate or brightness. I think they must have had a bit of a chuckle watching me walking in and out of the various rooms, wide-eyed as a child, as lights magically switched themselves on and off. Although everything really is cutting edge, Selkirk is also welcoming and warm-spirited and you are certainly encouraged to kick off your shoes and make full use of this splendiferous new creation. Just as I was about to leave a tortoise had made its way down the mountain and into the garden… the race is on!

Rooms: 5: 4 kings with en-s bath & shower & 1 twin with en-suite bath and shower.
Price: Low Season: 1st May 2013 – 31st Aug 2013 R650 pp sharing & R920 single. High Season: 1st Sept 2013 – 30th Apr 2014 R990 pp sharing & R1,300 single.
Meals: Full breakfast included, lunch & dinner on request.
Directions: From N2 take R43 into Hermanus, thru' village, pass Marine Hotel on R. After 1km at Shell Garage L into Fairways Ave towards mountain, 1st R, still Fairways Ave, next hairpin bend start of Fernkloof Dr, then 1st L Selkirk St.

Cliff Lodge

Gill O'Sullivan and Gideon Shapiro

6 Cliff St, De Kelders
Tel: 028-384-0983 Fax: 028-384-0228
Email: stay@clifflodge.co.za Web: www.clifflodge.co.za
Cell: 082-380-1676

This is the closest land-based whale-watching you could possibly find. I could see the whites of their eyes and the callosities on their heads. It was as though Gill and Gideon had paid them to put on a special show for me; blowing, breaching, spy-hopping, lob-tailing. I applauded delicately from the royal box. The viewing from my room and from the breakfast conservatory-balcony was don't-turn-your-eyes-away-for-a-minute magnetic. But the fun wasn't just in the looking. As soon as I walked through the door, Gideon whisked me down to the ocean for a swim through the cave (bring shoes you can swim in for the rocks) and Gill kindly booked me a whale-, sea-lion- and penguin-watching boat trip for the following morning. For the adventurous, there are also trips to view or cage-dive with great white sharks. The guest house is classy and modern and there are sea-view terraces for those rooms on the side of the house. The luxurious penthouse suite has a huge balcony and glass-fronted living room for whale-gazing in true style. On the cliff edge there is a swimming pool with loungers where you can unwind and languidly enjoy the hypnotic view. Gill, Gideon and the ever-smiling manager Nico are wonderfully hospitable hosts. They serve the best breakfast you could possibly have – exceptional loose-leaf teas, delicious barista coffee, fresh juices, a continental and hot breakfast spread. After breakfast indulge in a massage, nature reserve walks in front of the house and on a nearby flower farm, or spend the day on the unspoilt white beach a short walk from the lodge.

Rooms: 5: 1 twin/king with bath & shower; 1 twin/king with bath and outdoor shower; 1 luxury suite with king, separate living room, bath & shower; 2 twin/king with shower.
Price: R800 - R1,850 pp sharing. Single supplement +50%.
Meals: Full breakfast included.
Directions: N2, then R43 through Hermanus. Past Stanford towards Gansbaai. Turn right at first De Kelders turn-off, then right into De Villiers Rd, left into Kayser Rd and right into Cliff St.

Whalesong Lodge

Stanley and Lainy Carpenter
83 Cliff St, De Kelders
Tel: 028-384-1865
Email: stanley@whalesonglodge.co.za Web: www.whalesonglodge.co.za
Cell: 082-883-5793

"Almost forgot!" gasps Lainy, fleeing Whalesong's sun-soaked, cliff-hanging balcony for her eat-your-heart-out-Nigella kitchen. She skips back to a gaggle of performing whales, overflowing with fluffy cappuccinos and warm chocolate cookies: "wheat-free, I'm experimenting for food-intolerances". The Carpenters are foodies (and greenies) to a T: herbs'n'veg grow behind the pool, eggs come from "a little farm up the road", cheese from local cows and a compost worm farm ensures near zero waste. Anything not gobbled up by thousands of little wrigglers is recycled religiously. Lainy's ethical yummies, including her hand-made truffles, are for sale and guests are welcome to loiter in the kitchen where debates range from how to sweeten sugar-free apple cake to why their home-baked croissants and home-grown grenadilla jam are so lip-smacking. Upstairs, away from the long, homely breakfast table and open-fire lounge, Whalesong is all about the water. Bright, modern, elegant rooms (cleaned with nature-friendly orange oil, naturally) and clean-line bathrooms stare out to sea while cream walls are dotted with exposed brick and images of ocean life, boats, waves, breaching whales. Photo-filled welcome packs swell with shark-diving, whale-watching and kayaking suggestions for adventurous souls, but land-lovers should ask Stanley about fynbos trails and beach walks. This is a man who gets heart palpitations if he misses his daily walk and swim so has all the insider gossip. Well, how else could he burn off Lainy's puds?

Rooms: 5: 2 twins and 2 doubles, all en-suite shower and bath. 1 suite with king and en-suite shower and spa bath
Price: R750 - R1,350 pp sharing. See website for specials.
Meals: Full breakfast included.
Directions: From N2 take R43 through Hermanus and Stanford. Take first right signed to De Kelders and follow down to the sea. Turn right into Cliff Street. Third house on right.

Overberg, Western Cape

Sea Star Lodge

Ardi Hasenohrl
19 Ingang Street, De Kelders/Gansbaai
Tel: 028-384-0012 Fax: 086-602-4436
Email: info@seastar.co.za Web: www.seastar.co.za
Cell: 079-174-8548

Approaching Sea Star Lodge, Ardi whisked me straight onto the roof, bubbles in hand, to watch the sun set over the Atlantic. He said it would be special, but even he had to stifle chuckles as I stood gawping at the evolving hues of Walker Bay and the Fynbos Nature Reserve behind us. Darkness eventually won, but I would have happily lain under that glittering 360-degree blanket of sea stars all night had I not spied inside Sea Star's rooms en route to the rooftop and been nosy for more. Ardi is a former policeman-turned-private detective from Munich, which might explain why he is such a stickler for privacy and perfection; nothing less will do, particularly when it comes to his guests. Uber-slick, luxurious rooms are utterly mod-conified (mine boasted a fully-stocked Nespresso machine!) with blacked-out windows to stop peeping whales. Extravagant ocean panoramas made up for the fact that my Master Suite bath, though vast, was the only tub lacking a sea view, but Ardi apologised regardless by cracking open a bottle of vintage dessert wine to share on the sweeping verandah, an extension of the bright, open-plan guest living area. Joining Moulin the dog by a toasty fire, Ardi filled me in on De Kelders' clandestine pop-up restaurant, Klooks At Home; on the Durban artist whose fiery Kalahari paintings dot Sea Star's walls; on his pilot pal Evan who takes guests bird's-eye whale-spotting in his four-seater plane, African Wings.... I wonder if Ardi would place me under house arrest?

Rooms: 7: 6 kings with full en-suite; 1 self-catering beach house with two or three bedrooms. Rooftop suites have their own private terrace.
Price: R700 – R1,200 pp sharing. Singles +50%.
Meals: Full continental and cooked breakfast included; picnic baskets available on request. Complimentary mini-bar.
Directions: From N2 take R43 through Hermanus towards Gansbaai. Turn right at first De Kelders turn-off, then left into Hoof Weg. Take the second road on your right and turn into Ingang Street.

Klein Paradijs Country House

Susanne and Michael Fuchs
Pearly Beach, Gansbaai
Tel: 028-381-9760 Fax: 028-381-9803
Email: info@klein-paradijs.com Web: www.klein-paradijs.com

It's easy to dawdle over breakfast at Klein Paradijs. Munching crunchy home-made muesli (being Swiss, the Fuchs roll a mean honeyed oat) I was joined by an army of flapping, feathery friends who've made this expansive, colourful garden - a 140-hectare private nature reserve - their hunting ground. Susanne's chart shows 96 spottable species, but I was only quick enough to tag Cape weavers, pin-tailed whydahs and southern boubous. I'd certainly hang out here if I had wings: Klein Paradijs's ancient milkwoods are festooned with bird-feeders. Not that you need wings to enjoy this decadent pastoral paradise. For starters, there are the bedrooms. Sloping, thatched ceilings of local reed and dark wood beams smell terrific and tuck you into rustic luxury; wrought-iron beds draped in patchwork quilts are the definition of sturdy, homely elegance; soft lighting and weighty curtains ensure rooms are never anything but blissfully toasty. I prised myself away from a picturesque window, strolled past the doughnut pool with it's grassy island centre, peeked into the earthy double guest lounge neatly stocked with antiques, nature books, African artefacts and sleepy Rhodesian Ridgebacks, and contemplated rowing the dam before dinner. It's not just birds who get a good feeding here. Michael is a trained chef so don't fill up on breakfast - save room for his superb fish bobotie. Country living has seldom been so delicious.

Rooms: 5: 2 twins and 3 doubles all with en-suite bathrooms; 2 with bath and shower, 3 with showers.
Price: R500 - R1,250 pp sharing. Special prices for longer stays.
Meals: Full breakfast included. Light meals and dinner by arrangement. The restaurant is fully licensed.
Directions: From Hermanus take the R43 through Stanford and Gansbaai. Go left at Pearly Beach crossing, then 1st left again. The house is on the right. GPS S 34° 39' 23.5" E 19° 32' 05.7"

Farm 215 Nature Retreat and Fynbos Reserve

Maarten Groos

Farm 215, Hartebeeskloof, Fynbos Road, between Stanford and Bredasdorp
Tel: 028-388-0920 Email: book@farm215.co.za Web: www.farm215.co.za
Cell: 082-097-1655

Farm 215 perches neatly among the fynbos of this private nature reserve. As I stepped out of the car - my tired hot engine now at rest - silence prevailed. The individual cottages, angled to look rosy-faced into the sunset and onto sea and mountains, squat above the 35 different species of protea that contribute to the vast and wild garden. The conservation of the reserve here is a constant priority. The cottages were built with sustainability in mind and this is one of very few places in SA that are Fair Trade accredited. Testament to this is the yellow lichen, a sign of air purity, that paints the rock faces of this self-sufficient retreat. Maarten is constantly improving his fynbos world and speaks with eager animation of projects on the go, all in aid of restoring the land to its indigenous self and educating the local community (I learnt a thing or two myself!). The restaurant is capacious and contemporary with two fireplaces and folding doors that open onto a wooden deck. Dishes demonstrate a modern twist on country farmhouse style cooking; all of the ingredients are fresh, organic and either home-grown or locally-procured. The free-standing suites are luxurious, with cotton linen and large open-plan bathrooms of wood and black slate; or you can stay in the farmhouse rooms with their black-framed historic photographs and wide Persian rugs. With 20km of hiking trails radiating from the door of your cottage, an astonishing number of birds, horse trails on site and a spectacular, chlorine-free, 25m lap pool, there is every opportunity to earn yourself a slice of heaven.

Rooms: 6: 3 free-standing suites with kings, lounge area & en-suite bath & shower; 1 ground floor suite with private garden and 2 doubles in main house, each with en-s bath & shower.
Price: Homestead rooms R850 - R950. Fynbos suites R1300 pp sharing. Singles +30%. Discounts for longer stays (see website).
Meals: Full breakfast included. On-site restaurant for lunch & 3-course dinner. Picnic baskets also available.
Directions: A detailed route description will be mailed after reservation.

Entry Number: 95

Map Number: 4

Rothman Manor

Andreas and Franziska Gobel

268 Voortrek St, Swellendam
Tel: 028-514-2771 Fax: 086-664-6785
Email: info@rothmanmanor.co.za Web: www.rothmanmanor.co.za

With lily-littered dam, curvaceous salt-water pool and deck-bound jacuzzi overlooking a small eco-reserve of zebras and springbok, Rothman Manor boasts grounds of park-like calibre. The original Cape Dutch house and venerable oak tree (whose shady canopy acts as a parasol for your breakfast table) both date back to 1834, yet fresh, clipped interiors (born of Andreas and Franziska's combined flair for design) shift matters decisively into the present. With pale-blue or cream-hued walls and cloud-white curtain-swept beds, heavenly rooms are earthed by wooden flooring and canvas artworks, many of which are Franziska's own. Bathrooms sport chequered tiles and African-themed titbits seem to hang suspended in cubby-holes, unique reminders of the grounds and its outdoor inhabitants. Each generous room has its own view-treated patio opening out to the garden with its hidden nooks, hammocks, benches, romantic arbours and numerous statues. Perfectly situated with easy access to numerous nature reserves, the Robertson wine valley and Bontebok National Park, Rothman Manor is its own destination and a gateway to others.

Rooms: 6: 4 kings and 2 twins, 4 with full baths, 2 with shower only.
Price: R550 - R1100 pp sharing. Singles on request.
Meals: Full breakfast included. Restaurants nearby.
Directions: Turn off N2 onto R60 (signed Swellendam West), and then turn R into Swellendam. Rothman Manor on R.

Jan Harmsgat Country House

Willie Malherbe and Xolani Mhakananzi & Gerda De Lange

On R60 between Ashton and Swellendam
Tel: 023-616-3407 Fax: 086-523-9284
Email: reservations@janharmsgat.com Web: www.janharmsgat.com
Cell: 072-279-3138

The sight of Jan Harmsgat's thatched white-gabled houses on the road between Swellendam and the Robertson wine valley is enough to warm any weary traveller's heart. Willie and his business partner Xolani had dinner at JHG and fell in love with the guest-house. When they heard it was for sale they ended up buying the whole farm! Regulars, fear not. The four rooms in the old slave quarters, plus the vast honeymoon loft above the old wine cellar, retain their rustic authenticity, complete with hefty wooden beams, shutters and original clay walls. They've also installed five new garden suites, which occupy the 19th-century Van Eeden House. The large, elegant rooms continue Jan Harmsgat's open bathroom motif, while adding yet more opulence in elaborate chandeliers, chaises-longues, oversized showers and four-poster beds. Best of all, with a chef who's been in this kitchen for 14 years, Jan Harmsgat's foodie reputation is as sound as ever. The Cape gooseberry butterfish was the perfect candlelit prelude to peppercorn beef and a devilishly gooey chocolate tart. Moreover, if you overdo it during Jan Harmsgat's oh-so-civilised evening ritual - cocktails with your hosts at the bar - you can slink back to your boudoir through your own private entrance. And to open your shutters at dawn to a citron-scented zephyr breezing over an orchard of pecan trees is blissful.

Rooms: 10: 6 luxury suites with king-size bed, en-suite bath and shower, air-con; 4 standard (2 en-suite, 2 with en-suite loo and bath in room).
Price: R650 – R950 pp sharing; luxury suites R750 – R1,080 pp sharing. Children under 12 half price. Singles on request.
Meals: Full breakfast included. Restaurant on premises open for lunch and dinner.
Directions: From N1, take Worcester exit onto R62 through Robertson and Ashton, turn right onto the R60. House on left, 21km from Ashton. From N2, take Swellendam West exit onto R60. House on right after 24km.

Bloomestate

Maarten and Carla Van der Ven

276 Voortrekker Street, Swellendam
Tel: 028-514-2984 Fax: 028-514-3822
Email: info@bloomestate.com Web: www.bloomestate.com

If it weren't for the welcoming smiles on Carla and Maarten's faces and for the giant ridgebacks bounding across the lawn, I'd have been concerned that I'd stumbled off Swellendam's main street into a photo shoot for a design magazine. This house overflows with originality and is the quintessence of modern living (I-pod stations, wireless Internet a given). The seven enormous garden rooms are identical in size and furnishings, with super-soft beds looking through French windows either to a scented lavender patch or to the pool, with its one striking blue wall perfectly framing the mountains beyond. Each room is coded by season or element, with one dashingly-coloured wall, matching cushions and a spray-painted canvas. 'Spring' is a vibrant green, 'Summer' a sun-burnt orange, the honeymooners' 'Fire' a passionate red and the brand-new, very special Red Cloud Room has gadgets galore such as diffuse floor lighting when you step out of bed. In the lounge building an LED light projects the time onto the opposite wall, and shattered glass is encased in the bar. The stoep, equipped with bespoke furniture hand-made to the couple's own designs, provides a perfect viewing platform from which to watch the sun slipping down behind the mountains – or you could book a massage in the wellness room, or skip across to the jacuzzi, which overlooks a bird-filled dam in one corner of the garden. Maarten and Carla are the most charming of hosts and the whole experience is enchanting, not least the breakfast, which is as fresh, beautifully presented and utterly delicious as the place itself.

Rooms: 7: 3 kings, 3 twins and 1 luxury room, all with en-suite bath and shower.
Price: R575 - R900 pp sharing. Singles plus 50%.
Meals: Full breakfast included. Picnic baskets, cheese platters, seasonal salads and open sandwiches available on request from R90 pp.
Directions: From Cape Town and N2 take Swellendam West exit (R60) towards Ashton. At the crossroads turn right and Bloomestate is first building on the right.

Map Number: 2

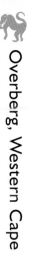

Augusta de Mist

Michel Platt and Henk Klijn

3 Human St, Swellendam
Tel: 028-514-2425
Email: info@augustademist.com Web: www.augustademist.com
Cell: 082-493-7971 (Michel) & 083-462-0969 (Henk)

Stranded in Swellendam, with no sign of torrential rains abating and far from my intended destination, I looked to the heavens. My prayers were duly answered as guardian angels, Henk and Michel, shepherded me into the alluring Augusta de Mist, a Cape Dutch National Monument (dating back to 1802) with yellowwood shutters and colonial-style verandah. Beneath the spansriet (Spanish reed) ceiling of my garden suite, Aloe, I toasted sodden toes by the open fire while supping on complimentary muscadel and indulging in a home-made hertzoggie. Aside from saving homeless GG inspectors, Henk and Michel are innovative hosts and master chefs as I was to discover at breakfast. Michel, a multilingual Montrealer, served up the full works complete with the perfect cappuccino, while Henk, of Afrikaner stock, initiated a tasting of kumquat chutney and biltong jelly with my continental cheese course! Besides these mouth-watering morsels I digested the Augusta Daily in-house news bulletin before Michel insisted on a tour of the gardens. Did I say gardens? More like indigenous wilderness! With Tucker the German shepherd as vanguard we gallivanted through prodigious foliage, past two lavish garden cottages and a lavender-banked swimming pool, before climbing the Augusta Valley Walk to reveal splendid sunlit views of Swellendam and a fairy-tale picnic spot. I only wish I could be stranded in Swellendam more often with 'La Belle Dame sans Chapeau', Augusta's new wine!

Rooms: 6: 2 garden cottages (2 kings); 2 garden suites (1 queen with 2 adjoining singles; 1 twin suite); 2 heritage accommodation (1 queen & 1 dble). All en-s & showers, most with separate oversize baths. Cot available.
Price: R550 – R930 pp sharing. Singles on request.
Meals: Full breakfast included. Set 4-course dinners at Augusta's African Kitchen on request R225. Wines specially blended.
Directions: On N2 take Swellendam East turn-off. Down hill. Past Stop. Over small bridge. Quick R up small hill. L then immediate R. Press white bell.

De Hoop Collection

Samantha Hughes (Reservations)

De Hoop Nature Reserve
Tel: 021-422-4522 Fax: 086-575-0405
Email: res@dehoopcollection.co.za Web: www.dehoopcollection.co.za

There are eighty-six mammal species in De Hoop Nature Reserve and, although I would have loved to see them all (and I did spot bontebok, eland, caracal and Cape mountain zebra), for the clarity of my sprawling notes it was a blessing we didn't. Hidden within the Cape Nature reserve, De Hoop Collection's accommodation is as eclectic as the wildlife. I stayed in the De Hoop Village, a suburban-style street made up of nine whitewashed three-bedroom cottages. The table in the rustic kitchen was already laid when I arrived and as I sat having supper a bontebok strolled past eating his. My double bed - covered in white linen and crowned by a handsome headboard - lay beneath a row of fynbos prints. Similar cottages and a few basic rondavels overlook the vlei, a stunning landmark that turns golden at dusk. Houses, with larger rooms, are dotted amongst the milkwood trees. Luxury lies at the other end of the vlei: a four-bedroom manor house done up to its former glory. Next door, the Fig Tree Restaurant serves food and drink all day, including an indispensible sundowner G&T. The song of some 260 species of birds was the only (!) sound.

Rooms: Cottages, houses, manor houses, rondavels and camping spots available. Ring or look at website for details.
Price: There are different accommodation types which range from R325 – R2,045 per person. There's a minimum charge on certain cottages.
Meals: Restaurant on-site for breakfast, lunch and dinner.
Directions: From Cape Town take N2 to Caledon. Head to Bredasdorp on R316, and then Swellendam on R319. After about 6km turn right at De Hoop/Malgas/Infanta sign. Follow dirt road for c. 35km to the reserve. For De Hoop Nature Reserve turn right at Buchu Bush sign.

Waterkloof Guesthouse

Hannes and Christine Uys

Waterkloof Farm, On R324 near Witsand
Tel: 028-722-1811 Fax: 028-722-1811
Email: info@waterkloofguesthouse.co.za
Web: www.waterkloofguesthouse.co.za Cell: 083-270-2348

Ever played chicken with an ostrich? Now's your chance. Admittedly I had the protection of a bull-barred pick-up truck but it was exciting stuff, rattling around the farm collecting still-warm eggs for the incubator and doing our best to avoid overly ruffling their fathers' feathers. Waterkloof is an ostrich farm through and through and there is nothing that Hannes (only the seventh generation of the Uys family to work this land!) doesn't know about these feisty fowl. They use the leather for bags, the eggs for breakfast, the eggshells for lampshades and the meat for supper (food is particularly good here - Christine makes sure of this). Sunk into rolling fields of barley and wheat, this is a hard-working farm but a great place to take it easy. The bathrooms have Victorian baths and separate showers, while cool, luxurious bedrooms open onto the garden and fountain. Wild fig trees shade benches built for reading on and the pool area has its own kitchen for help-yourself Sunday lunches. And if you feel like a change of scenery (and wildlife), Witsand is the place to see migrating whales. Back at the house Hannes patiently answered my babble of questions as we sank into ostrich-leather-covered armchairs and tucked into a traditional Afrikaner braai (ostrich sausages, of course) and Christine's utterly delicious and ostrich-free cheesecake. Leather goods made by Italian designers in Cape Town are sold here for a third of the price too!

Rooms: 4: 2 doubles and 1 twin all with bath and shower, 1 twin with shower.
Price: R350 - R480 pp sharing.
Meals: Full breakfast included. Traditional Afrikaner dinner on request.
Directions: From the CT and the N2 turn R onto R324 after Swellendam 32 to the farm. From Mossel Bay take R322 to Witsand. At the crossroads turn R. Farm is on the L after 17 km.

De Doornkraal Boutique Hotel

Christopher Peppas (Host) and Viviane Point (Hostess)
8 Long Street, Riversdale
Tel: 028-713-3838 Fax: 028-713-3050
Email: info@dedoornkraal.com Web: www.dedoornkraal.com
Cell: 082-958-0622

If the hectic pace of today's world leaves you feeling out of breath, I would prescribe a stay at the eco-friendly De Doornkraal. This Cape Dutch beauty (1746) is one of the earliest buildings in Riversdale. Also found here is a 200-year-old vine, the oldest on the Garden Route and still providing grapes for the breakfast jam. Listen carefully and you can almost hear the history echoing through the walls. The original yellowwood and Oregon pine floors and ceilings, blackwood furnishings and the stunning rosewood front door have all been restored to their former glory. Understatedly elegant rooms have simple, neutral-coloured upholstery so as not to upstage the beautiful woodwork. Original paintings by a well-known artist, Johannes Meintjies, who previously lived here, add splashes of colour. They also share a fine drawing room with honesty bar, the ideal place for an after-dinner nightcap. Across the road are two comfortable and airy cottages set by a large willow-shaded pond and the Syrah vineyard that rolls towards the river's bank. I sat listening happily to the fountain murmur in the tea garden, lost to the outside world. Its only reminder were hoots from the twice-daily steam-train that runs through an otherwise sleepy town. And now Host and Chef de Cuisine, Christopher, heads up the De Wingerdt Restaurant. The menu is a la carte, with most produce grown on the door step of the kitchen, and includes an extensive wine list. De Doornkraal is also home to the Aan't Vette Wine Estate, which produces award-winning wines.

Rooms: 15: Meintjes House (2Q/1T, all en-s bath/sh, sharing lounge); Annex (1Q/3D/5T, all en-s bath/sh, sharing lounge); Garden Cottage. (1Q, en-s sh, private lounge); Vineyard Cottage. (1Q, en-s bath/sh, 1T en-s sh, private lounge).
Price: R422.50 – R440 pp sharing. Cottages R440 – R750 pp sharing. Kids 7+ R280 - R315. Singles on request.
Meals: Full breakfast included. De Wingerdt Restaurant on the premises open for breakfast, lunch and dinner. *Special dietary requirements catered for.*
Directions: N2 from Cape Town to Riversdale, L into town at main entrance, follow signs. Turn L just before you leave town into Long St. 100m on LHS.

Map Number: 2

Entry Number: 102

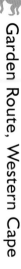

Riversong Farm

Piers Sibson

Goukou River Road, Stilbaai (Still Bay West)
Email: pierss@mweb.co.za Web: www.riversongfarm.co.za
Cell: 082-374-8274

Long after I've left South Africa, Riversong Farm will linger among my fondest memories. A winding dirt rollercoaster flecked with rocky outcrops, grinning dassies and patchwork farmland vistas runs alongside the Goukou River, coiling back towards the N2, away from the Still Bay coast. Some 12km along this track lies Piers' place, a supremely chilled-out farm (some friendly sheep here, a pic'n'mix orchard there) where nature gives you a great big hug. The child in me whooped for joy when I dropped down the hills, through the fynbos, towards the river and onto the farm. The adult in me did too... only with a little less grace. Two super-rustic log cabins sit happily side by side on a dewy, long-grass lawn, peeping through bushy reeds across the wide lolling river, the soothing scene occasionally fleetingly broken by a laughing water-skier, a swooshing rowboat, the splash of a golden retriever (or two) leaping off the jetty into the cool swimming water. It's a scene so soothing that Wilbur Smith penned a pile of novels while residing just three farms down. Piers - the epitome of a laid-back Englishman who swapped morning commute for morning kayak - built and occupies the rather more plush Kingfisher's Manor just a short pitch away. But he and his golden stick-chasers vacate should your party wish to commandeer the whole affair. And with a verandah and braai that size, every day here is a party. You'd be a fool to leave South Africa without sampling this exquisite patch of river magic. *Pets welcome!*

Rooms: 3: Kingfisher sleeps 8+ in 3 doubles & dormitory; Thames Chalet: 1 double & bunk & full en-s; Orange Chalet: 1 dble en-s shower, twins en-s loo.
Price: Thames and Orange chalets: R650 per chalet; Kingfisher: R2,600. Prices may vary depending on number of people. Discounts for booking whole farm.
Meals: Fully self-catering.
Directions: Betw' Riversdale & Albertinia on N2, take Stilbaai turn-off towards sea. In town R over bdge, then R into Goukou River Rd. Farm clearly named about 12km upriver.

Botlierskop Private Game Reserve

The Neethling Family
Little Brak River
Tel: 044-696-6055 Fax: 044-696-6272
Email: info@botlierskop.co.za Web: www.botlierskop.co.za
Cell: 082-563-8226

The Garden Route is best known for its scenery and sea life, so the last thing I expected to see as I navigated the back roads was a rhino. But there it was, chewing the cud like a contented cow. Botlierskop is a private game reserve that brings the big game south. It's not as wild as its northern counterparts (the lions are in a sanctuary) but it's a magical place to stay, set in 3,000 hectares of grassy plains and forested sandstone hills. The park is open to day visitors, though they use a separate day centre. Two real highlights are Sam, Tsotsi and Chima, orphaned elephants who are trained not only in giving rides but also as actors. Morning coffee with the rhino is also a must and personally I found nibbling on live termites pleasantly minty. Overnighters are appointed their own private guide - I had Billy, an animal almanac and rock art aficionado. From the cavernous hilltop restaurant, he ushered me into a dinghy and we drifted off down the wooded Moordkuil River before showing me to my tent. More marquee than tent, each is set above the river, giving a splendid view of both the water and the hills opposite. Inside it is luxury with a capital 'L'; deep armchairs, a writing desk and a room-for-two bath accompany the mosquito-netted four-poster. One tip though: zip it closed when you leave for the swimming pool (at the lodge) – the vervet monkeys have a penchant for coffee and cookies. Helicopter flights, horse-back safaris, catwalks and spa treatments are four more reasons to visit.

Rooms: 15 Luxury, Deluxe & Executive (with own lounge & splash pool) Tented Suites. All with a/c, en-s bath & outdoor shower. Self-catering rooms available suitable for kids of all ages.
Price: R2,107 - R3,112 pp sharing (inc. 2 game drives, meals & drinks). Singles R3,160 - R4,668. Child (6-12): 1/2 adult rate. 2-day stay incl. free horseback ride. 3-day stay incl. free helicopter flight.
Meals: Breakfast, lunch and dinner included.
Directions: From Mossel Bay and CT on N2 take Little Brak River exit (401). Heading inland turn R to Sorgfontein. Continue 4km and after causeway turn R for 4km along gravel road to Botlierskop.

Map Number: 2

Malvern Manor

Sandra and Michael Cook

Nr Fancourt, Blanco, George
Tel: 044-870-8788 Fax: 044-870-8790
Email: info@malvernmanor.co.za or malvernmanor@yahoo.co.uk
Web: www.malvernmanor.co.za Cell: 084-867-6470

If you are having any difficulty understanding why the area is called the Garden Route, well, have a trundle up Michael and Sandra's drive. Much more colourful and vibrant than anything visible from the public thoroughfares. I drove past cows and dams onto a redbrick road overflowing with thick tangles of foliage that hide Malvern from view - and all this perfectly framed by the imposing Outeniqua Mountains. Here is another English couple who fell in love with South Africa, upped sticks and bought their country idyll. They are both of farming stock, so this 21-hectare dairy farm was perfect. But despite being just a hop, skip and a jump from George, it was no easy task converting the Manor House, the keep at the heart of the farm, into a guest house. But it's all come together so nicely. My room opened onto the garden through French doors, and lavish Roman-style pillars pick out the bath – the perfect place to unwind after a round of golf at one of the many local courses. For non-golfers, there's endless scope for pre-breakfast walks and hikes... or you can sit and bird-watch in the tranquil gardens among proteas and roses. Play your cards right on your return and Michael might don his apron and prepare his speciality 'chocaccino'. Delightful people in an enchanting setting.

Rooms: 3: I queen, I twin or king, I double with single bed. All have en-suite bath and shower.
Price: R600 - R750 pp sharing. Singles on request.
Meals: Full breakfast included. Restaurants nearby and deliveries can be arranged.
Directions: From N2 take George airport exit onto R404 and follow signs to Oudtshoorn for approximately 8km. After Fancourt Golfing Estate, sign to Malvern Manor on left. Follow signs.

The Garden Villa

Gabriela Schlosser

35 Plantation Rd, George
Tel: 044-874-0391 Fax: 044-874-0391
Email: gardenvilla@isat.co.za Web: www.gardenvilla.co.za
Cell: 083-384-8499

In a frenzied hub such as George, upon which every Farmer Tomas, Henk and Willie descends for monthly supplies, what you truly need is a bit of peace and... shhh!... Gabriela's Garden Villa provides precisely that. The white Cape Dutch manor house sits at the base of the Outeniqua mountains, surrounded on all sides by lovingly manicured, luminously green lawn. I felt much more country mouse than city mouse here. A stroll round the hushed haven revealed bird baths, herb gardens, hydrangeas and bougainvillea so bright they seem to be plugged into a mains socket, tortoises (yes, two... Ernie and big Big Bertha), wild porcini mushrooms sprouting beneath the trees, cool stone furniture and pools (yes, two... a lap pool and a heated treat inside a greenhouse where hikers and golfers can soak weary limbs). Four softly furnished, pastel-coloured suites can be found teeming with freshly-cut flowers inside the main house which they share with two welcoming lounges, a handy communal kitchen and the sunny breakfast room which bubbly German Gabriela - who adores baking and, rumour has it, makes the best apricot jam in the world - uses if clouds keep her off the terracotta garden verandah. My favourite, however, was the intimate, pale blue loft room, Hortensia, peeping across garden and mountain and offering a kitchenette for couples who have no intention of leaving their toasty, pine-panelled hideaway. Just make sure you pop down for a cappuccino and slice of Gabriela's cheesecake - not to be missed!

Rooms: 5: 2 kings with full en-suite; 1 queen with en-suite shower; 1 twin with en-suite shower; 1 twin with en-suite shower and kitchenette.
Price: R550 - R795 pp sharing. Single +50%.
Meals: Full breakfast included. Restaurants nearby.
Directions: From Cape Town on N2 turn left onto R404 into George.

Moontide Guest Lodge

Maureen Mansfield
Southside Rd, Wilderness
Tel: 044-877-0361 Fax: 044-877-0124
Email: moontide@intekom.co.za Web: www.moontide.co.za

It's a rare pleasure for us to stay somewhere on holiday and to experience it over a period of days. And Moontide was a palpable hit with all five of us. Its position is hard to beat, right on the banks of the lagoon, its wooden decks shaded by 400-year-old milkwood trees. Here you can sit out for bountiful breakfasts or with an evening drink from your bar fridge and watch giant kingfishers diving for fish – well, we saw one anyway. Birdlife is profuse on the lagoon. The long, white-sanded Wilderness beach is only a two-minute walk from the house, but you can also take a canoe straight from Moontide up the lagoon into the Touw River and then walk along forest trails to waterfalls to swim in fresh-water rock pools. Whatever we did it was a pleasure to return, play cards in a relaxed sitting room or read in the cool of a bedroom. I was delighted with 'Milkwood' because I'm a sucker for dozing on a futon, in a loft, under thatched eaves, with river views by my head. But I would like to return and try them all. Since we descended en masse, Maureen has built herself a tree-top sanctuary. The deck, day-bed, even the free-standing bath, look out across thatched roofs to the river. Sportingly, she's decided it's too nice to keep for herself!

Rooms: 8: Moonriver Luxury Suite (king, 2 twins, bath, sh'r); Treetops (qu, bath, outside sh'r); Milkwood (king/twins & queen upstairs, bath, sh'r); Stone Cottage (king, 2 twins, bath, sh'r); The Boathouse (king, bath + sh'r); Moonshadow 1 & 2 (kings, baths & sh'rs); Moondance (king, bath, sh'r).
Price: R350 - R770 pp sharing. Single +60%.
Meals: Full breakfast included.
Directions: From George on N2 ignore Wilderness turn-off. Cross Touw River bridge, first left signed Southside Rd. Moontide at the end of cul-de-sac.

Serendipity

Phillip and Elsabé Kuypers

Freesia Avenue, Wilderness
Tel: 044-877-0433 Fax: 0866-717-992
Email: info@serendipitywilderness.com
Web: www.serendipitywilderness.com Cell: 082-4499-701

Where else can you dine in arguably the best restaurant on the Garden Route and then wander upstairs to snuggle into bed beneath goose-down duvets? This is a place whose name is breathed in quiet reverence all along the coast. Other Wilderness guesthouses flatly refuse to cater. "What's the point?" they say with community pride. Brushed up crisply for dinner after a three-chapter-long soak in the bath, I stepped from underfloor-heated tiles onto the shared balcony to watch geese flighting across a sunset lagoon. Then it was an easy meander down to the guest lounge for an apéritif, where Rudolf, husband to head-chef Lizelle (her culinary accolades, which hang in the loo, are very encouraging indeed), gave a sensuous description of a South African-inspired menu combined with European haute cuisine. Agonising, I finally plumped for snoek mousse and loin of springbok, variously interspersed by an *amuse-bouche* of kudu carpaccio and delicious butternut soup. The intimate restaurant discreetly backs onto a fireplace flanked by sheer windows looking out onto the water. For dessert I cracked into an exquisitely fruity crème brûlée, even as my waiter taught me the basics of Xhosa. Following a 3-course, crumpet-driven, meticulously-prepared breakfast (even the perfectly ripe strawberries are first brushed in a light almond syrup) in ebullient sunshine I found myself discussing semantics and champion deep-sea angling with owners Elsabé and Phillip, who had originally planned to run only a guesthouse…. That was before they invited their daughter to cook.

Rooms: 4: all twin/king with en-suite shower bathrooms.
Price: R480 - R640 pp sharing. Singles +50%
Meals: Full breakfast included. Five-course table d'hôte fine dining at R350 pp.
Directions: From N2 at Wilderness turn north at Caltex garage following George Road to T-junction in front of Protea Hotel. At T-junction turn right, travel along Waterside Road for 1.2km. Turn right into Freesia Avenue. Serendipity 4th house on right.

Wilderness Manor

Gerald Hoch and John-David (JD) Janse van Rensburg

397 Waterside Road, Wilderness
Tel: 044-877-0264 Fax: 044-877-0163
Email: info@wildernessmanor.co.za Web: www.manor.co.za
Cell: 083-441-1099

After 20+ years in the airline industry, Gerald and JD have visited most corners of the globe. Finally they have hung up their wings and decided that Wilderness is the pick of the bunch. And who can blame them - overlooking the lagoon, the glass-encased sitting room is crammed with African artefacts that have been begged, borrowed or bought: Ndebele pipes and beads, bartered-for carvings and stones from the Cradle of Mankind. An old billiard table is hiding there too, somewhere under a pile of maps. The large bedrooms have similar horn-and-hide hues, all the luxurious trappings you could wish for, and room for Indonesian chairs and chests, chocolate leather sofas, slipper baths and dark canopied beds with reading lights. Your hosts are discreet and attentive and after serving up a faultless (and greaseless) breakfast (you might even catch a glimpse of the visiting Knysna Loerie lured in by his daily apple), they will give you a map and bountiful beach-bag and send you on your way to explore your surrounds. Birdlife is rampant in the area and walks in the surrounding forests are a must. It is only a 10 to 15-minute stroll along lagoon-side boardwalks to the beach, village and some good restaurants.

Rooms: 4: 3 lagoon suites (2 kings and 1 king/twin with bath and shower en-s) and 1 garden room (king/twin with shower en-s).
Price: R400 – R700 per person sharing per night. Singles on request.
Meals: Full breakfast included.
Directions: Turn into village of Wilderness from N2 and follow road through village for approx 400 metres. At T-junction, turn right into Waterside Road and go along lagoon for 1 km. Wilderness Manor is a 3-storey house on left-hand side, 397 Waterside Road.

Lodge on the Lake

Frank Brauer

746 North Street, Wilderness
Tel: 044-877-1097 Fax: 044-877-1097
Email: info@lodgeonthelake.co.za Cell: 084-383-7766
Web: www.accommodation-wilderness.com

Übercool has come to Wilderness. Frank used to be in film production and his eye for precision design underlies every detail in this grandly Tuscan villa, which sits resplendent on its many pillars above the lake. As I skirted the central courtyard fountain and entered beneath the portico, something magic seemed to happen. The walls suddenly disappeared, the outside was inexplicably coming inside... but most mesmerising of all was the lake that had effortlessly risen, without a ripple, to the rim of the pool and forged a seamless sheet of the deepest liquid blue, only finally interrupted by the mountains. I suppose that's what you call German engineering. There's a Zen-like tranquillity here, a faraway sound of trickling water, which recently attracted a pair of authors; no one's sure whether they wrote anything. More than likely they discovered the delights of the in-house spa where three treatment rooms employ the mineral wealth of the sea to leave you feeling as fresh as the surf. Naturally the rooms, reached by a winding staircase, are mindful of weight, colour and proportion to the enth degree. Thick carpeting softens a solemnity of dark wooden bedsteads, cupboards and ingenious concertina doors, with a sense of playfulness creeping into striking patterns, stalactite pillars, open tubs and creative positioning of mirrors. Each has its own fabulous private balcony.

Rooms: 5: 4 doubles, 1 twin; all en-suite bath and shower.
Price: R400 - R1,000 pp sharing.
Meals: Full or continental breakfast included.
Directions: Emailed or faxed on booking.

Villa Castollini

Nan Raturat
Uitzicht, Brenton-on-Sea, Brenton, Knysna
Tel: 044-381-8200 Fax: 044-381-8239
Email: info@castollini.co.za Web: www.castollini.co.za
Cell: 083-460-2606

Here's a little piece of Italy picked up and tweezered onto 23 of the Garden Route finest hectares, a modern Tuscan villa set on top of Knysna's western head. I arrived through a grand mosaic entrance to be greeted by Nan and her friendly Bernese mountain dog cross grizzly bear... and I felt immediately reassured that I was in safe paws. Nan and her devilishly witty French husband Patrick run their guesthouse with rare affection and energy, constantly considering guests' needs. Do, however, allow Nan time to tend to her organic veggie garden. The rewards will be reaped at breakfast. Each bedroom has its own identity. Some have dressing rooms; others have sitting rooms. All are large and lead out to 180° view of Knysna town, the Outeniqua mountains and the oyster beds of the Knysna Estuary. Put aside time each day just to appreciate this view. In fact, make a point of having a drink at the pool after dark. The sparkling lights of Knysna below make this particularly atmospheric. I enjoyed the raised, open-plan, very Italian kitchen filled with tins of decadent treats, which guests are welcome to help themselves to. My favourite, though, has to be the Ferrari room. Clearly someone here is a Ferrari fanatic, hence the Ferrari-themed bar with its collection of miniatures (cars, not bottles) and Ferrari paraphernalia. Nan has personally overseen 83 weddings here, and with no neighbours, room for 16 guests... and the Ferrari room, this might be the perfect Garden Route wedding, honeymoon or other special occasion venue.

Rooms: 8: 3 king/twin with en-suite bath and shower, 2 king with en-suite bath and shower and 3 queen with en-suite shower.
Price: R500 - R1,200 pp sharing.
Meals: Full breakfast included. Dinner available on request.
Directions: From N2 take Brenton-on-Sea/Belvidere turn-off and continue for 5.2km. Villa Castollini is on the left side.

191 Nirvana

Madi Butler
191 Rheenendal Road, Rheenendal, Knysna
Tel: 044-386-0297 Fax: 086-606-0034
Email: madibutler@cyberperk.co.za Web: www.191nirvana.co.za
Cell: 084-826-2266

Who would have thought you could make a couple of self-catering cottages out of two water reservoirs? Evidently Madi Butler did. (First you have to empty out the water, of course.) Her two circular, thatched properties now stand proudly on the top of the hill. The position, at the hub of outstanding panoramic views that stretch from the end of the Outeniqua Mountains, across Knysna Lagoon and into the surrounding forest, was just too good to waste. You won't quite know where to gaze first. This is one self-catering place where you can be 100 per cent independent, yet still have the reassuring presence of a very friendly hostess just at the bottom of the hill. On top of all the added extras you require (Madi supplies beautiful white bed linen, towels, firewood and tit bits such as organic salad), a basket of home-grown herbs and veggies (depending on the season) will find its way onto your doorstep each morning. The indoor fireplace doubles up as a braai area which - and this is my favourite part - becomes virtually outdoors when you 'roll up' the walls (made of canvas blinds) at the front of the cottage. What's that? Roll up the walls? I assure you it's possible, you'll just have to come and see for yourself.

Rooms: 3 self-catering units.
Price: R350 – R500 pp sharing.
Meals: Self-catering.
Directions: Heading to Knysna from George on the N2. Before you enter Knysna turn left into Rheenendal Road. Follow the road for 1.6km and the entrance to 191 Nirvana is on your right.

Bamboo, the Guest House

Jaynie Court and Gordon Turrell
7 - 9 Bolton Street, Hunters Home, Knysna
Tel: 044-384-0937 Fax: 044-384-0937
Email: info@bambooguesthouse.co.za Web: www.bambooguesthouse.co.za
Cell: 082-812-8838

I had to call three times for directions (each time cringing a little more deeply), but Jaynie finally got through to me with, "and if you don't make it this time, you forgo the bottle of red under your pillow". Moments later I closed the door on the hubbub of Knysna. All around me wooden-slatted walkways divided a jungle of plants and fountains, pools and ponds. All the walkways spiral to the main house where breakfasting, lounging and evening merriment take place. Jaynie and Gordon have transformed an ordinary garden of lawns and flowerbeds into their own mini-Eden, burying fourteen spotless rooms in a relaxing garden that grabs the senses and deceives the eye. Watch out for the chickens. "There are so many, you may fall over them", Jaynie warns me! "There's nothing quite like a warm egg to start the process". Guests and hosts alike benefit from the tranquillity, manifest in Jaynie's smile (as warm as they come) and Gordon's obvious contentment as he braais away behind the bar. But beware: from his work-station come rustic feasts to challenge the most voracious appetite, wines to lure the most disciplined off task and stories to leave the most hardened traveller incredulous. There's something of Crocodile Dundee about Gordon and I felt a tad pale and urban next to him. This was not helped in any way by accepting a two-hour, full-body massage with an exceptional visiting masseuse. But I got over it. A night drifting to sleep on a mountain of cushy bed pillows, vaguely aware of frogs croaking one minute and birds chirping the next, made this weak urbanite feel terrific. Don't leave without visiting 'Granny's [Gordon's mother] Shop'.

Rooms: 14: I honeymoon suite & I honeymoon cottage, both with full bathrooms & wood-burning fireplaces; 7 en-suite family rooms/suites; 5 en-suite garden rooms. Self-catering options.
Price: R350 - R585 pp sharing. Singles rates available.
Meals: Full breakfast incl'. Other meals by arrangement.
Directions: From N2 in Knysna (heading to Plett) turn R down George Rex Drive. After lights take 2nd L into Howard St; at the golf club house take central road signed Bolton St, continue over 2 speed bumps and no.9 is on your R.

Villa Afrikana Guest Suites

Bianca Ackermann and Rossano Giunti

13 Watsonia Drive, Paradise, Knysna
Tel: 044-382-4989 Fax: 086-212-9966
Email: concierge@villaafrikana.com Web: www.villaafrikana.com
Cell: 082-940-0867

I'd barely hauled my car up the sloped driveway (and yanked on the handbrake) when smiley-eyed Bianca wondered if I'd like a world-famous (ok, maybe Knysna-famous) frothy coffee. Well, if they're as Italian as Ross and as plush as their guest house, I certainly would. Posited up in Paradise - I'm not gushing, that's truly the name of their locale - Villa Afrikana could put the swank into Hilary. Bianca (whose family live down the hill) and Ross (who hails from Florence) met working on a cruise liner - he in hospitality management, she in administration - and pooled their gifts for care and design into a tightly-run guest ship. White floors stretch through cool, clean living areas, parting for deep white sofas, zebra-skin rugs and floor-ceiling windows revealing panoramic lagoon vistas. I plumped for perusing the villa library in the starboard reading snug, propped in front of a porthole peeping out to the gleaming pool. Upstairs, in unfussy, roomy, balconied suites, things are no less glam. Subtle African touches tug at modern Euro-minimalism: local painter Niel Nieuwoudt's bespoke interpretations of Knysna grace each room while every pillow sparkles with a cheeky Ferrero Rocher (thanks Ross!). This stylish crow's nest towers over Knysna: from Bianca's pancake-prepping kitchen we watched yachts wriggle round the lagoon, ant-people exploring the Waterfront and a controlled fynbos fire billowing over the Heads. Releasing the handbrake and plunging my car back into reality, I knew I'd dream of Paradise that night.

Rooms: 6: 4 extra-length king with full en-suite; 1 extra-length king/twin with full en-suite; 1 extra-length king with shower over bath; 1 extra-length king/twin with shower over bath (can connect to family room & sleep 4).
Price: R850 - R1,150 pp sharing. Singles +60%.
Meals: Full breakfast included.
Directions: From Cape Town on the N2 entering Knysna turn left into Fletcher Road at Total Garage, left at top of Fletcher Road, right into Circular Drive. Watsonia Drive is on your right at the top of Circular Drive.

Map Number: 5

Entry Number: 114

Narnia Guest House

Richard and Stella Sohn
off Welbedacht Lane, Knysna
Tel: 044-382-1334 Fax: 044-382-2881
Email: narnia@pixie.co.za Web: www.narnia.co.za
Cell: 083-325-2581

Narnia combines just about every element we search for in a place to stay. It's defiantly itself - the style (luxuriously ethnic, but never overdone) is so unusual and so genuine that you know it is the extension of real people, not some pretentious interior design job. Stella (graphic design graduate, potter, mother of two) is one of those people and Richard (lawyer, 'architect' and father of four) the other. Narnia is entirely their creation, a dream slotted round one or two key requirements: the house should have a deck with a clear view to the Knysna Heads; and there should be a big, open, friendly entrance hall. Otherwise the house has grown organically into some mad ship with wooden decks, gangways and staircases, swing chairs, heavenly colours of tropical brilliance ("In a previous life I must have been a Mexican," says Stella), a prize-winning garden and smaller surprises everywhere. The decking-clad, black-painted pool (of swimming - as opposed to plunging - dimensions) shares the same long views in all directions as the fully-serviced self-catering cottages. Stella and Richard amaze me with their great energy and skill with people, despite holding down so many jobs. These qualities have evidently been inherited by their son Jaimi who is a qualified Swedish masseur and reiki master and offers treatments for guests. *Bushbuck are often spotted on the farm and visitors to the garden include porcupine, blue duiker, steenbuck, monkeys, bushpigs, lynx and 85 species of bird. Richard is happy to take guests deep-sea fishing and youngest son Mitch will take you bass fishing on their dam.*

Rooms: 2 self-catering cottages (both sleep 4): 1 with double & twin sharing bathroom; 1 with shr, queen & single in one bedroom and futon for child in lounge.
Price: B&B: R600 - R750. Self-catering: R100 less pp sharing. Children under 12 half-price.
Meals: Full breakfast is included for the B&B apartment. For self-catering full breakfast is R100, children R75, and continental is R50. Not available high season. Owners can recommend the best local restaurants.
Directions: On N2 from George turn into Welbedacht Lane just before Knysna. Then follow signs to Narnia.

Entry Number: 115

Packwood Country Estate

Vicky and Peter Gent

Fisanthoek, Nr Harkerville, Between Knysna and Plettenberg Bay
Tel: 044-532-7614
Email: vicky@packwood.co.za Web: www.packwood.co.za
Cell: 082-253-9621

"Rooney, off!" sighs Vicky, nudging her boisterous young collie off the cream sofa and out of the back door. Rooney, tumbling into 1,000 acres of pasture and vineyard, is not complaining. He bounds off to terrorise 900 dairy cattle. Cosseted between Knysna Forest and the ocean, Packwood offers a taste of country living at its best. Up here, wrapped in mountains, gazing onto the Robberg Peninsula, free-roaming Jerseys produce 5,000 litres of milk a day. But Vicky and Peter aren't a pair to rest on their laurels. 2009 heralded their crisp Maiden Vintage and now award-winning sauvignon blanc and first-release Blanc de Noir MCC bubbly. An array of Packwood produce - from the dairy, vineyard, farm and gardens - is available for your stay, including extra-mature cheddar and crisp garden salads. Plump for one of three summery self-catering cottages or treat yourself to the main country house. Ilsa, Packwood's full-time housekeeper and cook, is available by special arrangement. She will cook up a storm with her infamously fiery chicken curry and very naughty chocolate mousse cake. Guests really can have it all here: short drives lead to pristine beaches, world-class golf courses, local game parks and mountain treks; whilst relaxing days on the farm can include as much or as little as you feel up to, from farm tours, bike rides and walks to pool-side bathing. A stay at Packwood means an escape to the country for lazy mornings and heavenly peace. *Cheese and wine lunches & wine tastings available 11am – 3pm, Mon – Fri, excluding public holidays.*

Rooms: 6: main house: 3 kings with full en-suite; Family Cottage: 1 double & 2 twins, full bathroom, extra loo; Hill Cottage: 2 doubles (1 en-s shower, 1 separate shower); Bottlebrush Cottage: double, en-s bath.
Price: R800 per day – R3,500 per day. Long-term holiday lets negotiable. House-keeping Mon–Fri except public holidays. Minimum booking of 3 nights.
Meals: Self-catering: farm produce/dinner on day of arrival by request. Main house: housekeeper Ilsa available as cook with prior arrangement at extra cost.
Directions: From CT on N2, 25km from Knysna take Fisanthoek turn-off L & go 6km on good, untarred road.

Map Number: 5

Fynbos Ridge Country House and Cottages

Liz and Brian Phillips
Plettenberg Bay
Tel: 044-532-7862 Fax: 044-532-7855
Email: info@fynbosridge.co.za Web: www.fynbosridge.co.za
Cell: 083-448-0046

Fynbos Ridge is a botanical paradise where new owners Liz and Brian have continued an eco-conscious mission to remove all invasive alien vegetation. Painstakingly, a wide variety of indigenous trees and shrubs have been reinstated to create a haven where Cape flora (fynbos) and fauna can flourish. There are birds here that you will only see in the fynbos. These green-fingered nature lovers will cushion your stay with super-down duvets, pure cotton sheets and a hearty breakfast in the light-filled, alfresco-esque dining room. Lucky self-caterers can choose from newly-refurbished cottages in 'gazania' yellow, 'clivia' peach or 'aristea' blue, all inspired by indigenous flowers and fully and sensitively equipped to satisfy any modernist yearnings. I, for example, particularly liked the minimalist stone baths. They can also pick their own vegetables, but please do let Brian cook for you at least once. This private nature reserve cries out to be walked in, though unfortunately I only made it as far as the ozone-purified swimming pool (no chemicals here - just a weird-sounding contraption doing its bit to keep the establishment and all guests 100% carbon neutral). Follow the natural borders and discreet signposts to this oasis amongst the fynbos to take a dip. Hidden within the depths of a private nature reserve and contemplating the meeting of the Outeniqua and Tsitsikamma mountains, you could easily spend the whole day here languishing with a book. Now where did I pack my swimming togs? *Please ask about painting, cooking and birding holidays.*

Rooms: 9: 6 rooms in the house: 4 luxury doubles, 1 superior luxury double and 1 self-catering studio, all with en-suite bath and shower; 3 self-catering cottages, all sleeping 4-5 with 1 bathroom & 1 shower-room.
Price: B&B and self-catering from R900 pp sharing. Singles on request.
Meals: Full breakfast included in B&B price or R85 for self-catering. Lunch and dinner on request.
Directions: 7km along N2 from Plettenberg Bay heading towards Knysna. Take R into 'Blue Hills Bird Farm'. Bear L where road forks to Fynbos Ridge.

Cornerway House

Dee and Robin Pelham-Reid
61 Longships Drive, Plettenberg Bay
Tel: 044-533-3190 Fax: 044-533-3195
Email: cornerwayhouse@mweb.co.za Web: www.cornerwayhouse.co.za

Robin and Dee moved from Wiltshire, England some ten years ago to start Cornerway House... and fantastic hosts they make too. Robin will ably point you off to the beach or to the Robberg Peninsula walk, an exhilarating experience, and all that Plettenberg has to offer. Meanwhile Dee can give you a different and rewarding perspective on Plett as Chairman of The Plettaid Foundation. Her dedication has set in place home-care workers in the townships. Also a safe house for abused women and children (aptly named Invicta House) and an 8-bed hospice called Trinity House. I retired to my room - wooden antiques, comfy bed and sash windows looking onto the garden – and at dawn joined Ocean Blue to spot whales, dolphins and sharks, returning to a sumptuous breakfast (courtesy of the team) sprinkled with chives, parsley or whatever herb is on offer that day from the garden. Throughout the old house there are colourful, Dee-esque quirks (Robin would describe it no other way!), to wit the yellow-washed and lilac shutters of the house, the petunias bathing in a bath, a purple TV/sitting room with bright blue cushions and the pink and yellow mohair in the garden suite. The annex has a far more contemporary feel. I left Robin and Dee among the frangipani, gardenia and orange trees as I wrenched myself away. *See owner's website to make an online booking.*

Rooms: 8: 3 rooms in annex (2 a/c twin/king, en-suite shower/bath, 1 double, en-s sh'r); 4 twins and 1 d'ble; 2 en-s sh'r, 3 en-s sh'r/bath. 3 rms can be connected internally with own entrance suitable for families.
Price: R345 - R645. Singles +50% except high season. All rates include breakfast except for the self-catering unit option.
Meals: Full breakfast incl'. Self-catering available.
Directions: From N2 heading east, turn R into Plett. Continue to the circle and go straight over. Road descends to and crosses river. Over circle, turn R onto Longships Dr. Continue down 0.9km to Cornerway House on R. GPS: S34 04' 17'' E23 22' 4''

Map Number: 5

Beacon Lodge

Al and Clo Scheffer
57 Beacon Way,
Plettenberg Bay
Tel: 044-533-2614
Fax: 086-730-4037
Email:
info@beaconlodge.co.za
Web: www.beaconlodge.co.za

This is a small (just two rooms), personal, friendly and involving B&B – and I mean B&B in the proper sense where you share the house with your hosts. Both rooms have their own separate entrances, mind you, if you want to slip about more furtively. The patio, for breakfasts, garden bird-watching or reading, has long views out to sea and it's only a short walk to the beach and the lagoon, presumably where you will want to spend at least some of your time. To this end Al and Clo have all beach necessities at the ready – umbrellas, towels and the like. The larger of the two rooms was my favourite (and also the more expensive) with sea views through a huge window and anti-glare solar blinds. There is seagrass on floors, plenty of immaculate seaside white in walls and towels and colour is added in the form of fresh flowers. The Scheffers take the greatest care of their guests. *Fridge facilities provided. Great restaurants within walking distance. Whales and dolphins in season. Closed mid-Dec to mid-Jan and either June or July. Enquire first! Al and Clo also speak French, Dutch and German.*

Rooms: 2: 1 twin and 1 double, both with en-suite bathrooms with showers.
Price: R250 - R500 pp sharing. Singles on request.
Meals: Full breakfast included. There are good restaurants in town for other meals.
Directions: From Knysna take 3rd turn-off into Plett on right & from Port Elizabeth take 1st turn-off into Plett on left at Engen One-Stop Garage. The house is 600 metres further on the left.

Bitou River Lodge

Sue and Paul Scheepers

R340 Bitou Valley Road, Plettenberg Bay
Tel: 044-535-9577 Fax: 044-535-9577
Email: info@bitou.co.za Web: www.bitou.co.za
Cell: 082-978-6164

For well-heeled South Africans "Plett" is the place to summer and its sophisticated buzz can border on the frenetic. Which is why Bitou River Lodge is such a find. Just east of town, it's close to Plett's glass-plated beach houses, bijou shops and restaurants, yet feels a million miles away. Paul and Sue wanted to make the most of the natural environment and have created a peaceful haven for nature lovers. The drive sweeps past a citrus orchard and horse paddock to the whitewashed lodge, which sits on five hectares of neat flower-filled gardens, with pool, chipping-green and river frontage. Behind Cape ash trees and honeysuckle, stable-style bedrooms have river-facing patios, where dazzling sunbirds congregate. The lime-washed, painted-pine rooms have slate-floored kitchenettes and bathrooms, and sliding doors keep them light-filled. Farmhouse feasts are served in the breakfast room, which adjoins a warm lounge where you can settle into birding books (there are 134 species in the area to tick off). Outside, the liquid-smooth lawn gathers all before it – boulders, benches and flowerbeds – as it slips silently toward the lily-leafed river. While away some time out here on one of Sue's eco-strolls, or watch busy weaver birds build upside-down nests and lazy ones sway in the reeds, while the ripple of canoe paddles, the splash of a kingfisher and whizz of a fly-reel provide a soothing summer soundtrack.

Rooms: 5: 3 kings and 2 twins, all with en-suite bath and shower.
Price: R495 - R695 pp sharing. Singles on request.
Meals: Full farmhouse breakfast included. Plenty of restaurants in nearby Plett.
Directions: Head east from Plettenberg Bay on N2. Immediately after bridge, turn left onto the R340. Bitou River Lodge is signed on left, 4.2km from the N2.

Anlin Beach House

Dermot and Fran Molloy
33 Roche Bonne Avenue, Plettenberg Bay
Tel: 044-533-3694 Fax: 044-533-3394
Email: stay@anlinbeachhouse.co.za Web: www.anlinbeachhouse.co.za

Like a moth to a lamp, the first thing I did here after dropping off my bags was head to the beach, irresistibly close (100 metres away) and tantalizing from the top-floor balcony. A run along the soft sands all the way to the Robberg Peninsula was exhilarating at sunset. Beneath cobalt blue skies, I passed only seals and surfers cresting the smooth ocean rollers. The beach really does seem to slow you down as both Dermot (a wine-marketer) and Fran (a trained counsellor) will attest. As we passed the quirky outdoor shower, Fran commented that she always wanted the place to be ultra up-to-date in terms of design, but comfortable at the same time, "I don't want guests to think: 'I can't sit on that'". The style is therefore contemporary, with walls and furnishings in natural colours imitating the beach, the ocean and dramatic rocky outcrops. The bedrooms have tiled floors and cream-coloured furniture drenched in light from the private patios and vast windows. Dermot's an avid collector of South African art so expect to see some interesting pieces. If you can, book the upstairs apartment. The view, which sweeps across the ocean to the Outeniqua Mountains, finally persuaded Fran to go for the house; "when a school of dolphins swam past, I knew I had to sign!" The kitchens, with their polished-cement surfaces and hi-tech gas hobs, all come well stocked with tea, coffee and other goodies. Don't forget to ask Dermot for his autograph either. He once worked as an extra on *Zulu Dawn*!

Rooms: 4: 1 upstairs apartment (potentially 2 units) with 3 beds and 2 bathrooms, both with shower only; 2 garden apartments, both sleep 3 with 1 shower bathroom each.
Price: From R450 pp to R850 pp. Singles +25%.
Meals: Self-catering, but a full Continental breakfast can be served in your apartment or on private patio.
Directions: From N2 heading east, R into Plett. Continue to circle & go straight over. Road descends to river and crosses it. Over circle, R onto Longships Dr then left into Roche Bonne Avenue, which has a brown B&B sign. Anlin Beach House is 50m on R.

Piesang Valley Lodge

John Elliott
Piesang Valley Road, Plettenberg Bay
Tel: 044-533-6283 Fax: 086-260-2485
Email: info@pvl.co.za Web: www.pvl.co.za
Cell: 072-5190-244

If ever a place resembled its owner, this is it. Unpretentious, laid-back, friendly and personal, John has bestowed these qualities on a lodge, part of which he built with his own hands using a special vertical construction technique (just nod and make understanding grunts). These are also the rooms of choice where pine and timber frame a scene of dark wood furniture, inviting beds and earthy rugs, soothed by white-washed walls and alabaster bathrooms. All open breezily onto the garden. There's a refreshing youthful energy here as well, something else you'll notice about John, who leads a tremendously healthy life. I challenge anyone to guess his correct age. After many years in the hospitality industry, it was his dream to start his own guesthouse and where better than on family ground, whose hill-top seat looks all the way down the valley into Plett and out to the Indian Ocean. There are plenty of good restaurants in the town close by, but you're welcome to bring your own grub and cook lunch and dinner in the kitchen. That's if you're still hungry after a bonanza breakfast with the birds. The garden is a great place to kick back with a cold beer, from the pool side if you so wish, and enjoy a gently sloping verdant scene of fifteen acres worth of lawn, tree and untouched bush across which playful house hounds tumble. "It's convenient and tranquil," says John. It's very good value too. *Plettenberg Bay Country Club is a couple of minutes away.*

Rooms: 6 rooms: all queen doubles or twins (2 bath/shower and 4 shower en-suite).
Price: R340 - R570 pp sharing.
Meals: Full breakfast included. Guests are welcome to cook their own lunch and dinner in the kitchen.
Directions: Take Piesang Valley Road turn-off from N2 into Plettenberg Bay. 1.4km down the road the lodge is on your right-hand side.

Tamodi Lodge and Stables

Owen and Lynne Johnston
Tamodi Lodge and Stables, Keerboom Heights, Plettenberg Bay
Tel: 044-534-8071 Fax: 044-534-8073
Email: owen@tamodi.co.za Web: www.tamodi.co.za
Cell: 082-551-9313

I had only one evening at Tamodi and I wasn't going to waste a minute of it by dining out at the local beachside Italian or cosying up to a log fire on one of the lodge sofas, surfing the web and watching movies on DSTV (these luxuries are available for lucky guests staying more than one night). I planned and executed my evening, though I say it myself, to perfection. So, this is what I did. I nipped down the hill to fetch my take-away supper. Whilst waiting for my seafood pasta, I was briefly distracted by spy-hopping whales and a glorious African sunset. I made my way back up the dirt road (avoiding porcupines, bushbuck and baboons) complete with a portion of tiramisu. I sampled some wines from Owen's private wine cellar and plumped for a local red. I decanted pasta and wine into appropriate crockery. I made my way out on to the deck and watched darkness descend over the forested valley and the Tsitsikamma Mountains. After dinner I listened to the sounds of the African night and observed how different the stars look in the southern hemisphere. I contemplated a midnight swim in the infinity pool, but decided instead to retreat under thatch and take a long hot soak in my suite's free-standing stone bathtub. And then I drifted off to a deep sleep until breakfast. The whole evening was an exercise in precision self-pampering. But really I would have preferred several weeks at Tamodi.

Rooms: 3: 1 standard luxury queen, en-s bath & shower; 1 standard luxury king, en-s bath & shower (can split into 2 x 3-quarter beds); 1 honeymoon suite with king 4-poster & en-s bath, indoor/outdoor shr.
Price: R795 - R1,095 pp sharing. Singles on request: supplement 50%. Whole house available by arrangement.
Meals: Full cooked and continental breakfast.
Directions: From Cape Town take N2. Approx' 10km past Plettenberg Bay towards Port Elizabeth, go past 1st 2 turn-offs to Keurboomstrand & at top of hill find a Vodacom cellphone tower. Turn R at foot of tower & go 1.5 km.

That Place

Jo and David Butler

The Crags
Tel: 044-534-8886
Email: info@thatplace.co.za Web: www.thatplace.co.za
Cell: 082-578-1939 (Mon-Fri 8am-4:30pm)

This is "that place...," you know the one you talk about for years after you've been there. "Do you remember the time we went to South Africa and stayed in 'That Place' where we watched the elephants wandering through their paddock across the valley, where we hazily dreamt in the hand-crafted sauna. We braaied and feasted for hours on the deck, the kids duck-diving and splashing in the waters of the private pool - do you remember?" Jo and David have created a memory-building, self-catering home. And that's just what it is - a home. It's not grand or pretentious, just comfortable and happy to have you. I was shown around by a very modest David who failed to mention that the great wooden table and chairs, the sauna and the three cheeky fish sculptures suspended on the wall (amongst other details) had sprung from his own gifted fingers. I met the dogs too, all eight of them, from John Keats the Great Dane down to Robert the feisty Jack Russell. Don't worry, these chaps live next door and won't bother you unless you want them to. But if you want them to...! Also next door are elephants which can be seen from the house, along with monkeys and a huge variety of birds. "You named your dog after a poet?" I asked Jo. "David did," she replied, "he's very into his poetry." Sounds like the perfect man to me - unfortunately already taken by Jo who is equally wonderful.

Rooms: One 3-bedroom self-catering cottage let as a whole: 1 king with en-suite bath and shower and 2 twins (1 ideal for children).
Price: From R750 - R1,800 per night for the whole house.
Meals: Self-catering, but Bramon Wine Estate an easy walk away for lunch. Dinner can be arranged to be ready in fridge/oven for your arrival. Discuss with Jo when you book.
Directions: Travelling in the direction of Port Elizabeth on the N2, 20km east of Plettenberg Bay. At The Bramon Wine Shop, turn right off the N2 and follow the signs to 'That Place.'

Map Number: 5

Entry Number: 124

Lily Pond Country Lodge

Niels and Margret Hendriks
R102 Nature's Valley Road, The Crags
Tel: 044-534-8767 Fax: 044-534-8686
Email: info@lilypond.co.za Web: www.lilypond.co.za
Cell: 082-746-8782

From the moment I met Niels and Margret I was confident of a great stay. Whilst their lodge is a monument to mathematical modernity (straight lines and strong angles prevail), its slickness is balanced by the natural surroundings (beige and taupe walls contrast strikingly with the greenery of Nature's Valley). Everyone benefits from the tranquility and abundant birdlife here. The lily ponds provide a lush home to a mesmerising array of flora and fauna. The frogs serenaded me with their croaky chorus as I braved a mid-winter swim in the black infinity pool. I might go for the warmer option next time of the jacuzzi on the pond's edge. But any excuse to soak in my polished concrete bath and an opportunity to admire the garden suite's quirky design. Think African colonial (tribal paintings, gauzy curtains and kudu-skin rugs) with every bit of stuffiness surgically removed and replaced with funky exposed brickwork, slick crete-stone floors and a bright ochre-and-white colour scheme. In summer, the lilies outside are a carpet of colour and balmy evenings are set aside for drinks and nibbles followed by a many-coursed, mouth-watering meal in the (equally angular) restaurant. Margret, a supremely good cook, has trained a marvelous Xhosa chef, Vincent, who has a flair for flavour fusions; he crosses oriental and European dishes and is fond of South African bobotie wonton starters and sushi ice desserts. All the staff are friendly and, for people who "never meant to run a guest house," Niels and Margret are doing a seriously good job. *Massage treatments on request.*

Rooms: 10: 4 king/twins & 2 luxury suites, all en-s bath & sh'r; 3 luxury garden suites (extra-length king/tw) & 1 honeymoon suite (extra-length king/dble), all en-s bath & sh'r plus outdoor sh'r.
Price: R595 - R1,190 pp sharing (single supplement 50%).
Meals: Full breakfast included. Fusion kitchen with 4-course dinner R225 (vegetarian on request). Light lunches available.
Directions: 22km east of Plettenberg Bay and close to Nature's Valley. From CT take first exit to Nature's Valley. From Port Elizabeth take second exit Nature's Valley (14km after toll) to the left. Then follow R102 for 3km and turn right at the sign.

Redford House

Dr Clive Noble and Colleen Noble

12 Redford Road, The Crags
Tel: 044-534-8877 Fax: 044-534-8188
Email: redfordhouse@mweb.co.za Web: www.redfordhouse.co.za
Cell: 076-907-1019

Redford House, with its ploughs, wagon-wheels, rolling hills, meandering rivers and wizened, centuries-old oak trees, seems to exist in some previous and rather idyllic age; a rural haven to be found perhaps in the pages of a Thomas Hardy novel. If I had been staying longer I would surely have settled down on the verandah with a copy of Country Life to absorb some of this pure bucolic peace where only the reassuring buzz of a bee, the brief agitation of a rooster or the distant lowing of a cow might disrupt me. Instead I took in some polo and quaffed a glass of Pimms by the pool-house studio (Wednesday night is 'life drawing' night) before joining my hosts in the yellowwood-beamed Old Settler's dining room to hear stories of the buffalo and elephants that once roamed these pastures. Colleen, who is warm, gentle and caring and has spent a lifetime in conservancy, and Dr Clive, an orthopaedic surgeon, are a fascinating and erudite couple. Their home has become a sort of Garden Route Speakers' Corner where the Nobles host hot soup evenings at which you might learn about the history of global warming or perhaps Gondwanaland. Or you might just light a log fire and enjoy a cup of cocoa in the splendid pine-panelled drawing room before slipping off to the land of nod amid soft cotton in a cottage that Mrs Tiggywinkle would have loved.

Rooms: 4: 2 in Noble House (king bed, en-s bath & shr); 1 in Carriage House (queen bed, en-s with bath and shower); Mrs Tiggywinkle's self-catering cottage.
Price: Noble House: R600 - R700 pp sharing; Carriage House: R400 - R500 pp sh; Mrs Tiggywinkle's Cottage R600 - R700 for whole cottage. Single supp R50.
Meals: Full English breakfast included. Mrs Tiggywinkle's is self-catering. Dinner with stories by arrangement (R120 - R180). Breakfast R50.
Directions: On N2, 17km east of Plettenberg Bay L into Redford Rd. From PE, 16km from toll gate R into Redford Rd. 3km up Redford Rd, look for white poles & sign on L.

Map Number: 5

Entry Number: 126

Garden Route, Western Cape

The Fernery Lodge and Chalets

CJ Müller

Forest Ferns, Blueliliesbush,
Tsitsikamma
Tel: 042-280-3588
Fax: 041-394-5114
Email:
reservations@forestferns.co.za
Web: www.forestferns.co.za

You've heard us harping on about beautiful views before, but now I need an even stronger superlative! Cradling my welcome G&T, I watched an enormous waterfall relentlessly plummet 30 metres down a river gorge before making its way to the sea. Beyond the forest I could see all the way to the ocean. On certain clear days, whales and dolphins complete an impossibly picturesque scene here. Unsurprisingly, The Fernery focuses on their natural visual treasures, from lodge bedrooms to dining areas, jacuzzis and pools. Decks and towers offer yet more angles for kloof-gazing with sundowners. I stayed in the main lodge, the perfect place to relax (with a massage) after another leg-achingly long drive. Here you find yourself on the end of some serious pampering, with large inviting rooms leading to even larger bathrooms. Up the hill from the lodge, wooden chalets boast traditional wood-burning heaters and outdoor braais to give them a back-to-nature feel... and no TVs. But fear not, there is entertainment at hand for chalet guests, including a pub, pool, massage therapist, driving range and canopied jacuzzi overhanging the waterfall valley. And beyond these is Frans' gift to tandem couple travellers: the luxury twin self-catering chalet. Thought through to the last detail, two sleek suites branch off a central kitchen and dining area like arms off the nave of a church, while gliding walls allow each couple to retreat into plush privacy in one swift swoosh. At last travelling couples can have their cake and eat it.

Rooms: 16: 6 dbles en-s in lodge; 6 dble/twin B&B chalets en-s bathroom; 2 self-cater chalets with dbles & twins with 1 bathroom; 2 luxury S-C twin chalets with 2 full en-s bedrooms.

Price: B&B chalets R770 - R945 pp sharing; S-C family chalets (sleep 4) R1760 - R2120 per chalet; luxury S-C twin chalets: R3170 - R3800; B&B lodge suites: R1020 - R1200 pp sh. No extras for singles.

Meals: Full breakfast incl' for B&B chalets & lodge suites. 4-course dinner or 3-course dinner braai available for all guests.

Directions: Take Blueliliesbush turn-off, 4km from PE side of Storms River bridge, then continue 7.5km down signed track from road.

Thabile Lodge

Len Bornman
Vergelegen Road, between Oudtshoorn and De Rust
Tel: 044-251-6116 Fax: 044-251-6115
Email: info@thabilelodge.co.za Web: www.thabilelodge.co.za
Cell: 082-564-5295

Arriving at Thabile Lodge is like returning home after a long journey. Len, who's reformed the 110-year-old building into the welcoming house it is today, greets his guests with genuine delight. You'll then also be welcomed by Garfield, the largest cat you'll ever meet and who Len claims 'beat anorexia', and his best friend Pepsi, the alsation. The rooms have all been lovingly designed and built by Len. Simple and tastefully decorated each chalet has its own verandah, which is where you'll want to be as the sun is setting and the mountains make their way through all the autumn colours before turning dark. But the main house is where all the action happens. There's a spa with Jacuzzi and steam room; a fantastic bar area where you can cheer on the sports team of your choice and the beautiful, elevated verandah where I indulged in cooked-to-perfection ostrich steak and a blended red, chosen for me by Len, that went down way too easily. Before I knew it the Boegoe Blits was out and this signalled the start of a wonderful evening with new friends. What really makes this place special is Len and his amazing staff. As I enthusiastically waved goodbye to my new friend, I was already planning my next visit.

Rooms: 12: 10 king/twin en-suite with shower; 2 king/twin en-suite with bath and shower.
Price: R450 pp sharing per night; R650 for singles; R340 for children under 12 years. 10% discount for longer stays (2 nights plus).
Meals: Full breakfast included. A la carte dinner available every evening for R180.
Directions: Follow the N12 from Oudtsoorn to De Rust for 20km. Turn left at the Vergelegen sign. Thabile Lodge is well sign-posted on the right less than 2km down the road.

Rolbaken Guest House and Nature Reserve

Dick and Mary Carr
Daskop Road, Between Oudtshoorn and De Rust
Tel: 044-251-6191
Email: dickcarr@hilbert.co.za Web: www.rolbaken.co.za
Cell: 072-248-4830

It took Dick and Mary just half an hour to fall in love with this scenic, tranquil farm and gazing at the blend of Kammanassie Mountains and rolling green fields you can see why. Mary grew up in deepest Africa and Dick is a conservation biologist, so, all being well, most of their 500 hectares – recently designated a nature reserve – will soon see the introduction of game to go with their 103 recorded species of birds. Dick roared up to greet me on a quad bike, while Mary followed more sedately with a plate of home-baked muffins and organic strawberries. The farm's old schoolhouse, beautifully renovated and absolutely spankingly clean, is yours to enjoy. There are huge comfy sofas to collapse on in the high-beamed lounge and three private bedrooms lightly decorated with restored antiques and pastoral pictures – although the most spectacular pastoral scene is straight out of the large windows. The kitchen has all a cook could desire (plus a shaded outdoor braai by the splash pool), but your hosts are more than happy to cook up a breakfast of freshly-laid eggs or lay on a 3-course meal, tailored to your desires. If you wish to work off some energy, head up to the dam for a swim (so private, guests have been known to skinny dip) or take the kids down to say hello to the sheep, donkeys and other livestock. For the fitter and more adventurous among us, a guided 6km hike across beautiful, extensive farm land to ancient rock art sites can be arranged. As I trundled off down the road to Oudtshoorn I felt as if I was waving goodbye to old friends.... See you soon, Mary and Dick.

Rooms: 1 house: 3 bedrooms (1 queen, 1 twin, 1 double & bunk), all en-suite. Cot available. Pet-friendly.
Price: R350 - R400 pp sharing. Kids 4–14 years: R200. Under 4s free.
Meals: Fully-equipped kitchen & large braai in hse. Groceries on request at cost price. Full farm breakfast (R60) & 3-course evening meal, incl' wine (R175) by arrangement.
Directions: From Oudtshoorn, follow N12 twds De Rust. At Dysselsdorp turn R, then L after bridge. 1.6km (road becomes gravel), then R onto unsigned gravel road opposite stadium. Continue for 18.3km, past Leeublad farm. Rolbaken on L, just after cresting hill. GPS S33 40.33' E22 33.82'

De Zeekoe Guest Farm

Paula and Pottie Potgieter

Zeekoegat Farm, R328 (road to Mossel Bay), Oudtshoorn
Tel: 044-272-6721 Fax: 044-272-8534
Email: info@dezeekoe.co.za Web: www.dezeekoe.co.za
Cell: 082-551-3019 or 082-584-9957

Right in the heart of ostrich country you'll find De Zeekoe, whose dusty plains are ringed by mountains holding back the coastal cloud. I arrived on a sultry afternoon and took refuge in the cool, tile-floored farmhouse among soft leather chairs, vibrant oil landscapes and low Oregon pine windows. Next door, a large dining room overlooking the Outeniqua Mountains and river bed promised a memorable supper and the slickly luxurious main house rooms (refurbished this year) lured me in from the indigenous gardens, source of many of chef's ingredients. Beyond the saltwater pool is a wall of reeds where fish eagles nest and beyond that a river - the farm is named after the hippos once found here - where you can quietly canoe under a reliable summer sun. The farm stretches over 2,000 hectares, home to springbuck, ostriches, cattle and alfalfa stretching as far as the eye can see, so borrow a bike and introduce yourself. But I lost my heart to my rustic waterfront cabin - one of only four so ensure you ask for one of these early on! In a washed-blue dawn, the mountains now faintly outlined like mascara, bright birds busied about the reeds (there are 250 species to spot). I sat on the deck, its legs planted firmly in the dam, as my neighbour cast his line. So beautiful, so peaceful…. De Zeekoe completely relaxed me and I long to return. *Beauty therapies, small weddings and functions available. Wild meerkat (one of the 'shy-5') tours done on the reserve by guide Devey. All activities subject to weather conditions. Discounts for staying guests.*

Rooms: 20: 7 luxury, 8 superior in & around house, king/twin/dble with air-con & en-suite bath and/or shower; 4 rustic waterfront cabins with two bedrooms, shared showers and kitchenette.
Price: R470 – R1,300 pp.
Meals: Full breakfast incl'. A la carte menu available or set menu at R280 pp. All products free-range & fresh from farm. Light lunches avail' & wide variety wines.
Directions: Head west from Oudtshoorn (towards Calitzdorp) on R62. Turn L at sign to Mossel Bay on R328. After 7km turn R on dirt road, for 2km to De Zeekoe on L.

Map Number: 5

Entry Number: 130

Mooiplaas Guest House

Viljee and Hanlie Keller
Volmoed, Oudtshoorn
Tel: 044-279-4019
Fax: 086-508-2437
Email:
info@mooiplaasguesthouse.co.za
Web:
www.mooiplaasguesthouse.co.za
Cell: 082-504-7156

Mooiplaas is a family-run farm, dating back to the 1800s, and Viljee and Hanlie are the fourth generation of Kellers to live here. Their main focus is ostriches with some maize, alfalfa and cattle thrown into the mix too – this is a real working farm. Hanlie is a self-proclaimed perfectionist, so expect nothing less than luxury in the rooms. Large and airy with high ceilings, custom-made ostrich leather headboards (leather from their farm, of course) and a verandah with views overlooking the often snow-capped Swartberg Mountains, it didn't take me long to relax and unwind with a glass of Muscadel. Although one is spoilt for choice with the Swartberg in front and the Outeniqua Mountains behind, my attention was irresistibly drawn to the baby ostrich running around the lawn. While I was bombarding Hanlie with ostrich questions, Piet, her son, arrived back from school and started looking for a torch. His Friday job is to check the eggs in the incubator to see which ones have been fertilized. This I had to see. The set-up is incredible, but the best part was going to the nursery to see the new-borns. Mooiplaas is known for its delicious ostrich steaks, its warm hospitality and its elevated location with magnificent panoramic views of the mountains and the night skies. With so much to see, do and learn here, it was a real shame that I only had one night. *Personalised guided ostrich tours available (R85 pp) and ostrich products on offer.*

Rooms: 16: 4 superior/honeymoon suites; 8 luxury doubles (4 with self-catering options), 1 country house with 4 rooms. All rooms are en-suite with bath and shower.
Price: R491 - R860 pp/night. Singles on request.
Meals: Full breakfast included. BBQ dinner on request. Picnic baskets also available.
Directions: From R62 take the R328 to Mossel Bay. After 8km follow sign to right. After 1.1km the farm is on your left.

Boesmanskop

Tinie Bekker
Kruisrivier, near Calitzdorp
Tel: 044-213-3365 Fax: 044-213-3365
Email: info@boesmanskop.co.za Web: www.boesmanskop.co.za

It's amazing how many times I drove Route 62 without taking the Kruisrivier turn-off between Oudtshoorn and Calitzdorp. If you do you'll discover, along with the famed red stone hills and awesome Klein Karoo scenery, Tinie Bekker's small dairy and ostrich farm tucked neatly into the Swartberg mountain. Tinie is entirely modest about the two guest rooms he built on account of a billiards table (long story), calling 'simple farm accommodation' what more arty types might describe as 'rustic chic suites'. Rustic in the sense of reed ceilings, wonky wood floors and pebble-stoned showers – and the swallows which dart in and out in the evenings – but chic with their fine white linen and cleverly-restored old family furniture, like porcupine quill lampshades and a bathtub quirkily wrapped in a wine barrel. Wonderfully unkempt gardens are a kaleidoscope of colours with such novelties (in South Africa) as pansies, while the vegetable garden provides much of your evening meal. But he's modest about his green fingers... and modest, too, about his 'paint-by-numbers' cookery skills, which allowed him to conjure me up freshly-baked bread and a delicious four-course meal in the main farmhouse. Even better, Tinie's refreshingly reasonable with his rates. Early the next morning I was taken to see cows milked in the small dairy, then spent a memorable half-hour with a just-hatching baby ostrich... before tackling the only immodest thing around here, the towering Swartberg mountain with its famed helter-skelter pass.

Rooms: 2: 1 king with extra single, 1 king with 2 extra singles, both with en-suite shower and bath. Pet-friendly.
Price: R330 pp sharing for room only. Singles + R50. R580 pp for dinner, bed & breakfast.
Meals: Full breakfast R70. 4-course dinner R180 (excluding wine) by prior arrangement.
Directions: From Oudtshoorn, take R62 towards Calitzdorp for 30km, then turn R down gravel road to Kruisrivier. After 6km, turn R at T-junction, then continue for 13km. Farm on right.

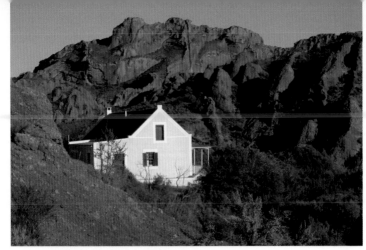

Red Stone Hills

Petro and Hermanus Potgieter
Oudtshoorn
Tel: 044-213-3783 Fax: 044-213-3291
Email: info@redstone.co.za Web: www.redstone.co.za

The humbling sense of the passage of time pervades this 3,000-hectare veld, whose desert colours swirl with Van Gogh vibrancy. The current Potgieters are the fifth generation to farm this land (ostrich, vineyards, cattle, fruit), but that lineage is put into perspective by the red stone hills. They date to the enon-conglomerate period, formed 120 million years ago when the earth twisted and a torrent of sanguine mud-stone settled and solidified; a few million years later, bushmen hid in the hills' stone pockets and painted wildlife; and in the 1790s Karoo cottages completed the picture. It's all been authenticated by erudite visitors: botanists, geologists and a chap from Roberts who identified 210 birds here, including eagles, black stork and five varieties of kingfisher. But you'll find Hermanus and Petro plenty knowledgeable themselves. We drove out along dusty tracks leading past the schoolhouse that his father donated to the mixed community (which still congregates there), through babbling brooks to Chinese lanterns and blankets of fynbos and medicinal succulents. Hermanus will name them all. Petro says he lives in the past, whereas she's an artist facing the future. Also on offer at certain times of year are geological, botanical and fossil tours. There are many ways to enjoy the scenery, cycling, hiking, horse-riding and ostrich farm tours… kids will love the morning tractor ride to feed the animals. When you're tired out, your sleepy cottage, with original Oregon pine doors and floors and farm-made furniture, awaits.

Rooms: 6 cottages: all fully self-contained with 1, 2 or 3 bedrooms & shared or en-s bathrooms, baths &/or shrs.
Price: R290 - R450 pp self-catering. Singles and special family rates on request.
Meals: Full breakfast R78, continental breakfast R60. 3-course farm dinners or semi-prepared braai packs on request.
Directions: Halfway between Calitzdorp & Oudtshoorn on R62. Head west from Oudtshoorn 28km, then Kruisrivier turn-off. Red Stone 6km down this road. Another entrance between foot of Swartberg mountain & Cango Caves via Matjiesrivier.

The Retreat at Groenfontein

Marie and Grant Burton
Calitzdorp
Tel: 044-213-3880 Fax: 086-271-5373
Email: info@groenfontein.com Web: www.groenfontein.com

A tiny gravel road twists along the sides of one idyllic to another yet more secluded valley, past old Cape Dutch farm buildings and jaw-dropping views, eventually arriving at the Burtons' Victorian-colonial homestead. Marie and Grant ran a popular wilderness lodge in Namibia before trawling southern Africa for a new Eden and it took years to find. It was worth the wait. The view from the verandah, where guest meals are served around one sociable table with your hosts (and where I sampled mouthwatering smoked snoek mousse and ostrich casserole), crosses a valley and climbs the Burtons' own mountain before joining the vast Swartberg Nature Reserve, now a World Heritage Site. What with paths winding up to intimate rock pools and excellent marked mountain trails, the opportunities for merry traipsing are limitless. When it gets hot, you can swim in the river, dam or pool, or collapse inside the gloriously cool house with its original marble fireplace and pine and yellowwood flooring. Take your pick from luxury rooms set apart from the homestead with slate floors, fabulous mountain views and surreal stoep stargazing, or more traditional bedrooms in the main house – equally inviting. It really is an incredible area to explore, with kloofs, mountain wilderness, half-forgotten roads and many animals and birds to look out for. But, best of all, you come back to award-winning hospitality: delicious table d'hôte dinners, welcoming hosts and a truly relaxed household. Give yourselves 2 nights at least!

Rooms: 8: 4 standard rooms in main house (king/qu/twin), 4 garden rooms (king/twin). All rooms have en-s shower &/or bath. All rooms pet-friendly.
Price: R480 - R980 pp sharing, including 3 or 4-course dinner and full breakfast. Singles on request.
Meals: Full breakfast & 3 or 4-course table d'hôte dinner (without wine) included. Fully licensed. Light lunches & picnics from R50.
Directions: From Oudtshoorn take R62 twds Calitzdorp 30km. Turn R onto dirt road signed Kruisrivier. After 17km keep L at fork as road gets narrower & follow 10.7km until sign for The Retreat to R. From Calitzdorp L at Groenfontein sign - 19km to house. Drive slowly.

Map Number: 2

Entry Number: 134

Bosch Luys Kloof Private Nature Reserve

Gerhard and Ans Rademeyer

Seweweekspoort, Off Route 62, Between Ladismith and Calitzdorp
Tel: 023-581-5046 Fax: 023-581-5038
Email: boschkloofpnr@telkomsa.net Web: www.boschluyskloof.co.za

The drive to Bosch Luys Kloof was an adventure in itself. Meandering through the Seweweekspoort with the swirling rocks above and then crawling down the original Bosch Luys Kloof Pass, built in 1860 for the width of a single wagon, I couldn't help but wonder what was waiting for me at the end. Sheer beauty, remoteness and tranquility would sum it up! Gerard and Ans have lovingly spent over 14 years returning the 14000ha back to its original form and creating a mini-refuge for nature-loving guests to explore. With 4x4 routes, walks of varying distances and difficulties, and game drives available too, you are guaranteed that no two days will be the same. The chalets built from natural materials with traditional thatched roofs are the perfect place to unwind with baths that boast spectacular views of the veld; or an outdoor shower if you want to get even closer to nature while you wash. The outstanding team prepares all your meals and before dinner Gerard and Ans welcome you at the bar, made from old sleepers, which opens onto the pool area. With a watering-hole mere metres away, your chances of combining sundowners and game-viewing are high. This really is a special place hidden away near the Gamkapoort Dam so make sure you give yourself enough time to explore the surroundings and enjoy Gerard and Ans's wonderful hospitality.

Rooms: 10 chalets: 4 twin/king en-s bath & outdoor sh'r; 5 dble chalets, twin/king en-s bath & outdoor sh'r in main bedroom & en-s sh'r in 2nd room; guest-house: 4 rooms en-s bathrooms, large lounge, sundeck, fireplace.
Price: Dinner, Bed & Breakfast: R1,040 pp. Full Day: R1,350 pp. Includes ALL meals. Nature drive included with Full Day tariff.
Meals: 2-course breakfast, 2-course lunch and 3-course dinner all inclusive.
Directions: Please contact us for directions or visit the website.

Mymering Guest House

Dr Andy & Penny Hillock
Mymering, Dwarsrivier, Ladismith
Tel: 028-5511-548 Fax: 028-551-1313
Email: penny@mymering.com Web: www.mymering.com
Cell: 082-891-2463

You'll hear Andy's laugh rolling through Dwarsrivier valley before you reach Mymering. And I'd bet two bunches of their home-grown table grapes - destined for Fortnum's, darling - that the joke was one of Penny's naughty ones. The Hillocks relocated from Port Elizabeth when surgeon Andy decided, reluctantly, to retire. "But look at this!" he announces, surveying his sublime, Cezannean kingdom after a brisk morning hike. "Stunning!" Andy co-owned the vineyard next door for aeons so the couple were frequent Ladismithers and know the area like natives. "Andy is tour guide," says Penny, showing off her shiny industrial kitchen after a wine-soaked supper of spicy butternut soup, soft salmon with minted peas, and creme brûlée, all served on zebra-print crockery. "I'm chef." Penny's glam taste is also on show in the glittering Mae West suite, one of three secluded chalets (the others being Madiba and Jacuzzi), each bedecked as their name implies. Lavender and Rosemary, two linked family chalets sharing a plunge pool where the others have their own, pay tribute to the farm's bygone days harvesting essential oils. Gravel paths through indigenous jungle unearth a thatched self-catering cottage, ideal if you want to spend a few days exploring the majestic Swartberg Pass and Seweweekspoort, both built by Thomas Bain, Andy's demi-god. Driving through the latter, pausing by a babbling brook to sup champagne, was my most exquisitely decadent Karoo moment! *Last year saw the launch of their boutique Hillock wines. Mymering is open for wine-tastings, lunch and teas every day.*

Rooms: 8: 2 king/twin with full en-s; 3 king with full en-s; 1 king with dble shr; 2 self-catering cottage with king/twin with en-s sh'r & queen with en-s sh'r.
Price: R600 pp sharing B&B. Cottage: R1,600 per night for whole cottage.
Meals: Full breakfast included. 3-course gourmet dinner, lunch & picnic baskets available on request.
Directions: On R62 between Ladismith and Barrydale. Take the Laingsburg road and follow clearly-marked signs. GPS S 33 29 55.26 E 21 10 18.65

Map Number: 2

Entry Number: 136

Les Hauts de Montagu Guest Lodge

Myriam and Eric Brillant

Route 62, Montagu
Tel: 023-614-2514 Fax: 023-614-3517
Email: info@leshautsdemontagu.co.za Web: www.leshautsdemontagu.co.za
Cell: 083-529-3389 (Myriam) 083-528-9250 (Eric)

If you set your sights solely on staying in Montagu itself you would completely miss this peaceful oasis, sitting contentedly on the green slopes of the Langeberg Mountains, just three kilometres further along the road. As I slunk slowly up the long driveway past the helipad (sadly the Greenwood chopper was in for a service), Les Hauts de Montagu revealed itself in all its glory. It is not difficult to see why Eric and Myriam (both Congolese by birth, but with years of Parisian industry experience) instantly fell *tête* over *talons* for this place; its setting is sensational. Perched high on the hillside it enjoys expansive views of the fynbos-clad valley and their 5-hectare plantation of olives. The main Cape Dutch farmhouse dates from 1865 and it has taken two years of painstaking restoration to bring the building back to life. These days, perfectly scrumptious breakfasts of lavish fruit platters and toasted treats are served under 21 huge beams that hold up the roof. At night, returning to the lodge after taking Myriam's excellent advice on Montagu's finest supper spots, I crunched along the loose stones leading the way to my cottage. A soaring chimney encourages the fire beneath on cold winter nights, while the huge glass doors allow refreshing breezes on hot summer ones. The glorious outside shower the following morning meant washing in the full view of Montagu…. I was thankful it was those three kilometres away! *There is a chapel for small weddings.*

Rooms: 10: 1 Honeymoon Suite and 1 Garden Suite, all with 4-posters; 4 superior suites (3 kings & 1 twin); 4 standard rooms (3 kings and 1 twin).
Price: R550 - R950 pp sharing. Singles on request.
Meals: Full breakfast included.
Directions: From Cape Town, take N1 to Worcester, then R60 + R62 to Montagu. Pass Montagu, stay on R62 for 3km. Hauts de Montagu signed on R. Helipad and airstrip also available.

Entry Number: 137

Map Number: 4

Onse Rus Guesthouse

Lisa Smith and Diana Jacobsz
47 Church St, Prince Albert
Tel: 023-541-1380 Fax: 086-548-9350
Email: info@onserus.co.za Web: www.onserus.co.za
Cell: 083-629-9196

You know you're staying in a historic house when the local tour guide stops by the verandah to enthuse about its archetypal Prince Albert gable. And you know you're in good hands when tea and home-made cake appear magically on your poolside table within minutes of your arrival. Restful in name, restful in nature, the 150-year-old Cape Dutch Onse Rus is the perfect place to experience Lisa Smith's particular brand of hospitality, which involves treating guests like friends from the moment they ring the bell. She fell in love with the house ten years ago and now runs it with the help of her wonderful mother Di. The five thatched bedrooms all have private entrances, high ceilings, white walls and simple Karoo furnishings. One used to be part of the bakery, another was the printing room for a local newspaper. The house has some history! The large living room, where breakfast is served around a sociable table, is hung with photos of Lisa's other love – her horses. Outside there's a swimming pool (a thing of beauty in such a hot climate) and shaded patio for relaxing over a good book. Explore the villagey delights of Prince Albert with its tea shops, galleries and award-winning dairy, take the unspeakably dramatic drive over the swirling Swartberg pass or the gentler (yet equally stunning) Meiringspoort towards Oudtshoorn, or try olive-tasting at the nearby farms. Superb. *Horse-riding available on the family farm, 30km from Prince Albert (R250 pp for a 2-hour ride).*

Rooms: 5: king/twin with private entrances, en-suite shower and/or bath; 3 have a lounge area and patio.
Price: R420 - R475 pp sharing. Singles on request.
Meals: Breakfast included. Snacks and meals for groups available on request.
Directions: On the corner of the main street (Kerk or Church St) and Bank Sts.

Karoo, Western Cape

Karoo View Cottages

Julie & Richard Waterston

Magrieta Prinsloo Road, Prince Albert
Tel: 023-541-1929 Fax: 086-689-7000
Email: julie@karooview.co.za Web: www.karooview.co.za
Cell: 082-882-5342

Julie and Richard have sampled CIY (cook it yourself) getaways the world over in the name of research and with Karoo View they've got it spot on. Their deluxe cottages sit poised gracefully on a koppie, just a hop, skip and a jump from Prince Albert's main street. With the sense of elevation on my private stoep, savouring the last of the evening's sun, I gazed idly (I moved in no other way during my stay) from the multi-coloured rooftops of the quaint town, across the rugged sandy veld and out to the imposing Swartberg mountains. The interior, that offers an equally tranquil space, conveys Julie's adulation for Karoo colours: dusty grey sofas, aloe-green blankets, off-white walls, deep brown fireplaces, complemented with vaulted reed ceilings and cool tiled floors. After a cosy night's sleep, comforted by my heated blanket (the winter months are few, but bitter), I awoke to admire the garden blossom as the sun began its journey once again. Keen to explore further than my stoep, I joined Richard for a nature walk through the neatly-labelled indigenous maze of plant life and secluded braai areas, one of which, hidden in a stone boma, is fully equipped to cook up a storm – there's even a plunge pool to dip in between courses. The cottages' kitchens also have it all, including panini toasters! Julie also offers braai hampers and will do your shopping. Spoilt is the word! Although, of course, it's up to you to pick your own from their veggie tunnel. A real Karoo view and experience not be missed.

Rooms: 4: 2 chalets, each comprising 2 private/interconnecting suites. Each sleeps max 3 in various bed arrangements. Two with full en-s bathrooms, two en-s bathrooms with showers only.
Price: R395 - R525 pp for 2 or more sharing. Children R250 pp sharing same suite as adult. Single rates upon request.
Meals: Continental breakfast provided in chalet. Full breakfast, lunch and braai baskets can be provided.
Directions: 350m off the main street of the village.

Entry Number: 139

Map Number: 2

Mai's Guest Lodge

Mai Shallow
81 Church Street, Prince Albert
Tel: 023-541-1188
Email: mais@telkomsa.net Web: www.maisbandb.co.za
Cell: 072-635-0902

'Open' read the sign on the gate… easier read than done, so it turned out. Finally I approached the front door, hoping my slightly humiliating tussle with the gate hadn't been witnessed. But Mai is a naturally warm and easy-going person and immediately put me at my ease. She arrived in South Africa from Ireland many moons ago - "I was only meant to be here for two years, but if you want to make God laugh, tell him your plans!" The tranquillity and slow pace of life is what attracted Mai to Prince Albert, qualities echoed within her traditional Cape Dutch home, although a generous dash of Irish charm and warmth is instantly felt when you enter the vibrant mod red lounge. Mai has created a variety of private spaces, all with a touch of colour and a quirky item or two; the bedrooms share all of this, as well as highlighting the original 19th-century features of the house: high ceilings, solid wooden floors and sash windows. I soon found my spot on the wooden bench on the front stoep watching village life go by. In the morning fresh and abundant breakfasts are laid out, filling the breakfast bar from head to toe, and served on the vine-sheltered terrace or the sun-filled dining room. Mai's love for her home and joy in sharing it with others is easy to participate in. "You never know who is going to knock on the door," she says. I suggest you be the next.

Rooms: 4: 2 queens with 1 single; 1 double with 1 single; 1 double with 1 single bunk. All with a/c and en-suite showers.
Price: R400 - R460 sharing. Singles R500 - R560.
Meals: Full breakfast included.
Directions: Prince Albert is 45km off N1 or from N12. Mai's Guest Lodge is on Main Street next to the Swartberg Hotel. GPS: 33o 13' 20.82 S 22o 01' 45.39 E

Map Number: 2

Entry Number: 140

Lemoenfontein Game Lodge

Ingrid Köster
Beaufort West
Tel: 023-415-2847 Fax: 086-650-9928
Email: lemoen@mweb.co.za Web: www.lemoenfontein.co.za

Lemoenfontein, at the foot of the Nuweveld Mountains, is one of those places where whatever your mood on arrival – and after a tiring drive down the N1, mine was ropey - a calmness envelops you like magic vapour. I was suddenly enjoying a cool drink on the vast wooden verandah, gazing over measureless miles of veld and chatting happily to Ingrid about the history of the place. It was built as a hunting lodge in 1850, then became a sanatorium for respiratory sufferers (the dry Karoo air was beneficial), a farm and finally (and still) a nature reserve. Everything has been done well here, no corners cut and the result is a most relaxing, hassle-free stay. Rooms are stylish and understated with top-quality fabrics and completely comfortable beds. Outside, lawns, a pool, bar and braai area and the veld are all segregated by high dry-stone walls. You *must* go on a game drive through the reserve before dinner - to look at all the buck, zebra and giraffe, of course, but also to be out in such scenery as the sun goes down. And one final thing: dinner when we got back was at first mouth-watering, then lip-smacking. A real South African experience. *All rooms are air-conditioned.*

Rooms: 14: 8 double all en-suite (4 bath/shower, 4 shower); 6 twin all en-suite (2 bath/shower, 4 shower).
Price: R445 – R645 pp.
Meals: Full breakfast available from R80 pp. 3-course dinner from R160 pp.
Directions: From the N1, 2km north of Beaufort West. Turn onto De Jagers Pass Road at the Lemoenfontein sign. After 1.5km turn left at the white Lemoenfontein gates. Go 4km up dirt track, following signs. GPS S32 18 59 E22 36 11.

Oyster Bay Lodge

Hans and Liesbeth Verstrate-Griffioen

Between Tsitsikamma & St Francis Bay, Oyster Bay
Tel: 042-297-0150 Fax: 042-297-0150
Email: info@oysterbaylodge.com Web: www.oysterbaylodge.com
Cell: 082-700-0553

Here's yet another film-set masquerading as a B&B… this one is for the beach scenes! Hans and Liesbeth have the very envy-inducing run of three and a half kilometres of pristine beach to themselves, the fine white sand of the dunes as pure as it is wind-driven (but for the odd vervet monkey footprint). As well as offering rollercoaster 4x4 dune safaris, Oyster Bay Lodge has fifteen horses, catering for every skill level, which roam free on the 235 hectare nature reserve. The first time I visited there simply wasn't time for a beach ride, so I dreamt hard for two weeks and managed to dream it into reality, returning to experience for real the wind in my hair, salt air in my face and sun shining down… amazing. But there's more: Hans and Liesbeth have made hiking trails from the sand dunes through the fynbos where you'll have a chance to see some of the 170 species of bird. I could hear them, but didn't quite catch a glimpse. Your stay is very personable and relaxing with use of the swimming pool and self-catering facilities if you choose. Otherwise, the restaurant serves up an absolute five-course treat, often with a fresh catch of the day. Come here for the empty beach, the horses and walks along an unspoilt coastline, the mountain bikes and the picnics at tables set upon the dunes overlooking the ocean. *Day-tours can be taken to nearby Tsitsikamma Nature Reserve and Baviaanskloof.*

Rooms: 14: 4 Luxury Chalets, 10 Comfortable Rooms (2 family; Honeymoon Suite: 2 rooms/4 beds). All extra-long kings, en-s bath & separate shower. Chalets: lounge, kitchenette, fire, verandah. All units bar 1 with sea view.
Price: All pp sharing. Luxury Chalets R1,080 B&B; Comfortable Rooms R750 B&B. Specials for people staying 3 nights or more. Ask about single and extra person rates and packages.
Meals: Full breakfast included. Lunches and dune picnics available through out the day. Five-course evening dinner at additional cost unless packaged deal.
Directions: From Cape Town on N2 turn off at exit number 632 Palmietvlei & follow signs to Oyster Bay Lodge. From Port Elizabeth take exit to Humansdorp, follow signs to Oyster Bay Lodge.

Cottage on the Hill Guest House

Anne and Rob Eaglesham

63 Assissi Drive, St. Francis Bay
Tel: 042-294-0761
Email: cottageonthehill@telkomsa.net Web: www.cottageonthehill.co.za
Cell: 076-563-5662

Cottage on the Hill has been awarded five stars, which, paradoxically, might have been quite off-putting for GG. But on this occasion we would award five stars too! This is because all the luxury is fully backed up by some very warm, attentive and characterful hosting from Anne and Rob. Leading me away from their sumptuous yellowwood bar, the ever-animated Eagleshams (followed closely by their two no-less-animated dachshunds) showed me to my enormous suite, Francolin. White furniture makes for a beachy atmosphere, as does the voile drape over the bed and the exposed thatched roof. You can absorb the sea view from the black-footed Victorian bath, although I remained dry and admired it from the expansive balcony. Then below there is Mongoose Suite with its dark granite surfaces on top of white cupboards and Persian rugs on the floor and original oil paintings. The shower has a door leading to an outside bath (always a sure-fire winner with me) and braai area. A sink thoughtfully placed next to the braai meant that I could prepare the record-breaking yellow-finned tuna I'd caught earlier that day. Further round, there's a bird hide hidden by indigenous plants. And across a courtyard, past the natural rock swimming pool and some metal heron sculptures, is Guinea-fowl Cottage with its mahogany bed and cane furniture. For golfers, you've got two courses within 1km, the friendly village course or the Jack Nicklaus-designed St Francis Links.

Rooms: 2 suites & 1 bedroom in cottage: 2 king/twins, 1 queen; All en-s bath & shower (bath outside in Mongoose).
Price: Guinea-fowl Cottage: R450 – R850 pp sharing. Mongoose & Francolin: R600 – R1,250 pp sh. Single rates on request. Check for winter specials.
Meals: Full breakfast & afternoon tea incl'. 3-course dinner on request: R250 pp incl' bottle of wine.
Directions: From N2, take St. Francis Bay/Humansdorp exist. Follow sign to St. Francis Bay onto R330. Go over roundabout, past golf course and drive for approx 600m. First road L into Homestead Rd. R onto Assisi - Cottage on the Hill is no. 63.

Map Number: 5

Entry Number: 143

Thunzi Bush Lodge

Mark and Trenwyth Pledger

Maitland Road, Maitlands, Port Elizabeth
Tel: 041-372-2082 Fax: 086-5030-698
Email: info@thunzi.co.za Web: www.thunzibushlodge.co.za
Cell: 072-597-4810

Ex-engineer Mark has been building treehouses since he was three (well, as soon as he could co-ordinate his hands with any intricacy) and Thunzi's flawlessly-planned and -finished chalets are standing proof of his skill. Many personal touches are integrated within; baths wrapped in wooden decking, sinks stationed on sealed, sniffle-free sneeze-wood (strangely enough, a beautiful wood that makes you sneeze when you work with it); and a medley of wholesome games and entertainments. The completely private cabins, linked only by gravel walkways, peep timidly through indigenous forest onto the De Stades River Wetlands where an abundance of birds have been listed. Over 352 wacky-named species flock to this eco-diverse area where coastal forest, thicket and wetlands meet (try narina trogon, African rail, Knysna loerie and the often-heard buff-spotted, red-chested and flufftails for size). Take a night walk through the forest and you'll be greeted by a hypnotic symphony of nocturnal sounds and even a few wandering antelope. By day relaxation comes easy (the spa packages sound blissful), but should you want a little more activity simply pop down the road to Maitland's impressive duned beach, the most isolated and untouched Port Elizabeth has to offer. Here you can hike, snorkel, whale-watch or sand-board (the dunes really are that big). Personally a lamp-lit dinner beneath the star-lined silhouette of canopy would be enough, but I suppose one really should work up an appetite first.

Rooms: 4 chalets: 2 twin/king B&Bs, both en-s bath & shr; 1 family B&B with 1 queen & 1 twin room en-s bath & shr. 1 self-catering unit with 1 queen & 1 twin room.
Price: B&B: R595 - R895 pp sharing. 40% supplement for singles. Self-catering chalet: R995 - R2,250.
Meals: Full breakfast incl' for B&B units. Gourmet picnics, light lunches & dinners (R100 - R265) on request; extra R165 for private open-air dining.
Directions: Take the exit marked Seaview from the N2. Thunzi Bush Lodge is signed after exit. More detailed directions can be emailed on request. GPS co-ordinates: S 33° 58' 43,6" E 25° 19' 11,1"

Lemon Tree Lane B&B

Ray and Dee Kemp
14 Mill Park Road, Mill Park, Port Elizabeth
Tel: 041-3734-103
Email: info@lemontreelane.co.za Web: www.lemontreelane.co.za
Cell: 082-7763-339

By the time I reached the charming Ray at charming Lemon Tree Lane I was all Port Elizabethed out, in need of a cuppa, a soak and some TLC... and who would have thought that out in the leafy suburb of Millpark I would find all three... and some unassuming luxury to boot! After 17 years receiving guests Ray and Dee are past masters at putting you at your ease (and they have a wall of accolades to prove it). Lemon Tree's eight impeccable rooms are stuffed full of antiques (antiques are Dee's guilty pleasure). Three of the suites are accessed via the shady courtyard they share. All are huge with handy kitchenette, sitting area and pristine en-suite bathrooms. Each room has its own individual feel with common features in polished wooden floors, ornate mirrors, elegant drapes and fresh flowers... and many useful comforts like air-con, heaters, microwaves, honesty bars, tea- and coffee-making facilities, hair-dryers, telephones, TVs and Wifi. Then there are the Villas, a recent addition, made up of two separate units, "Villa up" and "Villa Down". With Dee's love of PE's auction rooms, she has furnished them to be an extremely comfortable resting place. From eating spots to game parks, Ray can point you in the right direction. And, according to Ray, PE is a sports enthusiast's dream and golf and cricket (both within walking distance) are popular pastimes for visitors to Lemon Tree Lane. To think that it all started with that lovely oak dresser in the breakfast room bought for R230 many years ago....

Rooms: 8: all large double rooms all with en-suite bath and shower. Additional sleeper beds for children.
Price: R595 - R795 pp sharing. Singles on request.
Meals: Full breakfast included. Dinners on request.
Directions: See website for detailed map and directions.

Admiralty Beach House

Jo and Alan Byram

9 Admiralty Way, Summerstrand, Port Elizabeth
Tel: 041-583-1271 or 041-583-3720 Fax: 086-610-6770
Email: bookings@theadmiralty.co.za Web: www.theadmiralty.co.za
Cell: 083-555-6370

Breakfast was in full swing when I arrived at Admiralty Beach House and among the local art and curios on display (and for sale), as well as the intricate furnishings and ceramics (not for sale, although many have tried unsuccessfully to engage in friendly commerce with Jo!), I felt I had stumbled upon a very civilized, secret festival of feasting and creativity. Alan was quick to invite me to join their other guests, once I'd had a quick whirl around the pool and garden with its mosaics and kaleidoscopic colours. In the main house there are six modern suites, each with its own balcony or patio, fresh flowers, crisp white linens and bedrooms punctuated with bursts of colour in pretty plumped-up cushions and delicate cotton quilted throws. Jo personally chose the South African art that hangs on the walls, including, among much else, oil-painted lilies and local street scenes in bright acrylics. There are two other newly-built and very stylish suites, The Loft and a self-catering cottage, on Jo and Alan's home property, which is just a five-minute walk round the corner. These manifest the same artistic sentiment as the main house, but with the advantage of a little more space and privacy. Throughout Admiralty there are personal touches that together make it a home. Alan and Jo call Admiralty an evolution, an apt description for an establishment that started life as their home with a studio above the garage, where Jo used to teach ballet, and has since evolved into this wonderfully luxurious guest house.

Rooms: 8: 2 double suites, 4 double rooms, 2 family suites: 1 with 2 separate bedrooms and 1 self-catering cottage with sleeper-couch. All bathrooms with both bath and shower.
Price: R595 – R850 per person sharing. Children and family rates. Child and single supplement.
Meals: Full cooked and continental breakfast. Other meals on request. Light lunches on the patio.
Directions: See website for detailed map. GPS S 33 59. 526 E25 40. 446

Lupus Den Country House

Priscilla and Noel Walton
Addo/Sunland
Tel: 042-234-0447 Fax: 086-626-7380
Email: lupusden@srvalley.co.za Web: www.lupusden.co.za
Cell: 072-1814-750

Priscilla and Noel have not needed to learn any tricks about how to host. They are just naturally hospitable people who make you feel instantly at home and relaxed. When I arrived, lunch was waiting on the table and, with a home-made lemon drink in hand, I already felt part of the furniture. They have been living in their farmhouse for 40 years now – although the land it stands on has been in the family's hands since 1894 – and have made some adjustments to make the rooms all the more comfortable for their guests. The latest of these - three new large rooms, each with its private entrance - are in Garden Cottage. Two have outdoor showers and all have air-con. Their citrus and cattle farm is found on the friendly dirt roads between Addo and Kirkwood. And when I say friendly, I mean locals waved hello to me all the way there! The garden, surrounded by citrus groves, blooms with bougainvillaea and an abundance of other flowers and trees. The tiled swimming pool and an enormous tipuanu tree are two of the gardens' greatest assets, while vine-shaded terraces are the perfect places of repose after a rendezvous with the elephants in Addo (only 20 minutes away). When staying at Lupus Den you can be a tourist by day out in the parks and feel a local when back in the fold. A true farm B&B with home cooking – hard to beat.

Rooms: 6: Homestead: 1 twin, 1 dble, 1 twin/dble, 2 en-s bath & shower, 1 en-s sh'r; Garden Cottage: 3 doubles/twins, all en-s bathrooms, 2 outdoor shower. All rooms own entrance, patio & aircon.
Price: Homestead: R300 - R400 pp. Singles R390 - R520. Garden Cottage: R475 - R500 pp sharing. Singles R615 - R650. Children: under 5 free, reduced rate meals; 5 - 11 years half price.
Meals: Full breakfast incl'. Adults & kids 12+: light lunch R30 - R50 pp; set 3-course dinner R190 pp. Children under 12 years old - reduced meal rates.
Directions: From PE take R335 towards Addo. Cross railway in Addo, then L onto R336 towards Kirkwood. At Sunland R at Lupus Den B&B sign & follow signs.

Map Number: 6

The Elephant House

Clive and Anne Read
Addo
Tel: 042-233-2462 Fax: 042-233-0393
Email: info@elephanthouse.co.za Web: www.elephanthouse.co.za
Cell: 083-799-5671

The bush telegraph gave advance notice of the many charms at Elephant House. Many tourists and other guest house owners had urged us to visit with a sincerity you could not ignore. It's a stunning house, the brainchild of one night's sleepless pondering by Anne who mapped the whole thing out in her head – a small, lawned courtyard surrounded on three sides by thatched and shady verandahs. The house is, in a sense, inside out. The drawing room leads to a dining room outside on the verandah (with antiques and Persian rugs). All the bedrooms open onto the verandah too and dinner (advertised with an African gong) is served there on silver and crystal. Elegant evening meals are lit to stunning effect with lampshades made of Tuareg bowls. Lawns, indigenous trees and the racehorse stud (Clive used to run one in Natal) surround the house, though the gallopers were recently relocated to another paddock, just 1km away. The Elephant House bedrooms are luxurious affairs with antique furniture, carpets, thick duvets and deep beds; the Internet room is handy, as is the morning tea or coffee that's brought to your bed, if so desired. The Family Suite, which is separated from the main house, retains the same charm but is just a little cosier. The Elephant House also runs open-vehicle game drives in Addo, a few minutes away, morning and afternoon. *A seasonal on-site masseuse available for inside or outside treatments (Mon - Fri, Oct - May).*

Rooms: 8 rooms in the house; all king/twins with en-suite bath and shower and one family room that sleeps 5.
Price: R660 - R1,450 pp sharing.
Meals: Full breakfast included in Elephant House and Stable Cottages. Lunch & dinner provided. Three-course dinners R250.
Directions: From P.E. R335 through Addo 5km on the road towards the park - you will see a sign off to your left for The Elephant House.

Hopefield Country House

Kobus Buys and Gerhard Maritz

Off the R336, between Kirkwood and Addo, Sundays River Valley, Addo
Tel: 042-234-0333 Fax: 086-566-0152
Email: info@hopefield.co.za Web: www.hopefield.co.za

My mother, a conductor-pianist, would go absolutely bananas over Hopefield. Kobus actually has to pause and count when I ask how many pianos they have about the house (five… he thinks) and the soothing strains of chamber music, opera and choral melodies linger in the orange-blossom-sweet air of this 15-hectare citrus farm. Known throughout Addo as The Music Boys, Kobus and Gerhard did time in Gauteng's fast-paced record industry before repairing to Kobus's family home (along with their doting miniature schnauzers Horatio and Ophelia) to do what they love best: playing music, gardening and entertaining. And though the Beethoven busts, baby grands and roses named after composers (go on, give Edward Elgar and Benjamin Britten a sniff) will excite any musos among you, there's plenty here for everyone. Sun-worshippers may lounge in the rose-packed garden (52 varieties, to be precise), safe in the knowledge that Kobus is "happy to carry G 'n' T's to the pool on a regular basis"; disciples of design will adore one-off furniture pieces, unique bathtubs, private verandahs, the elegant Jack Vettriano prints dotted around one room, the chess-themed artwork of another; gastronomes mustn't miss orchard-fresh orange juice at breakfast or the gourmet dinners. Let's just say, you won't be getting a spatula of lasagne and a bag of chips, and Gerhard makes the best creme brûlée this side of the Mediterranean. Hopefield is a truly vibrant place to stay. And not just if you happen to be my Mum.

Rooms: 7: 3 king/twins with full en-suite bathroom; 1 king with full en-suite; 1 queen with en-suite bath; 1 queen with en-suite shower over bath; 1 king with en-suite shower.
Price: R445 - R645 pp sharing. Singles rates on request.
Meals: Full breakfast included. Packed lunches and set 3-course dinner available on request.
Directions: Signed from the R336 between Kirkwood and Addo. More detailed directions can be emailed.

Map Number: 6

Entry Number: 149

River Bend Lodge

Jayne Barlow

Off Zuurberg Road (R335), Addo Elephant National Park
Tel: 042-233-8000 Fax: 042-233-8028
Email: reservations@riverbendlodge.co.za Web: www.riverbendlodge.co.za

Within one hour of PE airport I was sipping a nectareously refreshing lemonade, squeezed from one of eight variants of citrus plantations near River Bend. Within another hour I'd moved on to vetkoek (a traditional 'doughnut' bread prepared with gourmet ingredients - irresistible!), followed by a fanned power kip and a reviving speed-dip in the pool. And now six of us, newly acquainted, were out spotting on a game drive, the sun, scent and space of the bush already working their magic, dissipating the rest of the world into the dust clouds behind us. I've been to Addo already and I've also been lucky enough to experience several other game drives up and down the country, but in this 400-odd-minute taster of the Nyathi section of the park - to which this lodge enjoys private access - I felt I could have been freshly landed from Heathrow. Under our super-approachable ranger, we learned anything from how the leopard tortoise is the only member of its family able to swim, to the cause for the genetic recession of female elephants' tusks in this area. We also fell into a trance at the beauty of a herd of 50+ ellies crossing grasslands under our noses. Folks don't come here for 'big five kills', nor is Addo comparable to Kruger or Botswana. This park knows its draw-cards and River Bend specializes in providing guests with an effortless, enchanting and affecting experience to take away with them. It is also very luxurious!

Rooms: 8: 7 Luxury Suites with private patios; 1 Honeymoon Suite, secluded patio & plunge pool; Long Hope Villa, exclusive use only, sleeps up to 6 (own garden, pool, look-out deck, personal chef & private guide).
Price: Luxury Suites: R2,800 - R3,600 pppn; Honeymoon Suite: R3,000 - R3,850 pppn; kids (3-11yrs): R1,800 – R1600; Long Hope Villa: R13,000 – R17,000 pn for 1st 4 guests. Rates inclusive of accommodation, daily game drives, meals, SANParks levies & charges.
Meals: A la carte menu for breakfast, lunch and dinner.
Directions: Allow a good hour from PE; see owner's website for detailed directions.

Idwala Game Lodge

Ernst and Alida Du Toit

Adjacent to Lalibela Game Reserve, Sidbury (40km from Grahamstown)
Tel: 046-622-2163
Email: enquiries@idwalalodge.com Web: www.idwalalodge.com
Cell: 083-277-7235

I was very excited when I first discovered Idwala. This was not just because of their introductory cocktail, complete with sunken pebble (in case you're wondering, it's because Idwala means 'rock'), but because this was a real family-run lodge, as luxurious as all its corporate competitors. Mother and daughter team Claudine and Alida have created their own unique take on bush lodge décor, hand-picking every detail of the rooms, right down to the rock soap dish. Carefully-chosen pieces of local art and craft adorn the walls. Animals made from wire paper and beads are lit from beneath, wardrobe knobs are shaped like tortoises' backs, and a beautifully gnarled knobwood tree branch wound its way to the top of my thatched ceiling. The glass doors in each room slide all the way back, so you can be completely open to the unfenced wilds beyond, and the shower has a glass wall out onto the bush. But you needn't worry about privacy. Every room is surrounded by greenery and reached by its own cliff-side walkway. The only creatures sneaking a peak through the curtains will be of the distinctly wild variety. And to get really close to them, Idwala's magnificent game drives are worth every minute of the early wake-up. *Airport transfers are available as well as star-gazing with trained ranger using on-site telescope. The lodge can also be rented out exclusively. Ask Alida for details.*

Rooms: 4: all can be double or twin with en-suite showers.
Price: R1,950 - R3,850 pp sharing. 50% supplement for singles.
Meals: All meals, local drinks and game drives are included.
Directions: Take the N2 from Port Elizabeth towards Grahamstown. Exit at the Sidbury/Kwantu/Bayete/Eagles Crag turn-off. Look out for the Idwala Lodge turn-off (to the right) 7km further down the gravel road.

Woodbury Lodge

Jennifer, Giles, Richard and Cathy Gush
Amakhala Game Reserve
Tel: 046-636-2750 Fax: 086-694-6895
Email: centralres@amakahala.co.za Web: www.amakahala.co.za

I'm more accustomed to being welcomed by barking dogs than by a giraffe nonchalantly chewing on the treetops. And was that an elephant doing its best to blend into the undergrowth? With Jennifer's eagle eye, more and more animals became apparent in the shimmering distance, and I'd hardly left the N2. Don't worry, though, you'd never know it. The stone-and-thatch buildings huddle against rocky hills and the rooms (reached via steps dug into the hillside) are hidden from each other by aloes and wild vegetation. The yellow walls of my simple room were dotted sparingly with local art, though the window offered the most striking sight – a 'dazzle' of zebra gently following the curves of the river while a raptor rode the thermal currents above. I knew I could never forget Amakhala. And all of this from my bed, whose crisp white linen promised a sound night's sleep later on. Heading back down to the deck outside the dining room, I feasted on the high tea with a ferocity that worried a fellow guest, impelling him to warn me against ruining my supper – how kind, but how mistaken, he was. After the game drive and drinks by the outside fire that had been lit in our absence, all three courses of supper were hungrily dispatched on the long dining table with Richard (Jennifer's cousin-in-law), our genial host. With the glowing embers of the fire slowly dimming before going out all together we made our way to bed. My new friend looked aghast when I expressed how much I was looking forward to breakfast.

Rooms: 6: all with twin/kings and en-suite baths and showers. Two of these can be family rooms.
Price: R2,480 - R3,180 pp sharing. 30% single supplement. Prices include meals, selected beverages and 2 safari activities.
Meals: Full breakfast, high tea and dinner included. Drinks also included.
Directions: 80km from Port Elizabeth on the N2 towards Grahamstown. Turn right at Woodbury Lodge sign.

The Cock House

Richard Anker-Simmons (Owner) Thoneka Bongo (Manager)

10 Market St, Grahamstown
Tel: 046-636-1287 Fax: 046-636-1287 Email: reservations@cockhouse.co.za
Web: www.cockhouse.co.za Cell: 082-820-5592

The Cock House offers a friendly welcome and fine dining in the setting of a historic old house in downtown Grahamstown. Nelson Mandela has stayed three times and former President Thabo Mbeki has also been a guest (their visits are recorded in photos on the entrance hall walls in case you don't believe me). Former owner Belinda Tudge worked hard with her late husband Peter to build up a business to be proud of, and it is really nice to see a staff who are so obviously genuinely proud to work there. With current owner Richard and his team carrying on the Cock House tradition of friendly hospitality there is always an opportunity to strike up a conversation in the delightful yellowwood bar. The house dates back to 1826 and was one of the first built in Grahamstown. A stone-floored verandah stretches along the front of the house (mirrored by a wooden balcony upstairs) and the interior is full of yellowwood beams and broad-planked floors. I can recommend Norden's restaurant, which offers an international cuisine with a South African flavour and has its own herb garden, using local and seasonal ingredients wherever possible. The home-made bread is a particular treat. The two large rooms in the main house have glass doors opening onto the balcony, while modern apartments and seven converted stables open onto the garden. Personal and fun.

Rooms: 13: 7 doubles, 2 twins; all en-suite; 4 x 2-bedroom self-catering apartments with bath and shower.
Price: R410 - R460 pp sharing. Singles R510 - R560.
Meals: Full breakfast included. Lunch and dinner available in Norden's restaurant (except Monday lunch). Dinners on request if not included.
Directions: From P.E. take 2nd exit from N2 signposted "Business District/George Street". Take off-ramp then turn L at bridge into George St. Continue down long hill into Grahamstown. At 4-way stop with Market St turn R & Cock House on R corner.

Fort D'Acre Reserve

Mel and Rory Gailey
Fish River Mouth, Port Alfred
Tel: 040-676-1091 Fax: 040-676-1095
Email: info@fortdacre.com Web: www.fortdacre.com
Cell: 082-092-3035

When the sun's gone down, you're running late and, whether you admit it or not, are ever so slightly lost, some sort of a signal is much appreciated. On cue, the Fish River Lighthouse that stands in the middle of the reserve lit up the night sky like a beacon to guide me in (or so I like to think). The lodge, where guests stay, is not actually a fort but a mammoth thatched affair, entered via heavy, sliding glass doors from a pretty redbrick garden path. It's immediately obvious that this was a lodge designed for hunters: the rustically tiled floor is strewn with animal skins and the local taxidermist has not been idle. Even the great central hearth is framed by elephant tusks. A galleried landing overlooks the communal lounge, where a cavernous leather sofa almost prevented me from making it to bed that night. The next morning I was able to see the Fort D'Acre Reserve in all its glory. Opening the curtains in the bay windows that dominated my bedroom, I looked beyond the milling herd of zebra to the Great Fish River stretching out below me towards the Indian Ocean and the reserve's private stretch of beach. I enjoyed my breakfast on the sun-drenched terrace, but the open-walled, thatched, outside bar could be equally appealing. Down on the beach is a new lapa from where whales can be watched, sundowners drunk and romantic picnics consumed.

Rooms: 4: 3 doubles and 1 twin, all with en-suite showers.
Price: R595 - R795 pp sharing. Whole lodge available for self-catering (sleeps 8, plus a kid's room): R3,750 - R4,000 per day, minimum 3 nights. Game drives an optional extra.
Meals: Full breakfast included (B&B). A selection of restaurants nearby.
Directions: On R72 20km from Port Alfred towards East London. First turning to right after Great Fish Point Lighthouse.

Crawford's Beach Lodge and Cabins

Mark, Ian and Lyn Crawford
Chintsa East
Tel: 043-738-5000 Fax: 043-738-5001
Email: crawfords@iafrica.com Web: www.crawfordsbeachlodge.com

I'd heard guests dine well here, so I arrived cunningly early, just in time for lunch. The hearty dining room buffet did not disappoint… and the sea view was spectacular: two humpbacks explosively breaching in the distance. A beach walkway ushered me forth for a postprandial closer look. My deep solitary footprints seemed to be the only sign of human life for kilometres in all directions. Plenty of marine life though! Right before me a pod of dolphins were surfing in the breakers and just beyond I could see the whales' huge propeller-shaped tails raise in salute before submerging once again. This natural idyll harmonises well with the naturalness of Crawford's itself, a lodge with chalet-style accommodation, perfect for families. The design can be attributed to Ian, while the interiors and décors are a credit to Lyn. Natural materials - wood, thatch, pine, bamboo, clay – very effectively set off the bright kilims, super-comfortable beds and studded leather sofas. As for things to do, boredom is just not on the menu here. The pool, horse-riding, tennis court, playground, guided hikes, spa treatments and games room will get the blood up and the muscles working. Plus there's big five Inkwenkwezi Game Park only 7km away, boat-based whale-watching and even wave-jumping for those that have an urge. But should you wish to simply unwind, consider the lounge, my favourite room, with its stacks of hardcover photography books and the telescope for studying the animated ocean life through the A-framed window. Essentially, there's something for everyone. This is a worthy wild coast gem.

Rooms: 30 lodge rooms, all kings and en-suite shower, some with bath; 2 self-catering, 3-bedroom cottages, all kings/twins with en-suite bathrooms.
Price: Lodge rooms: R650 - R1,150 pp sharing. Self-catering cottages: R1,000 - R5,000 per night. Ask about singles, children's and packaged rates.
Meals: In guest lodge full board included. Lunch buffet R120, dinner R150 - R195, braai R175.
Directions: Head north on N2 from East London for c. 28km, turn R at Schafi Rd/Chintsa turn-off, drive c. 7km to Chintsa East & follow Crawfords signs.

Kob Inn Beach Resort

Daan van Zyl
Willowvale Area, Wild Coast, Qhorha Mouth
Tel: 047-499-0011 Fax: 086-523-9354
Email: info@kobinn.co.za Web: www.kobinn.co.za
Cell: 083-452-0876

This is not called the Wild Coast for nothing. Barely thirty exhilarating metres from my chalet, waves pounded the rocks in huge swells and rips that have been the demise of many a stricken vessel. Xhosa chieftains have traditionally owned this unspoilt land, which, leased to the Kob Inn, ensures a close relationship with local communities. You may even recognise in your bedroom mural one of the village scenes that you pass on the 32km drive from the highway to get here… including wandering cattle, so go slowly. Soon after arriving I was guided through a labyrinth of thatch, firstly to the earthy comfort of my room… and then to a bar whose deck juts out like a prow. Sunday night was braai night and, having heaped my plate, I joined a Durban couple that come every year because they love the lack of commercialism. Waking from the sleep equivalent of the Mariana Trench, I took breakfast to the sound of laughter from a group of elderly travellers who epitomised the prevailing informal atmosphere. The Kob Inn staff are passionately keen and were only too happy to guide me to one of their favourite places, the mouth of the Jujura River. Honeymooners will love the privacy of deserted lagoons, but with so much to do on and off the water (kayaking, boating, quad-biking, games room, horse-riding etc), this is a brilliant place for families and children will be exceptionally well looked after.

Rooms: 45 rooms: 28 doubles (twin/king), 15 family and 2 honeymoon suites, 1 cottage. All en-suite bathrooms, mostly with bath and shower.
Price: R650 - R950 pp sharing. Full board. Certain activities extra. Children's rates: 1 year old 10%. 2 years old 20%. 3 years old 30% etc. 10 years old and above full rate. Pensioners special available.
Meals: All included. Lunch and dinner set menus. Saturday-night seafood buffet. Sunday-night braai.
Directions: Turn off N2 at Dutywa follow the tar road for 30km to Willowvale (Signposted). It's 32km from the highway along a dirt road to Kob Inn, which is signposted all the way. Make sure to branch right after 12km.

Umngazi River Bungalows & Spa

Michele and Graham Walker

Umngazi River Mouth, Wild Coast, Port St Johns
Tel: 047-564-1115/6/7 Fax: 047-564-1210
Email: stay@umngazi.co.za Web: www.umngazi.co.za
Cell: 082-321-5841

The wild coast may be South Africa's most spectacular and yet least touristy region with its rocky coastline, indigenous forests, secluded coves and many river mouths. And all this is on your doorstep at Umngazi, a lively family holiday resort where the only time you will spend indoors will be to sleep and eat. The relaxed and informal lodge is on the banks of the Umngazi Estuary so you can choose between swimming in the pool, the river or the sea, fishing off rocks or boats, and walking in the forests. Bird-watching cruises are also organised for sunset. Ferries transport guests over to the beach from a river jetty. Meanwhile, back at home you will be missing out on tennis, snooker and table tennis. I guarantee that a week here, however lazy you are, will see the colour back in your cheeks and a bit of muscle on the arms and legs. And your sense of time will go haywire. Children are well catered for with trampoline, fort, sandpit and designated dining room. You have a choice of sea-, river- or garden-front cottages, four honeymoon suites with spa baths and double outside showers, and the new Ntabeni (two luxury open-plan palapa suites with panoramic views across the estuary, a buggy service, in-house pampering and canapés served at 5pm). You can fly in from Durban at 500 feet above sea level along the coastline, a great start to a holiday. *The spa offers (among other things) the signature four-hand Pondo massage and an Umoja couples treatment (one for the romantics!) while you look out on 180-degree views of the Indian Ocean.*

Rooms: 69 bungalows: 67 twin or dble on request, all en/s bathrooms, most with baths & outdoor shrs; 2 luxury king suites, in-hse spa treatments, canapes & golf buggy service.
Price: Bungalows: R865 – R1,315 pppn sharing fully–inclusive 3 meals. Luxury Suites R1,560 – R1,870 pp sharing. Fly-in package R10,305 – R16,430 pp for flight, 7 nights, all meals & transfers from Port St Johns.
Meals: All included.
Directions: From south, Umngazi lies 90km due east of Umtata (Mthatha). From north, via Flagstaff & Lusikisiki to Port St Johns on tarred road. Also transfer service from Umtata (Mthatha) & private flight service betw' Durban & Port St Johns.

Map Number: 7

Entry Number: 157

Woodcliffe Country House and Cottage

Phyll Sephton-Borrowdale

Woodcliffe Farm, Maclear
Tel: 045-932-1550 Fax: 045-932-1550 / 088-045-932-1550
Email: info@woodcliffe.co.za Web: www.woodcliffe.co.za
Cell: 082-9251-030

A few hours' drive along the road less travelled you will eventually come to Woodcliffe Country House and Cottage, a farmhouse idyll smack bang in the middle of one of South Africa most staggering secret locations. After 24 years in business farmer Phyll has finally decided to let the cat out of the bag and take guests. The farm itself is a successful beef farm and herds of cattle rotate their way around the pastures and meadows. Guests can swim in the river or ramble around the lower fells and caves (Phyll is a qualified guide and is brimming with historical facts and figures about the area that won't fail to astonish). More experienced walkers can head up (up, up) into the majesty of the Eastern Cape's higher Drakensberg. Maps, routes and overnight stays on the mountains can be arranged too. Tread carefully as some of Africa's rarest and most beautiful species of fauna and flora are found here. Guests already in on the secret visit repeatedly, to indulge in Phyll's inspiring tales, genuine hospitality and lovingly-prepared grub, and because Woodcliffe Cottage is a far-flung outpost on the doorstep of the greatest of the great outdoors. You don't come to Woodcliffe Cottage for the luxury; the rooms are comfortable, the kitchen is well equipped, the water is hot and the wood-burner works hard. But if you are looking for somewhere wild and exciting that hardly anyone yet knows about and where you will be wonderfully well looked after, luxury will not matter. Woodcliffe is just what we are always looking for!

Rooms: Cottage: 2 x twin and 1 x double; shared bathroom with shower and bath.
Price: Self-catering cottage: R630 per night (2 sharing); for 3 or more R265 pp. B&B: R440 pp sharing. DB&B, R630 pp sharing. Singles on request. Prices exclude Easter and 1 Dec - 28 Feb where in-season rates apply.
Meals: B&B, fresh farmhouse breakfast incl' cooked breakfast. Or packed brunch. Dinner, meal of day - home-cooked seasonal meals. Lunches, packed lunches on request.
Directions: Woodcliffe signed from Maclear. Follow exit out of town for "Rhodes via Naude's Nek" for 14km, L at Woodcliffe Cave Trails sign & go 7km. GPS: 30° 59.671' S 28° 10.985' E.

Leliekloof Valley of Art

Dries and Minnie De Klerk
Burgersdorp (closer to Jamestown)
Tel: 087-550-0589 Fax: 086-579-8963
Email: sanart@nokwi.co.za Web: www.leliekloof.co.za
Cell: 083-760-7851 (please leave a message)

What a place! Magnificent Bushman art and high-altitude wilderness to nourish the soul; log fires and home-cooked meals to look after earthier parts. The river here has chiselled a tortuous gorge through the sandstone and ironstone hills and the many caves host thirteen remarkable sites of Bushman rock art, many of the paintings of indeterminable age. Dries took me for an exhilarating morning drive and we visited two of them, Eland and Dog Shelters. The quality of the paintings is superb, Dries a full reservoir of information about both the images and their artists. There is also a two-day scenic 19km hike around the valley, and two large dams for canoeing and trout/fly-fishing. Art apart, the countryside will extract from you superlatives you never knew you had. The De Klerks now live in the main house with their guests, but don't worry, they're great company and there's plenty of room for everyone! The magnificent main room is 22 metres long, with sitting area, DSTV, yellowwood bar, fireplace and huge antique Oregon pine dining table. You can self-cater, but given the stellar quality of Minnie's food (and the variety of things to do), I strongly suggest that you ask her to prepare your meals. *Two nights minimum stay recommended.*

Rooms: 1 farmhouse with 2 bedrooms (1 double with child's bed and 1 double with child's bed and 1 cot, 1 with en-suite bath, 1 en-s shower); plus a loft sleeping 4; also 1 extra bathroom with bath & shower. Only one couple/group booking at a time.
Price: Full board rates: R500 - R560 pp (for three or more). R530 - R590 pp for 2 people. Self-catering options available. Singles on request.
Meals: Breakfast, lunch and dinner included. Dinner is 3 courses - bring your own wine.
Directions: 6km south of Jamestown on N6 turn towards Burgersdorp. Turn R after 9.7km. After another 5.6km fork R again and Leliekloof is another 1km. Just follow Leliekloof signs. Map can be faxed.

Map Number: 6

Lowestoffe Country Lodge

Robyn Conroy, Neil Evens, Debra & Rolf Pretorius
Lowestoffe Country Lodge, Hogsback
Tel: 045-843-1716
Email: lowestoffe@hogsback.com Web: lowestoffecountrylodge.co.za
Cell: 083-651-9224

After a tricky drive through the early morning mountain fog of Hogsback it was a relief to see Debra waiting for me at the Rockford Farm entrance. Little did she know a gate was left open and the sheep, being the clever beasts they are, saw an opportunity to escape a shearing. It's chilly in the mountains when the sun's not out – I had some sympathy. After the sheep were rounded up (this is a holistic farm, they hadn't gone too far!), the mist had cleared and the gate had been closed, I was finally able to take in my surroundings: the well-fished Klipplaat River meandering through the green valley, the poplar trees on the ridge, the stunning Elandsberg Mountains and the bleating of defeated sheep putting the finishing touches to a perfect rural scene! Lowestoffe encompasses four farms, two of which have been in Neil's family for four generations (the fifth are in training) and it covers 5,500 hectares. The space and the setting is a veritable playground for outdoor folk: guided horse treks, a plethora of hiking trails and an abundance of birdlife (this is the meeting point for amur falcons before migration). For fly-fishermen there are three trout dams, one bass dam and the river, packed with trout and yellowfish. The lodges are simple, comfortable and, being situated on their own farms, private. Both come with open fires (essential when the snows descend!), braai facilities, fully-equipped kitchens and magnificent views in all directions… perfect for absorbing the day's adventures.

Rooms: 2: Trout Lodge sleeps 8: 2 doubles (1 en-suite) and 2 twins; Rockford Lodge sleeps 8: 1 double en-suite and 3 twins.
Price: R800 - R2,000 per lodge.
Meals: Available on special request
Directions: From Hogsback, continue north on R345, at T-junction turn right towards Cathcart and follow signs to Lowestoffe Country Lodge.

Cavers Country Guest House

Kenneth and Rozanne Ross

R63, Bedford
Tel: 046-685-0619 Fax: 086-545-8517
Email: info@cavers.co.za Web: www.cavers.co.za
Cell: 082-579-1807

I can't be the first to call Cavers an oasis, but it is irresistible. There in the distance a stand of tall oaks shimmers unconvincingly in the haze. And then suddenly you are among well-watered and mature gardens, an Eden of lawns and vivid flowers. The garden is one of only 20 to have been included in a beautiful coffee-table book, "Remarkable Gardens Of South Africa". The fine stone, ivy-encased farmhouse was built in 1840 and has been in Ken's family for four generations (now exclusively for guests). The bedrooms, with wooden floorboards, high ceilings and voluptuously draped windows, are refined and elegant. From one of the upstairs rooms I got an impression of living in the trees with an hadeda nesting at eye level and yellow orioles twittering and fluttering about. Two grand upstairs rooms with pressed-metal ceilings have balconies overlooking the profusion of flowers below. The thatched cottage also has long views over the lawns and up to the Winterberg Mountains. Rozanne is a maestro in the kitchen, cooking with fresh produce from the farm and the surrounding area and all her meals are mouth-watering feasts. The memory of that salmon cheesecake is even now a Pavlovian trigger that gets the mouth watering. There is a clay tennis court, hiking on rolling land inhabited with plains game, riding, cricket on the magnificent ground nearby; swimming is in the pool or a big round reservoir; and DSTV is on hand, should 'your team' be playing.

Rooms: 5: 4 rooms in the manor house: all king/twins, 2 en-suite shower, 1 bath, 1 shr & bath; 1 cottage has 1 twin & 1 double sharing bath & shower.
Price: R450 – R650 per person sharing.
Meals: Full breakfast included. Dinner and light lunches on request.
Directions: 8km from Bedford on the R63 towards Adelaide, turn left at the sign and follow the dirt road for 8km.

Die Tuishuise

Sandra Antrobus
Market St, Cradock
Tel: 048-881-1322 Fax: 048-881-5388
Email: info@tuishuise.co.za Web: www.tuishuise.co.za

Unique accommodation indeed! Sandra has a raptor's eye for historic detail, laced with an antique-dealer's nose and the heart of an interior designer - unparalleled in my experience of South Africa. There are 31 houses along Market Street, all antiquely furnished to reflect different styles, eras and professions. The houses were once lived in by bank managers, teachers, wagon makers etc and you step into their 19th-century shoes when you stay - although the bathrooms, perhaps, retain a little more modernity. Each house is an antique shop in its own right, but modern comforts include fans, heaters and fireplaces. I was lucky enough to visit them all and it is no exaggeration to say I was struck dumb - reason enough for Sandra to have gone to the effort (some might feel). The hotel, a Victorian manor at the end of the street, has a further 19 rooms similarly done out in the style of the time and sherry is served in the drawing room before buffet dinners (my Karoo lamb was delicious). Sandra and her daughter Lisa are dedicated to presenting South African history in a way you can touch and feel. *They do cultural performances epitomising the Xhosa and Afrikaner cultures - ask in advance. Closed 24th & 25th December. Karoo Spa and Wellness Studio offers treatments.*

Rooms: 31 restored 19th-century houses, each rented out as one 'unit'. There is also a hotel.
Price: R445 pp sharing to R550 pp sharing B&B.
Meals: Breakfast included (unless you choose to self-cater) and served 7 - 9am. Traditional dinners served between 7pm and 9pm.
Directions: From PE take N10. When you arrive in Cradock at 3-way stop turn left into Voortrekker St. Die Tuishuise is 4th block on left. Reception is at Victoria Manor.

Koffylaagte Game Lodge

Rebecca Axcell and Alistair McKerrow
Koffylaagte Game Lodge, Farm 284, Jansenville
Tel: 049-836-9188 Fax: 086-225-2220
Email: info@koffylaagtegamelodge.co.za
Web: www.koffylaagtegamelodge.co.za Cell: 073-457-3733

Twisting my way through rugged mountain ravines and across the open plains of the Karoo I half-expected to find myself in an African version of Doyle's 'The Lost World'. Suddenly, a kori bustard rose from the bush next to me and I was certain of it! Fortunately, Koffylaagte isn't an unforgiving plateau full of forgotten dinosaurs and ape-men. It is in fact a luxury game lodge in the Karoo heartland. Accommodation takes various forms: three lodge rooms, two self-catering suites in the settlers' homestead and five luxurious safari tents. The only tenty thing about these are the canvas walls; all have private verandahs looking out over the veld, thatched roofs, en-suite bathrooms, the best view from a bath tub imaginable and super-comfy beds. After a high-tea consisting of freshly-baked scones and the lodge's own blend of coffee, it was time for a game drive. I could have gone quad biking, swimming or horse-riding, but the buffalo are best seen from the (safety of a) safari vehicle! Afterwards we escaped the chilly evening in the sheltered boma; warmed our souls with banter, our feet with fire and our bellies with a delicious potjie, cooked to perfection by Rebecca. Feeling thoroughly content I strolled back to my tent marvelling at the stars and keeping a watchful eye out for wandering game. *Heritage trails through the Eastern Cape start from the lodge.*

Rooms: 14: 5 en-s luxury safari tents; 3 en-s lodge rooms; 2 self-catering farmhouse suites, each with 2 rooms (sleeps 8 altogether); 1 rustic bush cottage made up of 2 rooms (sleeps 8).
Price: Safari tents and lodge rooms from R1,500 pppn sharing. Self-catering farmhouse units from R1,300 per unit. Eco bush cottage from R1,500 for the unit.
Meals: All meals included (brunch, high tea, dinner) included with tents and lodge rooms. Self-caterers can purchase all daily meals by prior arrangement
Directions: Towards Graaff-Reinet on R75, look for brown Koffylaagte Game Lodge sign and turn onto gravel road. At T jct L, stay on this road, lodge on L after 20km. See website for alternative routes.

Map Number: 5

Wheatlands

Diana, Arthur, Kirsten and David Short
Route R75, Graaff-Reinet
Tel: 049-891-0422/4 Fax: 049-891-0422
Email: wheatlands@wam.co.za Web: www.wheatlands.co.za
Cell: 076-377-4026 or 072-251-9022

Welcome to Wheatlands, where if you're looking for flat-screens, iPod docks and high-speed wifi, you're in the wrong place. Wheatlands is for those who want antique, country-farm luxury and can't spell the word 'mod-con'. Built in 1912 on the profits of ostrich feathers (a so-called 'feather palace'), don't expect a humble farmhouse; I found a gigantic manor mingling Cape Dutch and Edwardian styles, a façade dominated by three extravagant gables and a lovely white-pillared rear verandah opening onto a green lake of lush lawn where heritage roses sprout like weeds. Haul your wagon into the huge sandy courtyard (to the strains of the goat chorus) and grace the long, cool, wood-panelled grand hall. It's a lofty pleasure after the desert heat of the Karoo and an appropriate home for Wheatlands' antique furniture and Persian rugs. Elsewhere, the bright, homely lounge, replete with cushioned windowsills, houses the grand piano. Corridors are lined with first editions, there's a snug for reading, and high-ceilinged guest bedrooms are not converted outhouses but an integral, lived-in part of the home. Wonderful wanders can be had in the sprawling back gardens and the Shorts are astoundingly nice people, brimful of the hostly arts. Kirsten and Diana cook decadent dinners, eaten at one large oak table, while David and Arthur are serious wool and mohair farmers. And cricketers. They even have their own ground. Of course, it's Aimee and Emma, David and Kirsten's tiny tots who really rule the manor.... Enjoy.

Rooms: 3 units: 1 king/twin with en-suite bath and shower. 1 twin with en-suite bath and shower. And 3 twin rooms with 2 shared bathrooms. Self-catering option on request for whole house.
Price: Dinner Bed and Breakfast: R500 - R600 pp sharing.
Meals: Full breakfast and dinner included (Karoo lamb a speciality).
Directions: 42km on the R75 south of Graaff-Reinet, Wheatlands turn-off to the left, 8km up a gravel road.

Cypress Cottages

Hillary Palmé
76 Donkin St, Graaff-Reinet
Tel: 049-892-3965 Fax: 0866-840-166
Email: info@cypresscottage.co.za Web: www.cypresscottage.co.za
Cell: 083-456-1795

After a hot and particularly bothersome drive to this historic Karoo town, it came as a huge relief to step wearily through Cypress Cottage's heavy wooden doors and immerse myself in the quiet coolness lurking within. Minutes later, cold beer in hand and propped up on a stoep with a magnificent mountain view, my recent hardships evaporated into the heat-hazed sky. Both cottages are of the beautiful early 1800s Cape Dutch variety and are understatedly decorated with a highly developed taste for the natural and comfortable. Thus, the bedrooms display high reed ceilings, solid pine and slate floors, antique chests, fresh flowers and free-standing baths. Fresh and perfectly wholesome breakfasts are laid up on the terraces - free-range eggs from the house chickens, succulent figs, peaches, prunes and apricots straight from the orchard. You can escape the heat by splashing in the bore-hole-fed reservoir that has been converted into a swimming pool. Across the sleepy street, a familiar smell wafted over from the other cottage, where guests were merrily braaiing under the shade of its vine-covered pergola. The main garden is an extraordinary feat of will and clever engineering - desert has been transformed into an oasis of lush vegetation despite the difficulties of brackish water. Historic Graaff-Reinet is worth at least a two-day stopover in my opinion.

Rooms: 2 cottages with 6 rooms: 4 doubles and 2 twins. All with en-suite bathrooms, wifi, DStv, air-con and heating.
Price: R400 - R550 pp sharing. Singles on request.
Meals: Full breakfast included. Self-catering possible.
Directions: From south enter town and pass police academy on L and go over bridge. Two filling stations on L - take road between them (West St). Follow to very end, turn R into Donkin St, guest house first on L. From north: R at T-jct (Caledon St). 4th Left is Donkin St. House last on R.

Abbotsbury

Sue Scott

Graaff-Reinet
Tel: 049-840-0201 Fax: 049-840-0201
Email: info@abbotsbury.co.za Web: www.abbotsbury.co.za
Cell: 072-486-8904

A three-kilometre drive on a dirt track takes you up into the land that time forgot, a small, perfectly-formed valley that Sue calls home. She is there to greet you in her improbably lush and well-tended garden, which seems immune to the Karoo sun's forbidding glare. An ingenious old water furrow running down from the dam must take some of the credit for this, although a fence has also been added to protect the garden's aloes and roses from midnight-feasting kudus… of which there are plenty, despite the privations. You can relax under the trees in the tranquil gardens or hike up the valley in search of the ten species of antelope and other Karoo wildlife on the farm. Back at base, guests either stay in a lovely old cottage, circa 1880; or a twin-bedded suite attached to Sue's own, even older house; or the luxury garden suite with its sweeping views of the garden and wild valley in the distance. None lack for character, with polished yellowwood floors, restored old furniture and photographic prints and artwork on the walls. Sue takes your supper orders when you book so as to have a fresh farm supply at the ready (springbok and Karoo lamb are specialities) and you are served in your own private dining room with solid silver cutlery, bone china and service bell! Breakfasts are also a royal affair. *Nearby: the sculpture garden of the Owl House, historic Graaff-Reinet and the awe-inspiring views of the Valley of Desolation.*

Rooms: 3 units: 1 cottage with twin en-suite shower & King with separate bath; 1 cottage, king & en-s shower; 1 twin/king suite, en-s bath & shower. All have private lounge/dining room.
Price: R480 - R550 pp sharing B&B.
Meals: Full breakfast included. Dinner available on request: R140. Meals are served privately to each cottage.
Directions: 27km north of Graaff-Reinet on N9, turn left onto 3km farm track to Abbotsbury.

The Stone Cottage

Michèle & Graham Hobson

Ebenezer Farm, Route 75, Graaff-Reinet
Tel: 049-8910-416 Fax: 049-8910-416
Email: info@thestonecottage.co.za Web: www.thestonecottage.co.za
Cell: 082-901-8309

I can hardly see The Stone Cottage for the butterflies. A thousand wings flit between lavender, African daisy and sunny aloe flower, all vying for the best spot outside The Stone Cottage, South Africa's family-friendliest farm-stay. It took a mighty spring clean to enable stays at Ebenezer Farm, explains lovely Michèle, piling my eager plate with roast farm chicken. "My husband Graham is the sixth generation of Hobson to work Ebenezer, but the cottage was a farm store for years." Two years of sprucing and one (almost) butterfly-proof stable door later, The Stone Cottage was born; a darling, shuttered den of warm, earthy tones, piled with furry rugs, Karoo-themed books and games, heaven for families fleeing city stress for wholesome farm fun. The cosy kitchen is armed for battle (stock up pre-arrival, no car likes tackling a 28km dirt road twice in one day!), but Michèle hates rumbling tummies and loves spoiling people since sons Leith and Stuart (whose Picasso-inspired artworks dot the cottage walls) started boarding school. She'll happily feed you, spicing things up daily. "A big guy who looked like he'd eat quite a hectic breakfast stayed, so I threw a lamb chop in with his full English," she reveals, apologising for not having made me her signature kudu pie. After lunch, Josh the collie leads us through the gardens to vast sheep and angora goat pastures, past the pool, tree-house, tennis court and mammoth jungle gym (surely I'm not too old for monkey bars?), down to the forest where real monkeys play. The Stone Cottage is a rustic Karoo paradise. Enjoy.

Rooms: 1: sleeps up to 7 adults & 1 child; 1 dble bedroom, 2 twins & sleeper-couch in family room, shared bathroom with shr; separate bedroom with en-s bathroom sleeps 3.
Price: Self-catering R300 – R350 pp sharing. B&B R350 – R400. Dinner, bed & breakfast R470 – R520. Kids under 3 no charge, 3-12 half-price.
Meals: Breakfast, lunch, picnic baskets country dinner on request.
Directions: From Graaff-Reinet 42km south on R75. Take 'Wheatlands' turn, then 28km on good gravel rd. From Somerset East go 47km on R63 to Pearston. As leave Pearston L onto R337 after little bridge. 27.5km on good gravel rd to Stone Cottage on R.

Map Number: 5

Entry Number: 167

De Kothuize

Peter Curle (owner), Christa Hahn (manager)
2 Parsonage Street, Graaff-Reinet
Tel: 082-571-6539
Email: info@dekothuize.co.za Web: www.dekothuize.co.za
Cell: 083-233-1227

It was one of those cloudless sunny Karoo days in Graaff-Reinet and I found myself, groceries in hand, strolling down Parsonage Street, one of the best-preserved and most historic streets in South Africa, lined with purple-flowering bougainvillea trees and home to the town's library. With a spring in my step and a smile on my face I headed for Number 10, my home for the night. On the corner, adjacent to the museum, you'll find Number 2, the hub of De Kothuize and the residence of Christa (on hand if you need anything) and her dogs. Most of the properties are national monuments and have been restored in detail to their original charming selves, but with a few modern creature comforts thrown in. Number 10 is a three-bedroom cottage, with a fully-equipped kitchen, dining room, lounge and courtyard. Most of the cottages are centrally located so you're within walking distance of the many fine eateries in town. I hadn't had the chance to cook for quite some time so I was itching to get into the kitchen and rustle up a feast. This I achieved and, suitably full from my culinary efforts, it was obviously time to put my feet up, pour a glass of wine and watch a film before losing myself in one of the very comfortable beds. Busy busy. The real joy of these cottages for me is that I didn't feel like a self-caterer overnighting in a bland, spiritless space; I felt like I was at home.

Rooms: 7 cottages, 6 with 2 bedrooms (4 en-suite, 2 with separate bathrooms); 1 with 3 bedrooms (all en-suite); 2 with own pools, 3 with access to pool. All air-conditioned.
Price: R330 - R600 pp sharing. Singles from R500.
Meals: Self-catering.
Directions: For Number 2 Parsonage Street, Turn into Parsonage Street (next to shell garage) from Church Street and drive to end. No. 2 is on your right.

KwaZulu Natal

Sunbirds

Liz and Jonathan Shaw

No. 54 (Lot 643) Outlook Road, Southbroom
Tel: 039-316-8202 Fax: 086-687-1991
Email: stay@sunbirds.co.za Web: www.sunbirds.co.za
Cell: 072-993-7902

Never one to resist temptation, when Jonathan insisted that I try a Sunbirds speciality breakfast I was happy to oblige. I assumed the position on the terrace overlooking the swimming pool, then palms and bush, and finally the distant ocean horizon. Today's 'mere starter' was honeyed papaya with a swirl of fresh yoghurt on the side. My galvanised tastebuds, like baby birds, craved for more and were answered commendably with a cooked breakfast and Liz's home-made almond and cranberry slices. In sympathy perhaps, the architect has created an effortlessly light interior. With the shutters thrown open, the outside floods in along white tiles and into an open-plan merging of living room, dining area, terrace and bar. The bedrooms, both in the house and in the cottage that overlooks a sub-tropical garden, have everything you'll need. Perhaps Liz and Jonathan's eye for detail developed during their lives in England as breeders and trainers of champion gundogs. Closer inspection of the little particulars give this away: a dalmatian doorstop, comedy canine figures at the bar, photographs of their prize spinone (not to mention the picture of a visiting Acadamy Award winning actress enjoying a cocktail with the Shaws at the honesty bar). If you're a golfer, the fifth hole is almost within putting distance, along with two good restaurants and the beach, all within a 3-minute walk - easy. And who's the actress? Her initials are J.C. Otherwise, sorry, you'll have to go and see for yourself.

Rooms: 4 rooms: twin/king (all en-suite 2 with bath and shower, 2 with shower only).
Price: From R575 upwards, pp sharing (singles +R100). Seasonal specials available.
Meals: Full breakfast included.
Directions: Driving along the R61 take the Southbroom South exit and after 400m turn right into Outlook Road. Sunbirds is 2.2km on the right-hand side.

Plumbago

Mick and Libby Goodall

546 St Ives Ave, Leisure Bay
Tel: 039-319-2665
Fax: 086-689-3993
Email:
info@plumbagokzn.co.za
Web:
www.plumbagokzn.co.za
Cell: 082-561-6993

I think the coast of KwaZulu Natal gets better and better the further south you head and Leisure Bay is testament to that. It's just stunning and, buried in the banana plantations between bush and beach, is easily missed by those hammering along the N2 to more on-the-beaten-track destinations. Plumbago itself is on the crest of a hill on sandy St Ives Avenue (just off Torquay Avenue, naturally), a gentle stroll from the sea. It's an airy double-storey home, hidden from its neighbours by the thick foliage of Libby's indigenous garden, indigenous that is "except the rosemary and the lemon tree for G&Ts," she admits. The birds are amazing and hop around right under your nose and while they chattered in the trees we chattered (over lunch) at a long, central dining table made from an old jetty post. Downstairs the house is open-plan with large windows, high ceilings and soft, blue walls – the perfect antidote to sizzling summer days. Upstairs a wrap-around verandah keeps the main bedroom equally cool and if you do get over-heated you can just jump in the outside shower. There are endless sea- or land-based activities to keep you busy in the area, but with a beautiful beach on hand, well, I'd be just as happy focusing on some serious R&R.

Rooms: 3: two kings with bath and shower, one king/twin with shower.
Price: From R410 pp sharing. Single supplement +R100.
Meals: Full breakfast included. Dinner on request.
Directions: Follow N2 & R61 south from Durban towards Port Edward. About 5km north of town take Torquay Ave/Leisure Bay turn-off. Follow Torquay Ave to crest of hill & L into St Ives Ave. Plumbago 100 yards down on R.

Coral Tree Colony B&B

Dave and Liz Page
593 Mandy Road, Southbroom
Tel: 039-316-6676
Email: coraltreecolony@gmail.com Web: www.thecoraltree.com
Cell: 083-771-6606

Conversational, culinary and golfing appetites will be well satisfied at Coral Tree Colony. I found myself, only moments after arriving, with beer in hand, peacefully chatting away to the Pages. From the breakfast terrace I was able to keep one malicious eye on the golfers below duffing their putts on Southbroom Golf Club's 12th green. I refrained from sledging, but they've no excuses – 'PGA Pro of the Year' Derek James coaches there. Liz is a fifth-generation coaster, speaks fluent Zulu and, as you'd expect, knows this area intimately. Dave, meanwhile, is a trained chef, so there's nothing amateurish about the cooking. And then there is daughter Emma who is the architect and whose talents are manifest in this handsome whitewashed home. With its verandahs and columns, it reminded me of a well-to-do home in the deep cotton-pickin' south of the United States. The green-grey rooms are simple and bright, with all the boutique hotel practicalities, fine linen and private terraces. As for the beds, well, they could win awards... more comfortable than your favourite slippers. The guest lounge is airy and bright, with its colonial, wicker, wing-backed chairs, books, DSTV and recycled Oregon pine floorboards. You're actually standing on the roof... which is confusing. Get Dave to explain that. He'll happily oblige. In fact, this is one obliging, stress-free place, especially with the salt-of-the-earth Pages, who made me feel so utterly welcome, at the helm.

Rooms: 6: all with extra-long kings/twins and en-suite bathrooms, 2 with bath and showers, 4 with showers.
Price: R500 - R550 per person sharing. Winter specials available on enquiry.
Meals: Full breakfast included. Dinner by arrangement. Dave and Liz can recommend excellent restaurants & coffee shops in area.
Directions: From Durban, take N2 south to Port Shepstone. At toll gate, carry on (N2 becomes R61). Turn L at Southbroom North exit, into Southbroom Ave. Pass Churchill, College and Berea Roads, over speed hump, then take first R into Berea Road (the second one). The next L is Mandy Road.

Yengele Paradise

Anna Jordan
68 Effingham Parade, Trafalgar
Tel: 071-422-0773 Fax: 039-313-0632
Email: info@yengeleparadise.co.za Web: www.yengeleparadise.co.za
Cell: 073-022-3329

Yengele is Zulu for spotted genet, a pretty cat-like creature which, along with a wide diversity of other wildlife, populates the forest bordering this property… so keep your eyes peeled when traipsing along the leaf-canopied walkway to the beach. The marine reserve waves roar ferociously here. The brave can snorkel the 90 million (give or take one or two)-year-old fossil beds at low tide, but blue-flagged Trafalgar Beach is only a scenic 25-minute stroll away for gentler swims. Significantly closer to home flows the Black Lake, a sleek, little-known horseshoe of flat water, as mysterious as its name suggests. The people who held it sacred many many years ago told the story that the stars originated from the lake. The house has been impressively reinvented with retro character and plenty of creature comfort. The autumn-coloured exterior is contrasted with bright interiors and family heirloom décor: Middle Eastern kilims, a red Victorian sofa, Zulu head-wear, a 1960's Xhosa skirt dyed in red river mud. The bathrooms are small, but bedrooms very homely. I longed to lie out on the substantial deck, sundowner in hand, gawping down at luscious indigenous gardens and an infinite Indian Ocean. The self-catering kitchen is ideal, although Anna specialises in vegan dishes, so give her a nod in that direction and expect something out of the ordinary. You should expect the extraordinary at Yengele anyway. *Kids 14+ welcome.*

Rooms: Beach House. One couple/group at a time. Accommodating groups of 2 to 6. Singles on request. All bedrooms en-suite, 2 with shr, 1 with bath and shower. Couple booking has full en-suite.
Price: B&B R650 – R470 pp sharing. Self-catering R480 – R300 pp sharing. Singles on request.
Meals: B&B includes continental breakfast. Home-cooked vegan meals by prior arrangement.
Directions: From Durban take N2 south. Halfway between Margate and Port Edward take Trafalgar exit. Continue 2 km to 2nd stop sign, turn R into Cunningham Ave. After 200m at T-junction turn R into Effingham Parade. No.68 is at end of cul-de-sac.

Lindsay Loft

Caroline and Pepi Jankovich

26 Lindsay Avenue, Morningside, Durban
Tel: 031-207-1634 Fax: 031-208-3227
Email: caroline@lindsayloft.co.za Web: www.lindsayloft.co.za
Cell: 083-490-0963

If your loft is anything like mine it's a dark and dusty dumping ground for old junk. Caroline's loft, I can enviously assure you, is NOTHING like mine. It's enormous. Walls are whitewashed and go up forever, floors are tiled to keep it cool in summer and there's a lengthy, decked verandah, of which more later. Actually no, I can't wait. The verandah is great, accessed from both the living- and bedrooms it peaks through the trees and across the city from its hill-top look-out. The stunning view stretches right up through the Umgeni Valley and gorge, which transforms into a starry, bright-lit cityscape by night. Back inside, the bedroom is cavernous and calming with (besides a bed, of course) caramel armchairs and a beautiful old writing desk. The living area too is dotted with mahogany antiques and separated from the kitchen by a breakfast bar. For the chef, there's all the cooking kit you need and Caroline will supply the essentials to get you started. This is a great base from which to explore KZN. The Drakensberg mountains are a few hours inland, the game reserves a short drive up the coast and there are excellent beaches and golf courses.

Rooms: 1 double/king with en-s combined bath and sh'r with optional spare single bed for extra family member in adjoining room. A/C. DSTV.
Price: R500 pp sharing. R950 singles.
Meals: Starter supplies and a health breakfast provided on arrival. Otherwise, fully self-catering.
Directions: From King Shaka Airport N2 to Durban. Take ramp L onto M27 Umdloti. L to Umdloti. R at M4 Umhlanga till pass stadium on R. Next R onto M17w Berea (Sandile Thusi Rd). Up hill becomes Springfield Rd. At lights before top of hill R into Essenwood /Stephen Dlamini Rd. At yield sign into Montpelier Rd. 100m ahead Lindsay Avenue.

Abalone Place

Sue and Donald Geddie

336 Cato Road, Glenwood, Durban
Tel: 031-205-6035 Fax: 0866-716-483
Email: info@abaloneplace.co.za Web: www.abaloneplace.co.za
Cell: 072-602-5052

"We wanted to create a serene and tranquil space", Sue explained, as she showed me past the near-century-old frangipani tree, up Indian-red steps, through a grand porch bedecked with urns of ornamental aloes and into immaculate Abalone Place. It took three years for Sue and Donald to refurbish to their impeccably high standards and to hand-pick furniture, lights and bathroom accoutrements from Durban's auction houses and antique shops. Every unique candelabrum, chandelier and retro light-shade is mounted on Donald's bespoke escutcheons. Stained-glass French doors, wall panelling and circular bay windows were also styled in Donald's workshop. There is so much to admire, from the pristine 1960's kitchen units and teak and Oregon staircase to the individual elegance of the six capacious suites. My personal favourites feature a giraffe-sized, mahogany four-poster bed, antique bureau and couch, a frond-caressed balcony with city and harbourscape views and an original black-and-white-tiled 1920's bathroom. Every room has its own distinctive tea set and even the bottles of water are chic. I accepted Sue's offer of Earl Grey under the verandah of purple-flowering petria, where guests can enjoy breakfast and sundowners among meticulously-planted indigenous gardens and tropical birdlife from the nearby Pigeon Valley Nature Reserve. If you're seeking originality, tranquillity and no small measure of luxury then Abalone is the place for you.

Rooms: Full suites: 1 king/twin with bath & shower, 1 queen with bath & shower, 2 queens with bath, all have own sitting rooms; 1 double with shower; 1 bachelor flat with king/twin & shower. All 6 have en-suite bathrooms & private balcony/garden.
Price: R500 - R700 pp sharing. Singles R700 - R900.
Meals: Full breakfast included. Lunch and dinner on request. Self-catering also available in bachelor flat.
Directions: From King Shaka airport, N2 to Durban. Before city, take 2nd M13 fly-off to Mazizi Kunene Rd (at tollgate bdge). R at lights over tollgate bdge. Thro 2 lights, past Entabeni hospital & St. Henry's school on R, over hill, L at bottom into Mazizi Kunene Rd. 1st L into Cato Rd. 336 1st house on L after Ellis Brown Ave.

The Grange Guest House

Annelie and Mutari Wada
1 Monteith Place, Durban North
Tel: 031-563-6826 Fax: 031-563-0072
Email: agrange@iafrica.com Web: www.thegrange.co.za
Cell: 072-324-1834

As I walked into the Grange I got that tingly excited feeling that GG researchers experience when they find somewhere particularly special! High ceilings create a feeling of vastness and you can't stop your eyes from wandering about the walls, which are adorned in exciting colours. The bewitching art around the house is from all parts of the African continent - my personal favourite was commissioned in Nigeria. And then, of course, there are your hosts. Mutari, who is Nigerian, met Annelie in her homeland of Australia. Never one to say no to a challenge, Annelie moved back to Nigeria with Mutari for 13 years before they decided on a new adventure in South Africa. You can chat to them for hours, which I did over a delectable steak from their local butcher, followed by a family favourite dish of warm strawberries with a dash of vodka. Listening to stories from their amazing life, it's clear that the inspiration for their home stems from their sense of adventure and passion for life. The Grange has been lovingly renovated into a very modern space, keeping in touch with the building's heritage in original wooden floors, but all the bathrooms, beds etc are super-luxurious. No expense has been spared. You'll be spoilt for choice with each room personally decorated – again, my favourite is the Indaba Tree room. With its own astroturf roof terrace overlooking the city, this is definitely the spot for sundowners.

Rooms: 6: 2 family rooms (1 full bathroom; 1 shower over bath); 2 queens (1 full bathroom; 1 shower); 2 king/twins, both with full bathrooms.
Price: R900 - R1,500 per room. Single R700 - R800.
Meals: Full breakfast included. Dinner and lunch available on request.
Directions: Drive north up Kenneth Kaunda (staduim on your left) and cross over the Umgeni River. Turn left into Norfolk up the hill. Cross over Grosvenor into Monteith. The Grange is the first property on your left.

Fairlight Beach House

Bruce and Michele Deeb

I Margaret Bacon Avenue, (Corner South Beach Rd), Umdloti Beach
Tel: 031-568-1835 Fax: 0866-128-658
Email: enquiries@fairlight.co.za Web: www.fairlight.co.za
Cell: 082-443-8529 or 082-775-9971

I got my first taste of Fairlight's laid-back hospitality as soon as I arrived. It was another hot KZN day and Bruce bustled me off for a joyous dip in the sea just across the road – "We can talk later." And we did. This newly-refreshed 'inspector' was soon sipping a fresh grenadilla juice by the pool and tucking into some of Fairlight's legendary scones. The garden behind the house is dominated by a large milkwood, a favourite hang-out for local vervet monkeys and a great place to shelter from the sun, although there are also sun-loungers around the swimming pool. The front of the house has a wooden deck running all along it, from where you can watch the surfers - six of the rooms open onto it. Dolphins love the surf too and if you're lucky you can swim with them. Bruce can lend you a boogie-board. Inside, it is effectively a family home and luxury guest house rolled into one – plenty of light and air as befits a beach house, family snaps on the wall and a warm, welcoming vibe to it. Rays of positive energy emanate from Michele and Bruce and from their very charming managers, Jaquie and Jenny. Soak it up, then go forth and fish, surf or swim with a big smile on your face. Ten miles of heaven, a.k.a. Umdloti Beach, are but 40 paces from the house while the Mount Moreland roost site for migrating swallows (Sept - April) is just ten minutes by car. *King Shaka International Airport is 8km from Fairlight and Durban 25 minutes drive. World-class golf courses nearby and great restaurants within easy walking distance.*

Rooms: 9: 5 rooms with en-suite bath & sh'r; 3 rooms with sh'r; I family room (sleeps 2 adults + 2 ch'n) with en-s bath & sh'r. All king/twin beds, fully air-conditioned & have sea views.
Price: R550 - R900 per person per night sharing. Family room: R1525-R2000. Singles: from R800.
Meals: Full breakfast included. Limited self-catering facilities available.
Directions: N2 exit to Umdloti. Follow down to roundabout. Keep right past Total garage and Fairlight is 500 metres along South Beach Rd. GPS S29O 40' 31.74" E31O 06' 53.98"

Comfort House

Ray Leitch
27 Dolphin Crescent, North Coast, Shaka's Rock, Umhali Beach
Tel: 032-525-5575 Fax: 086-649-9094
Email: comfort@iafrica.com Web: www.comforthouse.co.za
Cell: 082-556-9795

"I'm afraid I'm going to be a terrible host and ask you to get yourself a drink", was how Ray introduced herself to me. Within seconds I was drink in hand, utterly at ease and ready to get to know my terrible new host. As a former advocate for some years in the Cape, there's not much on the streets Ray hasn't seen or heard before ("everything you can possibly imagine… and also what you can't!"). She's certainly straight-talking, but also very down-to-earth, and in tandem with her manageress and niece, Debbie, who exudes calm, they have imbued Comfort House with an anything-goes, everybody's-family kind of a feel. This is a home and there's no attempt to conceal it. A Red Bear surfboard leans on a depiction of The Annunciation by the front door; family collages adorn the landing; greetings arrive in handfuls from the golden retriever and spaniel (with eyelashes longer than I believed possible). Even the four rooms are named after Ray's children (who fled the nest some time ago) and grandchild: Sarah, Jessica, Nicholas, Alexander and Anna. Yet none of this is overbearing. It's just what the label says: Comfort House. Each room opens on to a large communal balcony, so that guests fall into conversation and sun-loungers with equal ease, while taking in the turquoise pool below and the deep blue sea beyond. Honeymooners, of course, get the extra-special candle-lit treatment and I admired the gorgeous dark-wood sleigh bed and intimate Jacuzzi on the private verandah… almost worth getting married for!

Rooms: 5: 3 kings, 1 queen and 1 twin, all with en-suite baths and showers.
Price: R595 pppn sharing including breakfast. Singles R695. Please ask about winter specials from May to September.
Meals: Full breakfast included. Dinner on request from R150 for 2 courses.
Directions: From Durban take N2 north until off ramp 212 to Shaka's Rock Road. Turn towards the sea and continue 3.5km to a T-junction. Turn L into Ocean Drive and then 2nd L in to Dolphin Crescent. GPS: S29 30' 34.67 E31 13' 52.16

Seaforth Farm

Trevor and Sharneen Thompson
Seaforth Ave, off Old Fort Road, Foxhill, Umhlali
Tel: 032-525-5217 Fax: 032-525-4495
Email: info@seaforth.co.za Web: www.seaforth.co.za
Cell: 082-770-8376

Seaforth Farm is a full-blown treat of a guest house. Trevor and Sharneen have many interests, talents and motivations and Seaforth is a constant source of stimulation. Sharneen is a water-colourist and has also won medals for flower-arranging, so the house blooms with extravagant displays and paintings. Trevor is both an official tour guide and a skilled craftsman and much of the furniture has been made in his workshop (his latest piece, a huge lychee-wood bed) – and it is highly accomplished work. The garden is lush and wild and envelops everything at Seaforth in tropical colour. The produce from the organic garden will always make its way to the breakfast table, with a variety of fruit and veg wide enough to stock a greengrocers! Trevor's latest pastime is bee-keeping and after polishing off several slices of wild coastal honey cake I was duly shown around the apiary. In fact the entire working farm is a hive of activity. The cattle are now pure Nguni (the painted cattle of Africa), chickens run among the pawpaw and sweet and soursops trees and then there's the dam with its abundant bird life. Trevor is coaxing it in with a cunning plantation of pond weed, lilies and islets. The guest house provides large, well-equipped bedrooms, a pool and thatched summerhouse with dam- and sea-view for heavenly breakfasts and candle-lit curry evenings. Finally, the staff have a stake in the success of their venture. A pioneering guest house indeed…. *Zulu spoken.*

Rooms: 4: 1 family suite with 2 bedrooms, each with en/s shower; 2 doubles and 1 twin with en/s shower and bath.
Price: R430 - R580 pp sharing. Family suite from R325 pp (min R1,280). First child free.
Meals: Full breakfast included.
Directions: From Durban take the N2 north. Exit 214 east off the N2 signed Salt Rock. Go 200m and take the 1st right into Old Fort Road at the Foxhill sign, then 1st left into Seaforth Ave - the house is at the end.

Nalson's View

Wendy and Kelvin Nalson
10 Fairway Drive, Salt Rock
Tel: 032-525-5726 Fax: 032-525-5726
Email: nalsonsview@3i.co.za Web: www.nalsonsview.com
Cell: 083-303-1533

After a long, long (long, long) day on the road I finally emerged from my car at Nalson's, wild-eyed and mud-besmattered. I couldn't have pitched up anywhere more perfect. Kelvin and Wendy welcomed me as if I had been living there for years. This was my room, these my beers and friends… I owned the place didn't I? A fantastic shower washed off the mud (don't ask) and I was invited to dinner. I couldn't tell who were guests, who were family friends, such is the open-house air of friendship here, and the meal was out of this world. Kelvin and Wendy have an oyster and mussel licence (guests can go with them and pick their own) and these were by FAR the best I've had in SA. Nalson's is one of those places where guests stop over for one night and have to be prised out of the place days later. Breakfast was sensational (both local baker and butcher are true servants of the community!) and, joy oh joy, freshly-squeezed fruit juice. Guests who make the correct decision to stay more than one night will get involved in the sea activities – dolphin- and whale-watching on boats, fishing, bird-watching and the ten kilometres of beautiful Christmas Bay Beach. There's plenty to do on dry land too, including golf galore, walking-distance restaurants and the Sibaya casino 10 minutes down the road. With Durban's new King Shaka Airport just 20 minutes away, Nalson's View is a worthwhile first or last stop on any KZN adventure. *Ask about kids.*

Rooms: 4: 2 doubles, I family and I double/twin; 3 with en-suite shower, I with en-suite bath and shower.

Price: R400 - R500 pp sharing. Singles on request. Discounts for longer stays (2+ nights).

Meals: Full breakfast included and served when you want it. Dinners by prior arrangement. Price depends on what you have.

Directions: From Durban take N2 north. Take exit 214 (Salt Rock/Umhlali). Right at T-junction signed to Salt Rock, follow road round to the right past Salt Rock Hotel (on your left). Fairway Drive is next right.

One On Hely

Ann Walters

1 Hely Hutchinson, Mtunzini
Tel: 035-340-2498 Fax: 035-340-2499
Email: admin@oneonhely.co.za Web: www.oneonhely.co.za
Cell: 079-509-4256

Ann describes the Walters family's relocation to Mtunzini as a 'calling'. Swapping the industrial chimneys of Newcastle for the rolling Indian Ocean they have much to teach about bravely following your instincts. Mtunzini is an up-and-coming town on the tourist map. Its main street leads to the greenery of the Umlalazi Nature Reserve and on to miles and miles of virginal beach. "Oh dear, it's busy", Ann remarked as we walked onto the white sands and counted five people dotted between us and the horizon. With its burgeoning independent café and shop scene, Mtunzini is a gem waiting to be discovered. Here you can fish, surf, bird-spot, wind-surf, walk and water-ski to your heart's content – although if I were you I'd factor in some time flopping by the pool at One On Hely, which is set high above a flood of greenery. A stone's throw from town, this modern guest-house is surrounded by its own lovely garden, but from upstairs views are out over forest, reserve and sea. All the bedrooms have pristine beds and linen, while pictures of shells and wild flowers in dark wood frames remind you that the sea and green of the reserve is just outside your private balcony. As Mike owns The Fat Cat in town they frequently raid their own café for prawns, calamari, fresh fish and lamb. In fact, it seems, you can dine on pretty much whatever your belly is rumbling for. Get there before everybody else does.

Rooms: 6: all kings/twins with en-suite bathrooms.
Price: R600 - R700 pp sharing. Single R850 - R950.
Meals: Full breakfast included. All other meals on request.
Directions: Take N2 from Durban exit at Mtunzini toll plaza exit. Turn right and One on Hely is 1km on your right.

Chase Guest House

Jane and Jonathan Chennells

John Ross highway off R66, Eshowe
Tel: 035-474-5491 Fax: 035-474-1311
Email: thechase@netactive.co.za Web: www.thechase.co.za
Cell: 083-265-9629

Jane and Jonathan have so much to offer their guests that you hardly have to leave the premises. But leave the premises you must! Chase is in the heart of the Zulu kingdom and what better spot to catch up on the history of King Shaka or get tangled up in the Kings' Reed Dance. The Dlinza Forest Aerial Boardwalk is another highlight. Back at the ranch, the weather-boarded house is gargantuan (Mrs Chennells senior had a penchant for large, open spaces) with long views of the farm's sugar cane plantations on overlapping mounds of distant hills. On clear days you can even see 90 degrees of sea. They also have ducks, chickens and (Nguni) cows like a proper farm should, of course. Also a pair of resident spotted eagle owls. The garden is an orgy of barely controllable tropical growth, lush and colourful (check out the tulip tree and the Indian mahogany), its trees often weighed down by parasitic ferns and creepers. Birds are equally irrepressible and there are 80 species in the garden and 280 (!) in the Eshowe area. Kids will love the walled-in swimming pool (13 metres long) where you can swim by floodlight at night too. A hammock swings from a tree, a trampoline is stretched at ground level and there is a hard tennis court. Chase Guest House is an involving, very comfortable, incredibly good-value family home, with huge amounts of space inside and out. Pack a sense of humour and a pair of binoculars. *Bikes are available for use. They also do sugar farm and banana farm tours.*

Rooms: 4: 1 king with en-s bath; 1 twin with en-suite shower. 2 king/queen/twin self-catering garden cottages.
Price: B&B R400 - R450 pp sharing. Single rates available. Self-catering R650 - R700 per cottage.
Meals: Full breakfast incl' for B&B (& by arrangement only in garden cottages). Dinners on request.
Directions: From Durban take N2 north for 1 hour. Turn off at Dokodweni off-ramp R66 to Eshowe. 20 minutes to Eshowe. Take first left signed to Eshowe, Chase is 1.8km signed on left. GPS coordinates: S 28° 54.661' E 031° 28.292'

Birds of Paradise B&B

Delise Powell

45/49 Ulundi Street, Eshowe
Tel: 035-474-7738 Fax: 086-614-6709
Email: reservations@birdsofparadise.co.za Web: www.birdsofparadise.co.za
Cell: 082-532-4627

Delises's immediately and obviously friendly alsatians were bounding about chasing butterflies on the royal palm-flanked drive when I arrived at Birds of Paradise. Delise, who greeted me and showed me round, is a warm and caring, former nurse who met husband Quentin at school in Eshowe, so they know the area backwards. We strolled past the trampoline, vegetable patch and tennis court and on to the charming bedrooms with their dark, wooden headboards and, of course, avian sketches. This is a great base from which to explore the Zulu Kingdom. I went on a fascinating Zulu tour, that brought home vividly the perils that faced both the Zulus themselves and also our hobnail-booted, pith-helmeted predecessors. Later, exhausted from a day of adventure and cultural learning, I retreated to the verandah that forms part of the main house. From here I looked out onto a burgeoning garden, whose rich palette of Van Gogh-esque greens, purples and reds is borrowed from the nearby Dlinza forest. A roaring lapa fire, masterminded by Quentin, crackled around a traditional Afrikaner potjie cauldron. Cards were dealt and wine flowed. Good, old-fashioned, South African hospitality! I dozed off to the calls of the adorable bush-babies and awoke the next morning to the terrific sound of the resident trumpeter hornbills – they were probably just jealous of my croissants, piping-hot fresh coffee and full English breakfast! I was ready to take on another sunny day in the Zulu Kingdom.

Rooms: 10: 6 double/twin rooms; 2 luxury rooms; 2 self-catering rooms. All en-suite with ceiling fans and air-conditioning.
Price: R400 - R520 pp sharing. Singles R550. Self-catering R345 pp sharing.
Meals: Full breakfast included. Dinner on request (from R120 pp).
Directions: From Durban take N2 north for 1 hour. Turn off at Dokodweni off-ramp R66 to Eshowe for half an hour. Take second entrance to Eshowe at a set of traffic lights. Pass through next set & continue till hospital, turn right and follow 4 signs.

Map Number: 14

Entry Number: 182

Thula Thula Private Game Reserve

Françoise Malby-Anthony
D312 Buchanana Main Road, Heatonville
Tel: 035-792-8322/3/7065 Fax: 086-647-8357
Email: francoise@thulathula.com Web: www.thulathula.com
Cell: 082-259-9732 / 082-787-9991

Fresh fruit cocktail in hand, I was whisked into a 4x4 for an afternoon game drive only to find myself staring down the trunk of Nana the elephant, matriarch and star of Lawrence's best-seller, *The Elephant Whisperer*. Anyone who has read the book will know that Thula Thula is a special place where Lawrence worked closely with local Zulu communities. Today, Françoise and her team carry on the legacy of Lawrence's magnificent work. Both owner and staff are wonderfully entertaining and passionate conservationists. Here, human and animal lives are intimately intertwined as I discovered upon meeting Thabo and Ntombi (the not-so-small baby orphan rhinos). Thula Thula is also home to leopard, buffalo, giraffe, zebra, nyala, hyenas, crocodile, kudu, wildebeest and no fewer than 400 bird species. The tented camp with its outdoor showers, laid-back meals and luxury tents big enough for King Shaka and his entourage is perfect for families. A couple of kilometres through the bush, the lodge is equally breathtaking with cathedral-sized, African-themed rooms lavishly decked out with four-posters, zebra rugs and huge doors leading to the stoep. Not bad for the bush! Meeting other guests around a candlelit pool I was guided into the boma, complete with mesmerizing fire ("nature's TV" whispered Françoise) and presented with a four-course extravaganza of Franco-Zulu cuisine. While feasting on chicken with chilli chocolate sauce and a sensational impala pie, I conjured up a plan to stay longer... if only!

Rooms: 16: 8 lodges all king/ twin, 2 standard with sh'r, 4 luxury & 2 royal all en-s bath & sh'r. 8 luxury tents, 6 deluxe king/twin bath & shr & outside shr, 2 family bath & shr.
Price: Lodges: R2,200 - R3,000 pp sharing. Tents: R1,800 - R2,000. Full board & inclusive of all game drives & bush walks. See website for packages on offer all year round.
Meals: Includes all meals & gourmet Franco-Zulu 4-course dinner in Lodge or traditional SA home cooking in tented camp.
Directions: From N2 take R34 towards Empangeni. Thro' Empangeni turn R towards Heatonville. Follow 10km crossing 3 rail tracks. Turn L at next T-jct onto dirt rd for 8km. Turn R for 2km to Thula. 2 hrs from Durban. Map on website.

Macadamia Lodge

Lucy Williamson

1st Avenue, Monzi Village, Monzi
Tel: 035-550-4427
Email: enquiries@macadamialodge.co.za Web: www.macadamialodge.co.za
Cell: 072-424-1020

When I heard that Macadamia Lodge was overlooking a golf course I must admit I did have my doubts and had envisioned multiplex houses and characterless lawns. I'm now eating humble pie, as I could not have been more wrong. I was welcomed by Lucy with her infectious smile and bubbly personality and ushered into their family home where mum Pat (also known as 'Yogi Pat'), and dad Tim ('Farmer Tim') welcomed me with the same enthusiasm. The apple really doesn't fall far from the tree. Lucy has been in tourism her whole life and the family moved to South Africa with the dream of their welcoming lodge in mind. The two country cottages offer comfortable, private living and are the perfect place to unwind and forget about the rest of the world. Monzi is only 15 minutes from St Lucia but with all the activities going on around the farm you wouldn't be blamed for not wanting to leave. Pat is a dedicated yoga teacher with her own studio on the farm and is also the 'foodie' in the family. Expect delicious breakfasts and baked goods made from all their own produce. And, if you fancy learning about macadamia farming, let Tim take you on a tour around the macadamia orchard. Or take a stroll through Pat's butterfly garden and admire the farm's birdlife from Tim's hide that overlooks the pond, the perfect spot for a sundowner or a picnic. As I drove past the avo, mango and various citrus trees and through the winding pines that line their driveway, I understood why Lucy refers to home as magical Monzi.

Rooms: 2 self-catering cottages: 1 dble en-s shr; 1 with 2 bedrooms (1 dble; 1 twin) en-s bath & shower.
Price: Self-catering R400 pp; B&B R480 pp; DBB R630 pp. Kids 0-3 free. Under 16s ask re discounts.
Meals: Full breakfast included for B&B guests. 3-course dinner on request (24 hour notice required) served in the dining room. Home-made meals can be purchased for self-catering. Ask about costs.
Directions: From Durban take N2 pass Richards Bay. Turn off at exit 375 and head for Mtubatuba & St Lucia R618. Drive for approx 15km and turn right onto the P397 in the direction of Monzi. L into Monzi Village.

Map Number: 14

Entry Number: 184

Makakatana Bay Lodge

Hugh and Leigh-Ann Morrison
,iSimangaliso Wetland Park (formerly known as Greater St Lucia Wetland Park)
Tel: 035-550-4189 Fax: 035-550-4198
Email: maklodge@iafrica.com Web: www.makakatana.co.za
Cell: 082-573-5641

Makakatana Bay Lodge is sensational and I can do little to improve on these photos, which do not lie. If only we had space for ten shots, to show you every aspect of the lodge: the gleaming wooden interiors; the bedrooms (including the wonderful honeymoon suite), connected by walkways through the forest, with their gargantuan slabs of glass and warm, earthy African colours; the pool encased in decking and raised above the grasses of the wetlands; the lake itself and the extraordinary St Lucia Estuary and lake system. Guests are taken on drives into the wetlands to search for birds (360 species), crocodiles and hippos. You can also be taken on safaris to the beach for snorkelling and swimming or out on a game drive within the iSimangaliso Wetland Park before returning to a sumptuous dinner with your hosts in the outdoor boma. Safari drives to Hluhluwe Game Reserve are also available if you have a hankering to see the Big 5. The family's old 'Crab House' is the only part of the lodge not raised above the tall grasses. This was once a storeroom for crabs caught in the lake, now a wine cellar with a giant tree growing out of its roof. Huge sliding doors throughout the lodge open onto wooden decks and the absence of railings just adds to the feeling of openness to nature. The lodge is beautifully welded to its environment. An absolute treat.

Rooms: 6: 1 honeymoon suite with extra single bed, 2 king suites, 3 twin suites; all with en-suite bath and outside shower.
Price: R3,250 pp sharing, honeymoon suite R3,450 pp sharing. Singles R3,995, children (aged 8-12) R2,050. All meals and in-house activities included. Drinks for own account.
Meals: Fully inclusive of all meals and safaris.
Directions: Take N2 north from Durban for 250km to Charter's Creek. Follow road for 15km (14km on tar) to fork. Take R fork and follow signs to Makakatana Bay Lodge (4 more km or so).

Bushwillow Lodge

Julian and Liz Simon

PO Box 525, Hluhluwe
Tel: 035-562-0473 Fax: 035-562-0250; fax to email 086-650-2810
Email: info@bushwillow.com Web: www.bushwillow.com
Cell: 083-651-6777 (Julian), 073-151-6776 (Liz)

Game reserves can be an expensive stop-over, so for visitors on a tighter budget we've uncovered some more affordable gems that still offer great access to local highlights. Bushwillow, 'more of a passion than a business' to Julian and Liz, is one such. Set in Kuleni Game Park with 170 hectares to explore (on foot) you'll spot plenty of wildebeest, zebra, warthog and giraffe, setting the mood for the 'Big 5' at Hluhluwe-Umfolozi or the Isimangaliso Wetland Park just half an hour away. It's hidden in the sand forest and, while it can be reserved for your exclusive use, here you will always find an interesting array of people with whom to spend your time. I arrived on a blisteringly hot day and, passing a greedy 'sounder' of warthogs, was only too glad when Julian shepherded me inside to the cool of the fans. The three forest-green chalets blend into the bush perfectly, cunningly positioned a stone's throw from a small water-hole so you needn't go further than the deck (or plunge pool) to spot the local wildlife. Liz informed me that early risers can regularly witness giraffe stooping at their stoep. In fact, no need to rise. Just prop up a pillow and watch from your bed! The air-conditioned bedrooms are peaceful and private with basins set in jacaranda trunks and just a few steps along the boardwalk from the sociable living area. Here granite worktops and a eucalyptus dining table support Jabu and Victoria's excellent home-cooked meals. Or, have the whole kitchen to yourselves and self-cater in style! It seems they've thought of everything.

Rooms: 3 chalets (king or twin) with bath and shower. All bedrooms have air-con.
Price: R825 pp (B&B), R995 pp (DB&B). Singles & kids rates on request. 3-night packages available. Long stay discounts. Self-catering: R2,000 per night (up to 4 guests), R3,000 per night (up to 6 guests).
Meals: Meals: 3-course evening meals, continental or full-English breakfasts. Strictly no meals for self-caterers.
Directions: From N2 take Hluhluwe off-ramp & pass thro' Hluhluwe town. At bottom roundabout take R22 twds Sodwana Bay. Go 16km after crossing railway & Kuleni Game Park on L. Bushwillow signed in reserve.

Thonga Beach Lodge

Paige and Brett Gehren
Isibindi Africa Lodges, Mabibi, Greater St Lucia Wetland Park (now known as iSimangaliso Wetland Park)
Tel: 035-474-1473 Fax: 035-474-1490
Email: res@isibindi.co.za Web: www.isibindi.co.za Cell: 079-491-4422

I had been eagerly looking forward to my visit to Thonga Beach Lodge since before I had even left Cape Town. I knew it would be great because all the Gehrens' places are (see Isibindi Zulu Lodge, Kosi Forest Lodge and Rhino Walking Safaris) but I didn't expect it to be QUITE so beautiful! Thonga Beach is sandwiched between forested dunes and ocean, an hour's sandy drive and 4x4 trail from the nearest tar road. Huts are connected by snaking, wooden walkways and in each a huge mosquito net hangs from high rafters, separating the bed from the bathroom, a design marvel in itself. One single piece of sculpted concrete flows past glass-bowl sinks and chrome taps into an oval bath. After unpacking, I took a quick dip in the sea before being whisked out for a breath-taking sundowner on Lake Sibaya. An elegant supper followed and my perfectly light fish accompanied by a soft white wine sent me to my hut for a long, much-needed sleep. Come morning, I was raring to go for a sunrise stroll. The sky was a soft pink, the surf breaking onto footprint-free sand and, looking back to the lodge, I could just make out the thatched tops of each rounded room, twelve in all, poking out through milkwood brush. This is as luxurious and romantic a destination as you'll find anywhere, but it's super-relaxed too. All staff are hugely friendly, the birding, diving, walking and wildlife are superb and – a rare bonus – it's majority community-owned so your pennies help support the local economy.

Rooms: 12: 10 twins, 2 doubles, all with bath & sh'r, air-con, mosquito nets & sea or forest view.
Price: R2600 - R3440 pp sharing. Includes all meals, guided snorkelling, guided walks & kayaking. Spa treatments & scuba prices available on request.
Meals: Full board.
Directions: From Durban take N2 north to Hluhluwe, then follow signs to Kosi Bay (Kwa-Ngwanase). 30km beyond Mbazwana follow signs right to Coastal Forest Reserve. Thonga car park (& lodge pick-up point) now at Coastal Cashew factory, 4.7km from tar rd. For 4x4 vehicles you will have to go 32km on along sandy road.

Kosi Forest Lodge

Paige and Brett Gehren
Isibindi Africa Lodges, Kosi Bay Nature Reserve, Kosi Bay/KwaNgwanase
Tel: 035-474-1473 Fax: 035-474-1490
Email: res@isibindi.co.za Web: www.isibindi.co.za
Cell: 082-873-8874

Kosi Bay is the sort of place that novelists map out and then construct adventures in. You are picked up by a four-wheel drive, which can negotiate the sand tracks criss-crossing the region. You park up not just your car, but also the modern world you are now leaving. There is no tar and no electricity here. Instead you enter a landscape of raffia palm groves, primary sand forests, mangroves, water meadows, interconnecting lakes (yes, hippo and crocodile like it too and are regularly sighted). And then there are day trips to the sea and the mouth of the river for snorkelling, swimming and fishing in 'perfect, white sand coves with huge overhanging trees' (says the lodge brochure). The reed-thatched camp itself perfectly balances the wild (your chalet is in the middle of a boisterous forest) with the romantic (candlelit meals and outdoor baths and showers). I loved the deep stillness of the early-morning guided canoe trip and other activities include boat cruises across the lakes, turtle-tracking (seasonal), forest walks and bird safaris. I consider Kosi Forest Lodge one of the most rewarding (and therefore best-value) places I have stayed in SA. I recommend a minimum of two or three nights.

Rooms: 8: 1 family 'bush suite'; 5 twins and 2 honeymoon doubles; all with outdoor bath and shower.
Price: R1370 – R1790 per person per night sharing. Guided canoeing on the lakes, walks in raffia forest & sundowner excursion included.
Meals: All meals included.
Directions: From Durban take the N2 north to Hluhluwe and then follow signs to Kosi Bay (KwaNgwanase). From JHB pass Pongola and turn R at sign Jozini. In Jozini thru' town, L over the dam and follow for 37km. Turn R at T-jct and follow for 67km to Kwangwanase. Pass through town to end, go to Total Garage for pick from lodge (9km).

Ghost Mountain Inn

Craig Rutherfoord

Fish Eagle Rd, Mkuze
Tel: 035-573-1025 Fax: 035-573-1359
Email: gmi@ghostmountaininn.co.za Web: www.ghostmountaininn.co.za
Cell: 082-569-0596

I'd been looking forward to visiting Ghost Mountain, if only for the name, but how my excitement increased when I pulled into the car park and saw 26 pristine vintage Bentleys warming up for a day's adventure. NOT what I had expected to find deep in the heart of Zululand! This is definitely a hotel (50 rooms) and thus not a typical GG entry. But I have no doubts about its suitability for this guide. Craig, who is the very charming owner, will instantly make you feel at home. In fact, I cursed myself for not organizing to stay the night after he informed me, over a particularly rich and dark shot of coffee, that there was a boat trip to watch elephants drinking at nearby Lake Jozini or a trail in Hluhluwe-Umfolozi Park on offer if I wished to join them. I didn't even have time to sample a massage in the luxurious on-site health spa. Oh unhappy hour! I did, however, get to wander through the vast gardens that look up to Ghost Mountain (with its spooky history) and admire the fantastic double-trunked sycamore fig tree that stands next to a deep and inviting swimming pool. Naturally the rooms are also topnotch: flat-screen TV's for sports lovers, reed lampshades that cast gentle shadows across soft white linen and a private patio looking across to the Lebombo Mountains. I cast a green eye on those beautiful Bentleys as Craig escorted me back to my car. His phone rang and he apologetically made his excuses. A Zulu princess was expected for lunch and arrangements had to be made. *Bikes are available for guests' use.*

Rooms: 50: 1 Suite with extra-length bed (2 bathrooms en/s bath/sh'r + outside sh'r); 8 Garden Rooms with king (en-s bath and sh'r); 19 Superior Rooms with twin (en-s bath and sh'r); 22 Standard Rooms (en-s sh'r in bath).
Price: From R630 pp sharing. Singles from R895. 2- and 3-night packages from R2,151 and R3,370 pps.
Meals: Full breakfast included. Lunch and dinner a la carte or set menu from R190.
Directions: From N2 continue straight past Mkuze town to a T-junction. Turn left. After 400m the hotel will be on the right-hand side.

Shayamoya Tiger Fishing and Game Lodge

Lindy Blevin

Golela Road, Pongola District
Tel: 034-435-1110 Fax: 034-435-1008
Email: shayalodge@saol.com Web: www.shayamoya.co.za
Cell: 083-456-8423

At Shayamoya I was met by a broad-smiling Busi who ushered me through to a deck with spectacular views of Lake Jozini and the Lebombo Mountains and there I enjoyed a very welcome and peaceful afternoon tea. This treat of a view was shared by my thatched chalet, a hexagonal wood-and-stone affair with a cobbled outdoor shower. Eager to make use of the remaining daylight, I stretched my legs along the Idube Trail, where I encountered an antelope (I need to brush up on my antelopes – guide Muzi is the man to ask). My eyes were peeled for other animals when I came across a sign: 'BEWARE CHILDREN'. Children I can handle. Shayamoya is a family-built and -run lodge (ask to see the photo album), managed today by daughter Lindy on a reserve that once served as an extension of the family's cattle farm (another tale to tell). Alongside boat cruises, rhino walks and game drives (viewing a rich variety of animals and birds), the tiger fishing is a must. The occurence of tiger fish in Lake Jozini is what makes this a unique stretch of water. Come dusk, I was sharing pre-dinner drinks with two couples whose fishing holiday, planned by the husbands, had unearthed the wives' natural talent. At dawn I was woken by Nandi, the resident spotted eagle owl, who reminded me it was time to hit the road. Not before I booked my own return. *For the more adventurous, ask about their self-catering bush camp.*

Rooms: 10: 8 standard chalets; 1 family unit with bunk bed and pull-out couch; 1 honeymoon suite. All en-suite bathrooms, outdoor showers and viewing balconies.
Price: Standard & family unit: R600 pp sharing or R875 for singles. Honeymoon: R880 pp sharing or R1,155 for singles. All B&B.
Meals: Full breakfast included. Lunch: a light à la carte menu. Dinner (3 courses): R180 pp or a small à la carte menu suitable for last-minute arrivals.
Directions: Between the towns of Pongola and Mkuze, 2km off the N2 highway, on Golela/Swaziland border post road. 8km to border post.

Map Number: 14

Entry Number: 190

Dusk to Dawn

Johann and Gudrun Engelbrecht
Farm Wagendrift, Piet Retief
Tel: 017-821-0601 Fax: 086-514-0237
Email: dtd@ptr.dorea.co.za Web: www.dusktodawnbedandbreakfast.com
Cell: 083-627-6454

I'm ashamed to say that I saw neither the dusk nor the dawn on Johan and Gudrun's splendid farm. After missing sundown when my three-hour hop from Jo'burg turned into a five-hour slog, I was sorely tempted by Gudrun's description of sunrise over the distant Kommetjie-Kop seen from the balcony of my room, Egret's View. Unfortunately, my alarm clock failed me yet again! I blame the four-poster bed, with its soothing white linen, not to mention the in-room telescope, which had me glued to the startlingly starry night-sky far past my bedtime. The real culprit though, was the seriously deep bath complete with huge candles, bright enough to light a cathedral. Luckily breakfast is served until 10... and the whole pace of Dusk to Dawn is geared towards unwinding overnight, hence the name. It's the perfect stop-off point if you're travelling between KZN and the Kruger. The braai and verandah are large enough to cater for coach loads. And if you decide not to self-cater, breakfast is a healthy spread of smoothies, juices and, of course, fresh coffee - Gudrun is a trained nutritionist. Over dinner, meanwhile, I tasted some prime Dusk to Dawn pork. All the meat and most of the veggies come from the farm. Johan will happily show you around. He is also an expert on the Zulu Wars and the local German community which settled here over a century and a half ago. Use the farm as one-night stopover if you must, but if you can spare the time stay for two. *Mini-golf and mountain biking available on site.*

Rooms: 5: Egret: 1 twin, 1x4-poster en/s bath; Hadeda: twin en/s sh'r; Sunbirds: 4-poster en/s bath & sh; Barbet's (self-cater): queen en-s bath & sh; Robin's (self-cater): king en-s bath & sh, lounge.
Price: R690 pp sharing including dinner & breakfast. Single and self-catering rates available on request.
Meals: Full board. Barbet's/Robin's self-catering. Full English breakfast or healthy smoothies. Picnics on request.
Directions: Signed off N2, 35km south-east of Piet Retief & 65km north of Pongola. Please note Dusk to Dawn is in the province of Mpumalanga close to border of KZN.

Isandlwana Lodge

Pat Stubbs (owner)

Isandlwana
Tel: 034-271-8301/4/5 Fax: 034-271-8306
Email: lodge@isandlwana.co.za Web: www.isandlwana.co.za
Cell: 082-415-3679 or 082-789-9544

Isandlwana Lodge is 'the' place to relive Anglo-Zulu War history and approaching through the dust I could see its namesake hill from miles away. The rocky outcrop was throwing a long shadow across the valley, just as it did on January 22nd 1879 when 25,000 Zulus attacked the British soldiers encamped on the hill's eastern slope. The story of the ensuing battle is fascinating and the lodge eats and sleeps it. Rob Gerrard, an ex-Gordon Highlander (or one of his trusty sidekicks), leads tours that include nearby Rorke's Drift. Even the lodge itself is designed around a Zulu shield, a thatched, tapered structure that wraps around the hillside and looks across the Isandlwana battlefield. Though steeped in history, it has a refreshingly modern feel. Upstairs, the lounge and bar have leather sofas, ceiling fans and high-backed, Nguni dining chairs. All twelve rooms are downstairs off a winding, rocky corridor, with very private balconies for enjoying the incredible view. Pat has furnished the lodge in a pleasingly subtle blend of hand-printed bedspreads, copper lampshades and slate-tiled, chrome-tapped bathrooms. Having arrived here from Florida and a life of "peanuts and insurance" she has taken to hosting as a duck takes to water. Once you've waltzed through her to-do list of battlefield tours, walking trails, 300 bird species, cultural tours, horse-riding, swimming and gourmet dining, you'll have happily spent at least three nights here. Cultural tours are now available visiting local communities.

Rooms: 12: 5 doubles & 7 twins all with shwrs. Also a separate guesthouse: 3 bedrooms sleeps up to 6.
Price: Lodge (full board) R1775 - R2205 pppn sharing in lodge. Single supp R950. Guesthouse (excl meals) R2200 per night (6 people). Ask for rates for 2 or 4. Battlefield tours R450 pp. Ask re other activities.
Meals: Price includes full breakfast, lunch & 4-course dinner.
Directions: From Durban take N2 north to Eshowe then R68 thro Melmouth & Babanango. L at 4-way stop in Babanango. Travel c 45km to turn-off to Isandlwana Lodge, then another 9km on dirt road.

Isibindi Zulu Lodge

Paige and Brett Gehren
Isibindi Africa Lodges, Rorke's Drift/Battlefields, Dundee
Tel: 035-474-1473 Fax: 035-474-1490
Email: res@isibindi.co.za Web: www.isibindi.co.za
Cell: 082-896-0332

Driving up to Isibindi in the early evening, the way ahead was intermittently illuminated by a spectacular thunderstorm. It seemed to be following me. Ignoring the portents, I pressed on Homerically to claim my prize, a night at the wonderful (the first line of my notes just reads 'Wow!') Isibindi Zulu Lodge. It's on a hill in the middle of a 2,000-hectare nature reserve on the Buffalo River, with six secluded chalets looking out over the bush, a modern spin on the traditional Zulu beehive hut. The best view is reserved for the pool, a great place for daytime dozing before an afternoon game drive with lodge managers who are extremely passionate about the bush. The game wasn't playing ball on our evening outing but we heard plenty of snuffling about in the twilight as we walked back under the stars to the lodge. For those not barmy about the bush there are Zulu dancing evenings laid on. Personally though, the tour of the nearby Isandlwana and Rorke's Drift battlefields are the highlight. Walking the 50 yards of Rorke's Drift, having the battle described to me as the rain fell and the local Zulu choir had their weekly rehearsal in the church on the battlefield itself, was a highlight not just of my trip, but will remain one of the most extraordinary experiences of my life. Nature, history and culture… Isibindi has it all.

Rooms: 6: 4 twins, 1 double, 1 honeymoon suite; all in the traditional beehive shape with en-suite bath and shower.
Price: R1,370 – R1,790 pp sharing. Singles plus 30%. Price includes 3 meals & 1 game activity per day plus a Zulu Boma Evening for a 2-night stay. Battlefield tours, Zulu homestead visits & panoramic day trips optional extras.
Meals: Full board includes breakfast, lunch and dinner and all teas and coffees.
Directions: Take R33 from Dundee towards Greytown for 42km, then turn left onto dirt road at Isibindi Eco Reserve/Elandskraal sign. Follow signs to Isibindi which is 21km from main road.

Sneezewood Farm

Paul and Karen Theunissen

Dundee/Wasbank Road (P33), Dundee
Tel: 034-212-1260 Fax: 088-034-212-1260
Email: info@sneezewood.co.za Web: www.sneezewood.co.za
Cell: 082-611-3560

Karen, Paul and Jubejube, their loyal Jack Russell, gave me a wonderful welcome to Sneezewood! Jubejube – fondly known as PR – ushered me to my room where she quickly made herself at home. She loves to look after new arrivals and Karen often has a difficult time extracting her when the time comes. The Theunissens managed a resort in the Seychelles for three years (poor things!), before deciding to create their own perfect B&B. They have clearly poured their heart and soul into the project. There is a modern crispness to the bedrooms and bathrooms, which are neat and compact, the walls painted in soft natural tones. Each room has its own colour theme and fabrics have been chosen in traditional floral patterns and linens - you can disappear into the scatter cushions on the beds. They have included original family furniture in the B&B and another nice touch was the collection of new battlefield history books in the sitting room for guests to browse through. Sneezewood is within easy reach of most of the major battlefields and just 10km away from the 20-acre Talana Museum, devoted, unsurprisingly, to the Battle of Talana and the broader history of Dundee. Paul and Karen are natural hosts, kind and caring people, and they will make you feel like you have known them for years.

Rooms: 6 double rooms: 5 en-suite with shower & 1 en-suite with bath and hand shower.
Price: Mar 2013 - Mar 2014: rates per room per night: king/twin room: R1,100; queen room: R990; singles: R660. Children over 10 years welcome.
Meals: Dinner and packed lunches are available by prior arrangement.
Directions: Enter the traffic circle on Dundee's main road (Karel Landmann Str). Exit over the railway bridge signposted "Wasbank". Travel 5km along Victoria Street to Sneezewood sign on right-hand side.

Esiweni Lodge

Natie and Magda LeRoux
Nambiti Private Game Reserve,
Elandslaagte/Ladysmith
Tel: 036-636-9002/3
Fax: 086-546-4045
Email:
information@esiweni.co.za
Web: www.esiweni.co.za

I was greeted at my car and whisked off into the wild to join other Esiweni guests already viewing the abundance of wildlife that roams this historic land. After sundowners – keeping one wary eye on the lioness across the river - we migrated lodgewards, outflanking a herd of wildebeest en route. This lodge manages the neat trick of providing professional hospitality and exciting game drives while also feeling like an involving home. Natie and Magda are your wise and welcoming parents and the big five are your pets! Speaking of pets, you must meet 'Wild', the lodge's new mascot and African wild cat. Dinner is an intimate affair where I revelled in some hysterical 'bush' stories, asked Magda about the 'lizards' and wrung Natie's brain for top tips on wildlife photography, an art form requiring technical skill and patience... two talents I may never possess. Esiweni is known for its outstanding location and views and next morning, with the rise of the sun, I saw why. Sitting on my private balcony at the edge of a cliff, I looked down on the Sundays River meandering through an immense valley with its waterfalls and game animals. Between my perch and the valley floor a myriad of birds swooped and glided, wings glinting in the early morning sun. With 265 species of birds, Esiweni is Birdlife South Africa accredited and the only big five game reserve in the area. I later settled myself above these same views on the martini seat in the rim-flow swimming pool. Esiweni is a real treat!

Rooms: 5: all king/twins with open bathroom and outdoor shower, 1 with outdoor bath. All chalets have their own private balconies overlooking the Sundays River.
Price: R2,050 - R2,450 pp. Singles on request. All meals and game drives included. Excluding beverages.
Meals: All meals included.
Directions: Heading north up the N3 take the N11 and then the R602. After 2.3km turn R onto P555. Follow Battle of Elandslaagte signboards to Nambiti Game Reserve.

Mawelawela Game and Fishing Lodge

George and Herta Mitchell-Innes

Fodo Farm, Elandslaagte
Email: mitchellinnes@mweb.co.za Web: www.mawelawela.co.za
Cell: 083-259-6394 or 073-486-8694

George and Herta are a natural, down-to-earth couple whose veins of hospitality run deep… and staying with them is to enjoy a few days awash with incidental pleasures. Herta, a bubbly Austrian, moved out to South Africa some 38 years ago and married George, who is a beef farmer – his boerewors is delicious. He is also a keen historian and leads tours out to the site of the battle of Elandslaagte. His study is full of Anglo-Boer war prints and weighty tomes including a collection of the London Illustrated News. (Ask him to show you his father's beautiful collection of bird-eggs too.) If you stay in the main house the rooms are very comfortable and the bungalow across the jacaranda-filled garden is perfect for families or groups. A short drive away from the farm itself you'll find the thatched hunters' cottage on 1500 wild hectares set aside for game. There is a trout dam at the front into which George has built a waterfall and there's a shower and a plunge pool to one side. The cane-sided shady braai area faces dam-wards and you can watch the eland and kudu come to drink in the evenings and with the Nambiti 'big five', malaria-free conservancy just a short drive away from the lodge, you won't forget you're in animal country. Finally a toast to Herta's cooking which is wonderful! Many of the ingredients are home-grown and all is served on her collection of fine china and family silver.

Rooms: 4: 2 twins (1 en/s bath, 1 en/s bath & shr); 1 apartment with dble, twins & single (self-catering or B&B); 1 self-catering game lodge sleeps 7.
Price: R300 - R450 pp sharing B&B. Singles on request. Self-catering R250 pppn. Booking essential.
Meals: All meals are in the main house. Full breakfast included. Meals on request (prior arrangement).
Directions: On N11, 35km from Ladysmith, 70km from Newcastle. Also entrance on R602, 35km from Dundee towards Ladysmith. For B&B look for sign to Fodo Farm. GPS 28 22' 13.00 S 29 58' 15.00 E.

Map Number: 13

Three Trees at Spioenkop

Simon and Cheryl Blackburn

Rhenosterfontein Farm, Bergville
Tel: 036-448-1171
Email: reservations@threetreehill.co.za Web: www.threetreehill.co.za

This is the comfortable way to experience the Boer War and one of its most famous battlefields, Spioenkop Hill. The lodge sits in complete isolation on an opposing hill with views that flood out across the green valley and down to the Spioenkop Nature Reserve. The chalets are little colonial havens where the emphasis is on simple good quality, rather than elaborate decoration. Each overlooks the reserve and rhino, giraffe, eland, warthog, various species of buck and plentiful bird life can be seen from the rooms. If you can pull yourself away from your unobserved verandah there's plenty to do. Croquet over a glass of home-made lemonade, a tour of the battlefields, horse-riding, exhilarating guided walks tracking rhino with guide and owner Simon… or losing yourself for hours in the lounge which is steeped in history with paintings, books and a wonderful collection of artifacts. Simon and Cheryl clearly have a love of life and a deep care for the environment. This is the first Fair Trade guesthouse in Natal no less; they make their own firelighters out of teabags; they have a wormery; a wonderful veggie garden where kids are encouraged to get dirty; and a newly-purchased solar cooker. So, whether it's relaxing at the sunset spot overlooking the Amphitheatre and Spioenkop Dam, trekking Spioenkop Mountain and hearing the story of the battle, or making your way through a gauntlet of dalek-like aloes to the decked pool perched precariously on the hip of the valley for a little lie down, Three Trees will surely have at least one box for you to put a big tick in!

Rooms: 8: 1 family chalet (chn under 12) with 2 bedrooms (1 dble, 1 bunk + single); 1 self contained family chalet (children 12+) with 2 bedrooms both en-s; 6 dble chalets with en-s bath + sh'r.
Price: R1,950 pp per night sharing, including all meals and guided walks.
Meals: All meals included. Meals available for self-catering on request.
Directions: From Durban take the N3 north for 260km - take the R616 L for 19km towards Bergville. Go L onto the D564 for 8km.

Spion Kop Lodge

Lynette and Raymond Heron

R600, Drakensberg and Battlefields Region, Ladysmith/Winterton
Tel: 036-488-1404 Fax: 086-647-8134
Email: spionkop@futurenet.co.za Web: www.spionkop.co.za
Cell: 082-573-0224/5

Soon after arriving, we were off on a late-afternoon game drive in the reserve next to the farm, winding our way through thick grasses towards a vast lake, then glowing pink-blue under the setting sun. We had the place to ourselves, if you don't count the animals, who seemed to be everywhere, including a nonchalant rhinoceros, who munched his way uncomfortably close to our vehicle. Safely back at base, I began exploring. The lodge is a 700-hectare working farm and eco-reserve with 295 bird species and a mass of flowering aloes in June and July. You can stay either in stone cottages, which are snug with fireplaces for winter and verandahs for summer; or in the colonial farmhouse with its original Oregon-pine floors and library full of history books. But the main heart of the lodge is the 108-year-old stone converted barn, now a massive glass-walled dining room with sinuous blonde branches creeping from floor to ceiling... and breath-taking views. After an excellent dinner with much red wine and merry-making, we embarked on a night safari in search of leopards and porcupines. Raymond Heron (FRGS) and his son Alastair are registered Battlefield, Culture and Birding guides. Raymond is also a raconteur par excellence and an expert on the tragic movements on the Battle of Spionskop. His battlefield tours are so riveting that they are often reported as highlights of people's whole trips in South Africa. Both Raymond and Lynette are wonderful hosts, assisted by family members Alastair and Hester, who will ensure that you have an eventful stay. *Horse-riding, boat cruises, fishing, birding and San Rock art, Drakensberg Boys' Choir.*

Rooms: 8 dbles/twins, all en-s bath & shr. Plus 2 self-catering cottages: Aloe has 1 dble, 1 twin & a bath; Acacia has 2 dble bedrooms & 2 bathrooms, plus 1 small single room.
Price: R990 – R1,650 full board pp sharing. Aloe R1,100 per night; Acacia R1,500 pn. B&B on request.
Meals: Full breakfast, lunch & 5-course dinner.
Directions: On R600 between N11 from Ladysmith & Winterton. Signed off R74 & N11. Gravel rd for 1.5km. (Close to N3: 2.5 hrs from Durban, 3.5 hrs from Jo'burg). See website for map. GPS: 28 42 19.6 South and 29 31 48.7 East.

Montusi Mountain Lodge

The Carte Family
Off D119, Near Alpine Heath, Bergville
Tel: 036-438-6243 Fax: 036-438-6566
Email: montusi@iafrica.com Web: www.montusi.co.za

Montusi feels a bit like a hotel, which just happens to be run by your aunt and uncle. You know… you haven't seen them for years, but no sooner have you stepped from the car than they've got your bed sorted (well, your thatched, Conran-style, country cottage complete with fireplace, selected DSTV and view!) and are fixing you a sundowner on the patio. Ant bought wattle-strangled Montusi Farm in the early 1990s. Being a man of X-ray vision, he saw through the undergrowth to a lodge perfectly positioned to catch the surrounding view, he saw fields of galloping horses and he saw lakes to fish in. So he did away with the wattles and a new Montusi emerged. Meals are superb… some examples: red wine-glazed lamb with balsamic cognac, braised butternut with tomato, onion and grilled mozzarella, milk tartlet, chocolate mousse. There are many ways to burn off the calories with limitless and fabulous Drakensberg hiking on your doorstep (we walked up stunning Tugela Gorge, but the Cartes can help with suggestions). There's also horse-riding for all levels of experience, mountain-biking (bring your own bike), swimming in the wonderful pool and fishing. And just ten minutes down the road is son-in-law Chris's Adventure Centre with high-adrenaline activities ranging from zip line to quad biking. Montusi impressed me because it's a happy, family-run place with plenty of style. *Relaxation massages are offered by local ladies as part of a successful community project. Picnics at waterfalls can be arranged.*

Rooms: 14 cottages: 4 are kings with en-suite bath and another twin with en-suite shower next door. 10 are kings with shower and bath.
Price: From R1,250 pp sharing per night. Singles R1,450. Rate includes dinner and breakfast.
Meals: Full breakfast and 4-course dinner included (wine extra).
Directions: If coming from the south head north through Pietermaritzburg, Estcourt and turn L signed Northern Drakensberg. Continue for 80km thro' Winterton and Bergville on R74. Follow signs (some small) to Montusi. From north use Harrismith & R74.

Zingela Safaris

Mark and Linda Calverley

3 Bloukrans St, Weenen
Tel: 087-802-0050 Fax: 086-650-8950
Email: zingela@futurenet.co.za Web: www.zingelasafaris.co.za
Cell: 079-134-3168

Hiking, fly-fishing, abseiling, rafting, swimming, game-viewing… perhaps I'd be better off listing the things you can't do at Zingela. Mark and Linda are delightful and, over thirty years or so, have built up their home/riverside bush camp to offer everything and anything, all the more astonishing given their location. This really is wild country. From a rendezvous in the wee village of Weenen it was an hour's 4x4 drive (not for the faint-hearted) past isolated Zulu villages and down to the Tugela River - worth every bump. There are five palatial reed and canvas units overlooking the river, all open to the elements. Showers are more outside than in, branches provide the towel rails and each "room" has hefty, iron-framed beds and beautiful wooden furniture from Zanzibar. Those on the romance beat will love the "hitching post" with doubtless the world's largest headboard, a vast, mattress-to-canvas slab of sandstone. There's electricity and gallons of hot water but Zingela is essentially bush living ("don't-forget-the-loo-roll-or-matches kind of country," says Linda). When I visited the place was alive with families (there are zillions of kids' beds in extra dormitory tents). Some youngsters were preparing for a rafting adventure and everyone was thoroughly enjoying the endless fresh air, filling grub and lashings of good, wholesome fun. *The thatched self-catering camp is now open!*

Rooms: 5 bush units: 3 doubles and 2 twins, all with shower (one with a bath). Self-catering option available.
Price: R850 - R950 for leisure. R500 for all adventure activities, including game walks, abseiling & rafting. 4x4 transfer from Weenen: R400 per vehicle.
Meals: Full board.
Directions: Faxed or emailed on booking.

Ardmore Farm

Paul and Sue Ross

Champagne Valley, Central Drakensberg
Tel: 036-468-1314 Fax: 086-503-3453
Email: info@ardmore.co.za Web: www.ardmore.co.za

Just in time for scones and tea on the lawn, the rain clouds parted and I was able to savour the stunning views of the three highest peaks in South Africa: Mafadi (highest at 3450m), Injisuti Dome (second highest at 3410m) and the majestic Champagne Castle (third highest at 3377m). The Drakensberg National Park begins just down the road so bring your hiking boots. Ardmore is a super-relaxed, free-wheeling sort of place. Paul (who bears an uncanny resemblance to Tom Hanks) is always working on something new - a deck, a tree-house or, when I got there, he was in the process of moving his wife's prized cabbage tree. He enthusiastically showed me around the Zulu cotton-weaving factory, run by Sue with the help of the local Zulu community, and the new on-site museum celebrating the renowned pottery of the Ardmore Ceramic Art Studio, which was founded here in 1985 (although the pottery itself was relocated to a new site a few years ago). Sociable and delicious dinners, eaten by lantern light in the yellowwood dining room, draw on the farm's organic produce - eggs from happy, roaming chickens and fruit, vegetables and herbs from a pesticide-free garden. There is masses to do at Ardmore: hike to waterfalls and mountain peaks; watch the rare bald ibis that makes its home here; fish, canoe, mountain-bike or, if you're lucky, catch the Drakensberg Boys' Choir. There are many rock art sites in the area too. The small, thatched rondavels complete with fireplaces are sweet and cosy. Ardmore has a few rough edges, but it's very sociable, great fun... and really good value too.

Rooms: 9: 6 cottages and 3 rondavels: 2 cottages with 2 en-s bedrooms with queen 4-posters; 4 cottages with 1 queen 4-poster, 1 double/twin & 1 twin; 2 en-s. Rondavels all queen; all with shower & sep' bath. All units have fireplaces and own spa-bath/Jacuzzi.
Price: R545 - R695 pp sharing. DBB.
Meals: Full breakfast & 4-course dinner with wine incl'.
Directions: From the N3 take the R74 to Winterton and go south along the R600 towards the Central Drakensberg for 18km. You'll see a sign on your left, 5km up partly dirt road for Ardmore.

Entry Number: 201

Map Number: 13

Sewula Gorge Lodge

Graham McIntosh and Jacquie Geldart

Off R103, 18km from Estcourt
Email: info@sewula.co.za Web: www.sewula.co.za
Cell: 082-824-0329

The pictures do not exaggerate. This glorious thatched lodge lives within a rocky-river gorge filled with cascading waterfalls (the main one is 20 metres high) and swimming pools. As soon as I arrived I realised I had made a significant mistake. I had not organised to stay the night at Sewula and had missed my opportunity to swim under the waterfall looking at the stars. A group of botanists and ornithologists were far wiser and subsequently had a field day on this national heritage site. The emphasis is on relaxation and seclusion (staff are close by when needed) and only one party stays at a time. For this far-too-low-really price, you can pretend you own this truly heavenly place – your 'summer home'! It is self-catering, but with any domestic hardship extracted. For here, not only does nature spoil you, but the staff do too, by washing up, servicing the rooms and lighting the log fires. Under the thatched pitch of the main lodge roof are the kitchen, bush-chic sunken sitting room, a giant fireplace, an oversized chess set and much wildly original carpentry and functional sculpture. Similarly lovely are the cottages, which have sleeping lofts for children and face the river gorge. You can walk to an iron-age settlement, battle memorials and great fishing spots. Jacquie is a stellar host and constantly thoughtful. 100% (as the locals say)! *The rock art sites and white-water rafting are within an hour's drive. Mountain biking trails on the farm (contact in advance to check availability).*

Rooms: 4 cottages (max 8 adults & 10 children): 3 have en-s shower, 2 of which have outdoor shower too; 1 cottage has en-s shower and bath. One booking at a time.
Price: R450 pp per night self catering (min 2 people). 20% discount for groups with 6 adults or more. Children are half price.
Meals: Restaurants are nearby (within 10km).
Directions: Exit 143 on N3 from Durban to Mooi River. Take R103 to Estcourt, 20.3km from off-ramp, take right turn onto dirt road to Malanspruit and follow signs to Sewula Gorge Camp.

Hartford House

Mick and Cheryl Goss

Hartford House, Mooi River
Tel: 033-263-2713 Fax: 033-263-2818
Email: info@hartford.co.za Web: www.hartford.co.za

The Gosses, owners of Hartford House, humbly refer to themselves as "custodians of one of Africa's most treasured legacies". General Botha assumed command of the Boer forces here in 1899 and it was also home to the family of Sir Frederick Moor, the last prime minister of the Colony of Natal. The deputy prime minister, Colonel Richards, established the world-renowned Summerhill Stud on the property, which today hosts stallions for the rulers of Dubai. Aside from all this history, the Gosses also rightly revel in the beauty of this spectacular place… and so will you. Spread across seemingly endless landscaped gardens, the fourteen rooms have been decorated with dark wood antiques from India and West Africa. Scraping my jaw off the floor, I surveyed the four lakeside suites which are nothing short of spectacular. I was especially taken with the aptly-named "Siyabonga" ("thank you" in Zulu) with its twin egg baths and private pool. The beaded chair, the wooden cow heads on the wall and the building materials are all locally sourced. An emperor-sized round bed dominates the Inkanyesi Suite, while "Nhlanhla" ("good luck") combines Burmese antiques with bold green and rich red furnishings and a bright copper bath glints in the bathroom. Made entirely out of hay bales, this amazing example of sustainable luxury accommodation is so close to the dam it is practically floating. Oh, and by the way, the restaurant I dined in (after my Swedish massage) was the South African House and Leisure restaurant of the year. Just go.

Rooms: 15: 4 lakeside suites all king with bath and wet room; 4 garden/ pool suites all with bath and shower; 3 standard kings with bath and shower; 2 twins bath only; 1 twin bath and shower; 1 double bath only.
Price: R840 – R1,555 pp. Wellness Centre offers a variety of treatments.
Meals: Full 3 course breakfast included. A la carte lunch and 5 course set dinner. Restaurant in Eat Out top 20.
Directions: Please refer to website.

Sandstone Cottage

Graham and Sue Armstrong

Kamberg Valley, Nr Rosetta and Nottingham Road
Tel: 033-267-7218 Email: sandstone@bundunet.com
Web: www.sandstonecottage.wordpress.com
Cell: 082-854-5746 (Graham) 082-854-2338 (Sue)

"Now, where are you headed next? I will work on a route and Sue can be your tour guide", insisted Graham. I had met my surrogate SA parents! While Graham retrieved his maps, Sue led me to Sandstone Cottage, set on the grounds of the Armstrongs' home and sharing the same beautiful view overlooking trout-filled dams and beyond to the foothills of the Drakensberg. We'd only made it as far as the stoep when I found a quirky item of interest – a lion's paw-print ashtray. This sort of unusual detail is typical. See the stuffed otter from their previous home in Ireland that sits proudly above the open fire. We shared many enthusiasms, so the tour took quite a while. "Everything is reclaimed," Sue explained. The sash windows, for example, came from a cattle shed. When I admired the material in the bedrooms, Sue educated me on two English fabrics, Jane Churchill and Crowson, and I later learned that Sue is a textile designer by trade. We were soon joined by Graham, a farmer born and bred, who led us to his pride and joy, the wine cellar where bottles are strategically stacked in mangers. "Do guests have access to this?" I asked, to which he replied, "I would love the company!" As well as accommodating guests, the Armstrongs have retired champion thoroughbreds at livery. Sandstone offers hiking and fishing... but this is just a great place to relax, safe in the strong arms of the Armstrongs.

Rooms: 1 cottage with 2 doubles with bath and shower en-suite.
Price: Self-catering R435 pn. Bed and breakfast R540 pn.
Meals: Full English breakfast, Continental by request. Meat "braai" packs in the freezer for guests who don't want to go to a restaurant.
Directions: From Durban/Jo'burg, take Mooi River Toll Plaza off N3. L onto R103 to Rosetta, then R onto Kamberg for 11km. R onto D450 for 1km. "Sandstone" is the first house on the L.

Inversanda Farm Cottages

Tom and Lucinda Bate

Howick
Tel: 082-772-1621 Fax: 086-650-5622
Email: info@inversanda.co.za Web: www.inversanda.co.za
Cell: 082-781-3875

It's true that GG owners are a welcoming bunch, but the Bates go far beyond the call of duty. Actually, I don't think they see it as a duty at all. In fact, I know they don't! Hemmed in by mountains and a meander of the Mgeni River, the farm is in a world of its own, but in easy reach of the major routes. All four Bates (plus assorted hounds) are utterly charming and you're encouraged to participate in their farm and life as much or as little as you like. Talk about a welcome! We were hardly out of the car before we had a greedy calf and a bottle of milk in hand. Half an hour later we were bringing the horses in for feeding. Then just time for a bobble over the fields looking at pregnant cows before a delicious and greatly entertaining dinner with the family. Tom and Lucinda are serious horse-lovers, breeding and schooling polo ponies. Polo players are more than welcome for a weekend knock-about on the makeshift riverside pitch. Otherwise you can fish, walk or swim pretty much anywhere you want. If you've got a 4x4, you're encouraged to hit the trail that will take you to a fantastic waterfall and leave you with breathtaking views of the Midmar Dam and Dargle Valley. The farmhouse itself (1800s) goes on forever and guests have the choice of their own wing, a pot-planted patio with stunning views across the valley, good-sized bedrooms and a basic kitchen; or a cottage which also has a large verandah with a commanding view over the valley and two large bedrooms. But even if you had to lie on a bed of spikes, I'd still recommend Inversanda! This is a place that allows you to unburden yourself of the tourist mantle and truly feel part of what's going on.

Rooms: 1 self-catering wing with 1 double room & 1 twin room, shared bath & shower; 1 cottage with 1 double & 1 family room that sleeps 4. Both have en-suite bathrooms, 1 with shower & 1 with bath & shower.
Price: From R330 pp self-catering.
Meals: Meals available on request.
Directions: Faxed or emailed on booking.

Penwarn Country Lodge

Peter and Barbara Dommett

Bushmen's Nek Road, Southern Drakensberg, Underberg
Tel: 033-701-1368 Fax: 086-611-6439
Email: info@penwarn.com Web: www.penwarn.com
Cell: 076-790-2419

Negotiating my way past an inquisitive eland, I was ushered straight to the bar by Peter and Barbara, a couple who care passionately about the countryside and its conservation. And now they have taken up the reins at Penwarn alongside their neighbouring dairy farm and stud. All very good news for us! The lodge boasts dark-beamed sitting rooms and bedrooms so large they make you want to run amok. Reclining on a deep leather divan in 'Nimrod' (dedicated to a much-loved otter) I goggled at a lake caressed by willows and supervised by cranes. Dinner was a buffet extravaganza. Venison pie went down a treat after my afternoon horse ride with Mondi (they call him Mondi Roberts, the Zulu horse-whisperer). The horse-back game rides are a must, through breathtaking landscapes past droves of zebras, springbok, wildebeest and hartebeest and up to the Bushmen cave figures painted a millennium ago. A couple of GG devotees insisted I visit them at the separate Mthini Lodge. From its stellar position above the dam, overlooking foothills grazed by antelope, we watched the sun set behind the mountains beyond. The sense of space is liberating, the ideal spot to escape and enjoy the gentle pursuits of fishing, paddling, a tour of the draft horse stud (8 different breeds!), flower walks in season and excellent bird-watching at the 'Vulture Restaurant'. A magical place. *Penwarn is part of the Waterford Estate with access to 3500ha, 50 fishing dams and a World Heritage site.*

Rooms: 15: 4 dbles & 3 suites at Indabushe Ldge; 4 suites at Mthini Ldge. All en-s bath &/or sh. 3 s/c cottages: Riverside Cottage (8); Kudu Lodge (6); Log Cabin (4).
Price: R950 - R1,220 pp sharing DBB. R250 - R400 pp for self-catering cottages. Kids under 12 half price. See website for list of activities.
Meals: Full breakfast, 3-course buffet dinner & afternoon tea included. S/c in cottages, but meals available in lodge.
Directions: Exit 99 off N3 to Underberg & Howick Sth. 110km west on R617, thro' Boston & Bulwer. 5km thro Underberg direction Kokstad/Swartberg, R onto Bushmansnek Rd (dirt track). After 16km L to Penwarn (drive 4km on dirt track.)

Map Number: 13

Entry Number: 206

Free State

The View

Ryk and Bea and Sasha Becker

20 Bell Street, Harrismith Tel: 058-623-0961 Fax: 058-623-0961
Email: rmbecker@internext.co.za
Web: www.harrismithaccommodation.co.za
Cell: 082-775-7381 (Bea); 082-921-3624 (Ryk)

How better to while away a sticky afternoon than by nesting in a rocking chair behind teak pillars on a shady verandah, overlooking a lush garden, slowly draining a pot of tea? Bea and Ryk have found a magic formula simply by being themselves at home! The actual view of the title is now interrupted by an abundance of verdure, but I for one was glad of the green shade and the peaceful sounds of twittering birds hidden among the branches. Inside, a portrait of Bea's big-bearded great-grandfather, President of the Free State (deceased, of course), overlooks the social epicentre of this family home. The lounge, complete with creaking wooden floorboards, vibrant rugs and daringly bright sofas, sweeps through folded-back doors into the dining room where the heavy table awaits those staying in for dinner. And I thoroughly recommend you are among them. You would travel a long way to find a better meal and you'll miss out on Ryk spilling the beans on what to do in this area where he grew up. Before heading up to my goose-feathered bed for my best night's sleep in years, no visit to The View would be complete without being introduced to the rest of the family: two springer and three cocker spaniels. *Son-in-law Simon can arrange star-gazing visits to his farm and battlefield tours through local historian and Boer War expert, Leon.*

Rooms: 2: 1 double with en-suite shower; 1 twin with en-suite bath & shower over bath.
Price: R450 - R500 pp sharing. Singles R460.
Meals: Full breakfast included. Dinners on request from R165 pp.
Directions: From Jo'burg side into Warden Street (main street) go around church. 7 blocks from church turn R into Bell Street. From Durban & Bloem, on entering Harrismith turn away from Spur/Engen garage into King Street. Turn L into Warden Street at 1st stop-street. Bell Street is about 10 blocks from here on L.

Map Number: 13

Entry Number: 207

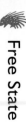

Artists' Colony B&B

Robert and Susan Jewell
3 Church Street, Smithfield
Tel: 051-683-1138 Fax: 051-683-1138
Email: colony@global.co.za Web: www.artistscolony.co.za

For service to weary travellers like me, Robert and Susan deserve knighthoods. After a long trip through the Free State mountains, I reached the serene 'oasis' of Smithfield and spotted, with relief, the calming yellow-and-white walls of the Artists' Colony peeping out from behind verdant greenery, heralding the end of my day's journey. Along with the welcoming tea Susan slipped into my hand, the house's high yellowwood ceilings and wooden floors were as soothing balms to my hotness and bother. The original settlers knew all the tricks to keeping a Karoo-style house cool. Three of the rooms are across the wide road behind a rich curtain of roses, lilies and irises in a building declared a national monument. Each has its own little quirk, whether the maroons and greens of the Birdcage Room, or the East African hair salon advert for all manner of (slightly outdated) haircuts in the Barber Shop room. The original Oregon floorboards creak as you walk on them and the door frames have their own shape! But don't worry – tie rods hold the sun-baked bricks firmly together. All this is part of the delightful charm of Artists' Colony - true 1848 heritage accommodation transformed into a real gem by the wonderfully hospitable and aptly-named Jewells - and I fell instantly in love with it. Being almost exactly in the centre of South Africa, close to the N1 and on the Friendly N6, you will undoubtedly have passed by on some trip or another. Next time don't pass by, drop in. This is a special place to stay.

Rooms: 4: 2 queens, with en-s bath & shower; 2 twins, 1 with en-s bath & shower, 1 with shr only. All rooms have aircon, fridges, fans & tea and coffee.
Price: R400 - R425 per person sharing. Single rate on application.
Meals: Full breakfast included.3 course dinner, available on request R110. Local restaurants nearby.
Directions: South on N1, take exit 177 at Bloemfontein onto Friendly N6 & approx. 120km to Smithfield. North on N1, take exit 8 to Gariep Dam & then onto R701 & approx 115km to Smithfield. In Smithfield, turn into Church St opposite church.

De Oude Kraal Country Estate & Spa

Gerhard and Marie Lombard

35km south of Bloemfontein on N1, exit 153, 6km off N1
Bloemfontein District
Tel: 051-5640-733 Fax: 051-5640-635
Email: info@deoudekraal.com Web: www.deoudekraal.com

I promise you, I had every intention of hiking in the 2,400 hectares of De Oude Kraal, searching out remnants of the Boer War, stalking game or even visiting the Voortrekker graves. But one look at my suite with reclaimed veld fire branches sprouting out of the headboard, the sumptuous bed, sofa, TV and an amazing Balinese bathroom, with spa-tub and super-shower, I knew I wasn't going anywhere! An indulgent few hours of relaxation ensued before I settled for the simple luxury of my verandah and the unspoiled view of the sun setting over the veld, a silhouetted wind pump off-centre completing the perfect picture. Feeling thoroughly content I strolled through the picturesque gardens to the bar for a pre-dinner drink. Fortunately I wasn't wearing my best tie as I feel it may have been confiscated and added to Gerhard's collection on the wall. Thirst quenched, I was led through the main house – in the family for six generations – to the dining room for five courses of candle-lit deliciousness. The food, a fusion of fine dining and hearty farmhouse, has won many an award, as has the wine list, and it's worth having a good look round the cellar. It would have been prudent for me to enjoy a pre-boer-breakfast stretch of the legs, but that didn't happen either; the setting and comfort lend itself to an altogether more leisurely mind-set. *On site spa treatments available.*

Rooms: 11: 1 family suite, 2 standard rooms, 3 luxury rooms, 6 suites.
Price: R605 – R980 pp sharing including breakfast.
Meals: 5-course fine dining dinner R325 pp. Light lunch menu available. Booking essential.
Directions: 35km south of Bloemfontein on N1 take 153 offramp towards Koppieskraal/Riversford. Travel towards Riversford. Turn left at T junction and look for sign.

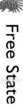

Liedjiesbos Guesthouse

Henning De Bruin
13 Frans Kleynhans Road, Groenvlei, Bloemfontein
Tel: 083-282-5701
Email: info@liedjiesbos.co.za Web: www.liedjiesbos.co.za
Cell: 083-282-5701

Liedjiesbos – meaning song bush in Afrikaans – is an ode to the beauty of the Free State and South Africa: abundant bird life, pristine lawns, indigenous gardens full of rare and wonderful plants, tin roofs and the roar of a lion (housed in the nearby cheetah experience!). What used to be a barn and a shed is now a piece of very intelligent architecture and a very special place to stay. The old barn, with butterfly roof, now has two chic-but-cosy en-suite bedrooms, the kitchen (which I'll come back to) and the main living space, filled with art, curios and furniture from Henning and Dawie's travels. Outside on the shaded stoep is the large restored dining table with a chandelier made from fig tree twigs hanging above it. There's no waste here… everything can be recycled, from the old roof turned into a storage unit to unwanted wood used for fertilizer. They all live on. Now for the kitchen: you won't find frantic chefs, sizzling pans or fast food here. This is home to true aficionados of the slow cooking movement. Local, seasonal produce - mostly from the garden - is cooked slowly and lovingly so you'll need to give plenty of warning if you want feeding. For those with less time, be sure to pick up some of the Liedjiebos' delicious preserves and chutneys. I was rather upset when I ran out… I think I may have to go back!

Rooms: 4 doubles/twins with en-suite bathrooms, AC, DSTV.
Price: 440 pp sharing 650 singles including breakfast.
Meals: Slow food: R180 2 courses, R210 3 courses.
Directions: From N1 take Nelson Mandela off-ramp towards Dealesville (west). After 2.7km turn R at Tempe/Kenilworth turn-off. Continue for 2.7km, R into Frans Kleynhans Rd (Frans Kleynhans sign currently missing). Continue 2km & R into Liedjiesbos at orange wall.

Lesotho

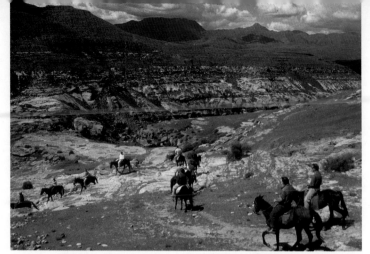

Malealea Lodge and Pony Trek Centre

Michael & Debbie Deutschmann
Malealea, Lesotho
Tel: 082-552-4215 Fax: 0866-481-815
Email: info@malealealodge.com Web: www.malealea.co.LS
Cell: 082-552-4215

"Where are you heading?" asked the border official. "Malealea," I replied nervously. She smiled, "You'll enjoy it there." Here in the heartland of mountainous Lesotho where blanket-clad shepherds watch over their flocks, the Jones family have created a fascinating environment through a combination of their own personal warmth, native knowledge and a wealth of natural and cultural attractions. Malealea thrives on its genuine interaction with the neighbouring village and I arrived just as the choir was starting up, followed by a band playing home-made instruments with wonderful exuberance. The pony trekking centre is run entirely by the locals, who will take you on treks for up to six days (you stay in the villages you visit), and children lead you to waterfalls and rock art. Communal suppers are served canteen style - backpackers and ambassadors rub comradely shoulders – before the pub and Glenn's singing around the fire lure you away. When the generator stops, your torch guides you back to thatched rondavel or farmhouse-style accommodation. I woke to the unmistakable cries of peacocks ringing out of the early-morning mist lying low in the valleys. I loved this place. Suddenly your trip just got longer.

Rooms: 40 Basotho rondavels & farmhouse en-suite rooms, 12 doubles & 28 twins, all with shower en-s.
Price: Rondavels R300 - R330 pp sharing, farmhouses R240 - R275 pp sharing. Single supplement 50%. Overnight horse treks R400 - R450 pp per day. Village accommodation R80 - R90 pp. Day rides R200 - R220 pp.
Meals: Breakfast R75 pp. Lunch R85 pp. Dinner R125 pp. Four communal kitchens available.
Directions: Faxed or emailed on booking.

Northern Cape

Kuilfontein Stable Cottages

Penny and Leigh Southey
Kuilfontein Farm, Route N1, Colesberg
Tel: 051-753-1364 Fax: 051-753-0200
Email: kuil@mweb.co.za Web: www.kuilfontein.co.za
Cell: 082-552-2488

A drink is always welcome in the middle of the blazing Karoo and I was gasping when Penny poured mine in the chilled-out guest lounge. Kuilfontein has been in Leigh's family for five generations and is still a busy dairy and sheep farm. Surrounded by a vast hinterland of arid fields it's hard to believe it's only 1.2 kilometres from the N1. The white-washed Stable bedrooms are all named after racehorses, the theme continuing inside with newspaper clippings and framed shots of 'Danny Boy' or 'Equilateral' (among others) in action. French doors lead from your own verandah onto gleaming screed floors sporting locally-made furniture, as well as the odd family heirloom, while brightly-coloured walls and fine-quality linen create a homely feeling. The 'Feed Room' has been appropriately converted into a dining/breakfast room where resident chef, Maryke, produces tantalising meals from the organic produce on the farm. 'Home-grown' Karoo lamb, venison and fresh cream from the dairy are used in conjunction with cactus fruit and other Karoo specialities. Pre-dinner drinks are taken in the bar with its upside-down trough counter and a great selection of wines are available in an old feed bin. A tall wicker stool is the perfect spot to park yourself for cheerful banter, beverages and hilarity. Coffee and liqueurs are served under the spectacular starry skies. For the more energetic there is a spring-water swimming pool, boules and bird-watching. A popular stop-over point, but this farmstead is worth staying a lot longer for.

Rooms: 8: 5 standard double bedrooms, 2 luxury double rooms and 1 family suite, all with en-suite showers.
Price: R420 – R495p.p. R90 single supplement. Children 6+ on request.
Meals: Full 'health' breakfast included. 3-course dinners: R160 - R170.
Directions: 12km south of Colesberg, 60km north of Hanover on N1. Look for Kuilfontein sign. If you are flying they have a 1300m airstrip on the property. The runway co-ordinates are as follows. Kuilfontein, S 30 49 04,86 E 024 59 37,05.

Papkuilsfontein Guest Farm

Willem and Mariëtte van Wyk

Nieuwoudtville
Tel: 027-218-1246 Fax: 086-573-1246
Email: info@papkuilsfontein.com Web: www.papkuilsfontein.com

Well, this is certainly up there among the most memorable places to stay in South Africa! For starters, you stay in an old stone cottage, high up on the summit of a wild mountain plateau, surrounded by rich geological rock formations, fynbos vegetation (including huge taaibos and kraaibos shrubs, wild olives, restios, sonkwas reeds) and bouncing dassies, not another human in sight and no mountains to break the golden horizon. The quality of peace and stillness defeats description. Gas-fired plumbing for baths, hurricane lamps for light - many guests have refused to return if the van Wyks installs electricity (although there's a restored corrugated-iron cottage for those who can't do without). Then there's the small matter of the gorge and waterfall. Your jaw will drop 180 metres into the canyon. In winter, when the water runs, take picnics to the swimmable rock pools above the falls. Alternatively, opt for a quick plunge in the bore-hole water dam between the cottages. Spring's wild flowers are sensational here even by Namaqualand standards; the plantlife - part Cape fynbos, part Karoo succulent - a botanist's dream; steenbok, klipspringer and porcupine can be sighted hopping about if you look carefully. Alrie and her mother Petru are excellent cooks (breakfast is a string of surprises) and can set up hearty farm suppers in your cottage. It's a magically secluded retreat that few people know about and the van Wyks are lovely, helpful hosts. Stay at least two nights.

Rooms: 3 stone cottages: Rondekraal sleeps 2 (1 double) bath & outside shr; De Hoop sleeps 4 bath & outside shr; Gert Boom sleeps 4 (2 more beds for kids), with 2 bathrooms, shr only.
Price: From Aug 2012: R350 pp sharing. Minimum per cottage pn in flower season (without meals): Gert Boom R1,400, De Hoop R850 & Rondekraal R820; kids under 12 half-tariff, under 2 free.
Meals: Full breakfast R110. 3-course dinners R215, 2-course dinners R160. Self-catering facilities in cottages.
Directions: From CT N1 then N7 to Vanrhynsdorp. Turn onto R27 to Nieuwoudtville. R into town, straight thro onto dirt rd 22km. Farm signed to R. GPS S31 33.548 E19 10.978

Map Number: 1

Entry Number: 213

Naries Namakwa Retreat

Julene Hamman

27km from Springbok (N7), on the way to Kleinzee (on R355),
Namakwaland Tel: 027-712-2462 (reception) or 0861-991-118
(reservations) Fax: 021-872-6099 Email: reservations@naries.co.za
Web: www.naries.co.za

27km from Springbok, Naries is set in the heart of Namaqualand, with its beautiful plains scenery, its arid mountains and its magical seasonal flower display – 600 species. Among the varied options for accommodation, the most spectacular are the three Namakwa Mountain Suites, which have been constructed on the edge of a high escarpment with an eagle's eye view of the dramatic and barren mountains that march off to the sea 70km away at Kleinzee. The architecture is in the form of a domed Nama-dwelling-styled cottage and is perfectly integrated with the round granite kopies of the area. Their exterior simplicity, however, is deceptive, for the interiors are vast and luxurious, while retaining some natural features: the almost woven texture of the walls of the cottage, for example, and the bare rocks which erupt into the space as bed-heads or in the sublime bathrooms. The old Cape Dutch manor, where dinners are served, also houses some fine bedrooms. The house is painted in plain colours, which offset the 1930s furniture perfectly. A short stroll from the manor, two new family self-catering cottages offer a cape country style and an embarrassment of space, mountain views and braai facilities. Naries recommends various day excursions to explore the beauty of Namakwaland: 4x4 Shipwreck Experience, Goegap Nature Reserve, Namakwa and Richtersveld National Parks. Also, make sure you book well in advance for the desert flower season! But advance booking is always essential.

Rooms: 10: 3 Namakwa Mountain Suites with en-suite bathrooms; 5 Manor House rooms with en-suite bathrooms; 2 family self contained cottages with en-suite bath & shower, sleeps max 4.
Price: Dinner B&B: Mountain Suites R1,185 – R1,750 pp sharing; Manor House R750 – R1,110 pp; self-contained family cottages: R340 – R455 pp (aged 5 - 11 R185 – R210). Ask for singles & specials.
Meals: 3-course dinner & breakfast included in rates of Namakwa Mountain Suites & Manor House.
Directions: 27km from Springbok (N7), on your way to Kleinzee on tarred road (R355).

A la Fugue

Jacqueline Castella
40 Jangroentjieweg, Upington
Tel: 054-338-0424 Fax: 054-338-0084
Email: a-la-fugue@mweb.co.za Web: www.lafugue-guesthouse.com
Cell: 082-789-9324

Chaud, hot, heiss! Upington was knocking on almost 40°C when I visited, so Jacqueline definitely had the right idea, meeting me at the car in a pink swimming costume and sarong. Positively melting after hours on the road I was invited to flump myself down on a plant-shaded pillow by the pool and was fed a glass of iced tea. What initially struck me about A la Fugue, as I was led along a rose-lined and plant-dotted path, was the tropical garden, absolutely dazzling in the intense sunshine. Named after great composers, each of La Fugue's bungalows has their own unique identity. Rossini and Rusticana, two quaint wooden chalets, seem to originate from the Swiss element of your host, while studio bungalow Mozart and family unit Vivaldi perhaps embody the classic French side. The two B&B rooms in the house (Chopin and Bach), soothing in golds and creams, are found along a short landing where Jacqueline's stunning model daughter beams warmly from the wall. Jacqui's gourmet dinners and breakfasts, touched with a little foreign pizazz, are served outside on one of the bright mosaic tables (your hostess has a distinct flair for mosaics and you will find examples in many unexpected places). It's a good thing that each room has its own outdoor seating area as with such a garden you won't want to sit inside. Personally I would rarely be found far from the thatched African-themed poolside lapa and loungers. *Jacqueline is fluent in French, English and German.*

Rooms: 5: 2 self-catering studios, 1 self-catering family unit & 2 B&B dble rooms. All en-s shr & own entrances.
Price: R250 – R400 pp sharing for B&B. Ask re singles & self-catering prices. Breakfast-brunch for self-caterers: additional 80 pp. Extra bed R80.
Meals: Full breakfast incl' in B&B rate. For self-caterers, breakfast/brunch on request at R80 pp. Gourmet dinners on request (with 24 hrs notice), R340 pp incl' all wine & drinks.
Directions: In Upington take Schröder St towards Olifantshoek, N14 under rail bridge past Gordonia hospital. 1.7 km after hospital R at Engen garage. L (Groenpunt Rd). From Bi-Lo, count 4 streets on R till Jangtroentjieweg. GPS: 28d26m25.1s E / 21d17m40.8s S

Map Number: 10

Entry Number: 215

African Vineyard

Dr Elmarie De Bruin

Plot 79, Kanoneiland, Upington
Tel: 083-461-1724 Fax: 086-650-8572
Email: elmariedeb@vodamail.co.za Web: www.africanvineyard.co.za
Cell: 083-461-1724

Driving over the bridge onto the verdant Kanoneiland, the largest inhabited inland island in the country, I had to remind myself I was still in the Northern Cape! With a day on desert roads, the site of bountiful vineyards and the flowing water of the Orange River was a site for sore and decidedly dusty eyes. Leaving the car in the giant parking barn I was met by the lovely Elmarie and shown to my room, Ruby Cabernet. When I say 'room' I actually mean converted stable… all to myself! The space is filled with unique and ingenious designs crafted by Elmarie's husband Theuns: the long dining table made from reclaimed seringa wood using pipes for legs, bare copper piping in the bathroom - a blue pebble indicating the cold taps, the bed made from wild olive with stumps as side tables; and it's all enhanced by an intelligent use of lighting, elegant antiques and leather sofas. There are cosier suites on the other side of the house, furnished in the same style and all with their own personality. To complement the hand-crafted nature of this working raisin farm, Elmarie, an advocate of the slow cooking movement, is a genius in the kitchen. Joined by my fellow guests and sitting round another of Theuns' masterpieces, we enjoyed wine from the local area along with sampmeal and a hearty oxtail stew. To really relax into some slow living, stay for a few days.

Rooms: 6 aircon rooms, all with en-suite bath & shower.
Price: R490 - R600 pp sharing. R650 - R750 for singles. Includes breakfast.
Meals: Dinner on request: R135 - R195. Lunch on request: R85 - R125.
Directions: Take Kanoneiland turn-off from N14, travel 3km, turn right into town and left into main street. Just before end of tar road, turn right onto gravel. African Vineyard is 500m on right-hand side.

Gauteng

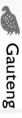

Melrose Place Guest Lodge

Sue Truter

12a North St, Melrose, Johannesburg
Tel: 011-442-5231 Fax: 011-880-2371
Email: info@melroseplace.co.za Web: www.melroseplace.co.za
Cell: 083-457-4021

Once ensconced behind the electric gates at Melrose you have entered an Eden-in-the-city. The verandah overlooks a large flower garden and enormous swimming pool, all shaded by trees. Eight new rooms don't crowd it at all. It is such a pleasant environment that you may find yourself shelving projected tasks for a day's lounging about. My room was a suite attached to the main house, with mounted TV, huge bed (built up with cushions and pillows), a big bathroom and double doors onto the garden. The high levels of luxury in all the rooms are not reflected in the rates. Sue is the sweetest of hostesses, quick to smiles and reacting sensitively to the mood and wishes of each guest. On the night I stayed we had a braai with an amazing array of meat dishes and salads which appeared from nowhere, and Sue's team will cook dinner or, if the mood dictates, a braai for anyone who wants it. Her aim is to maximise the number of happy campers staying. This is her home after all. With guest contentment running at 100 per cent and visitors from all over the world coming back again and again (including us), it's difficult to see what else she can do. *Laundry provided on request. Complimentary gym access and unlimited Internet access available. Nearby: Wanderers cricket ground, Melrose Arch, Rosebank and Sandton shopping/business precincts and many restaurants. Airport transfers arranged by Sue.*

Rooms: 30: 12 premium suites; 18 classic rooms. All king/twin. All en-suite. All with garden patios/balconies.
Price: R700 - R900 pp sharing. Singles R1,150 - R1,500. Airport transfers arranged by Sue.
Meals: Full breakfast included. Lunches and dinners by arrangement. Rosebank and Sandton shopping precincts and many restaurants nearby.
Directions: Ask for a map when booking. Or a map is on the web site.

The Residence Boutique Hotel

Edgar Rudge (owner) & Sanet van der Westhuizen (Manager)

17 Fourth Avenue, Houghton, Johannesburg Tel: 011-853-2480
Fax: 011-483-1303 Email: info@theresidence.co.za
Web: www.theresidence.co.za Hotel cell: 076-038-3016

The jacaranda-lined streets and avenues of Houghton are a pleasure to drive around in and it's an even greater pleasure when you're greeted at the gate of The Residence by a smiley chap in a top hat! Before I knew it my bags had been whisked away to my room and I was presented with a much-needed iced tea (there was sherry on offer if you prefer). Entering my suite, each step produced a wow of ascending volume! Firstly: the huge bed, antique furniture, colonial décor and super-indulgent bathroom; another stride and I was marvelling at the twin outdoor shower on my private terrace. My fellow guests could surely by now hear my 'wowing' in the opposite wing. By the time I saw the Jacuzzi I'd almost lost my voice! "What time is dinner served" I croaked. "Whenever you'd like, sir". "Splendid"! Satisfied I'd lounged in every available space in the suite I dragged myself away and pottered downstairs feeling very Bertie Wooster-ish. As I entered the piano bar two immaculately-dressed barmen almost simultaneously appeared, snacks were laid out and very cold beer was poured. I made my way through to the dining room for an amazing Thai curry; the rest of the menu looked just as delicious. Content and full, I returned to my suite with ideas of baths and movies…. But in the end the bed proved far too alluring, so I opted for sleep instead!

Rooms: 11 rooms (including 1 penthouse & Madiba Suite). All rooms have full en-s bathrooms & outdoor showers & outdoor bath or outdoor Jacuzzi (some have all 3!). Some rooms also have fireplaces.
Price: Rates per room: Luxury Room R2,263; Luxury Suite R2,830; Penthouse R3,800; Madiba Suite R4,250. Rates include breakfast, soft drinks in mini bar & wifi.
Meals: Full dining menu (breakfast, lunch, dinner, snack menu, room service until 11pm): starters R45, mains R60 – R140, desserts R45.
Directions: On M1 (south) take Riviera Rd off-ramp (keep L), L into West (becomes Central), then 1st R into 4th Ave. Hse on LHS. Website has full directions.

Map Number: 12, 13 & 16

Entry Number: 218

Kashan Country House

Peter Curle (owner), Paulina Banda (manager)
Portion 1 Farm, Steynshoop, Hekpoort
Tel: 014-576-1035
Email: reservations@kashanhouse.co.za Web: www.kashanhouse.co.za
Cell: 082-552-4876

From the Cradle of Humankind I followed the steep and winding track up to civilisation. And you don't get much more civilised than Kashan. A pretty thatched house sitting beneath the Magaliesberg mountains with topnotch views of the lush and very ancient valley. I had come home (not just historically!) or so I was made to feel by Paulina and the team. Within minutes my bags had been unloaded into my pristine, white, four-postered bedroom and I was gliding around in no fewer than 22 metres of infinity pool. Peter's friends thought he was 'mad' to install such a massively luxurious pool. Well I think he's a genius! I wiled away the afternoon spying on birds and monkeys through the lodge telescope, toyed with the idea of investigating the hiking trail up the mountain or having a game of croquet out on the lawn (I told you it was civilised here). But instead I opted for a sprawling chill-out on the sofa with books, movies and tea (I felt totally at home). An unforgettable sunset brought nightfall, together with a nocturnal amphibian choir, Peter, back from the city, and a three-course gourmet dinner prepared by the highly-skilled resident chef – cigar optional! Peter hand-picked the delicate yellowwood furnishings, commissioned the construction of two outside showers and insisted on high-spec mattresses to ensure his guests the best night's sleep this side of the equator. It's not often you come across perfect equilibrium, but Kashan House with its luxury, relaxed hospitality, historic views, proximity to Johannesburg and fantastic food might just have achieved it.

Rooms: 9: 4 luxury rooms with king-size extra-length beds & en-s bath & shower (2 rooms have additional outside shower); 5 standard doubles (3 en-s bath & shower, 2 en-s shower).
Price: R730 – R905 pp sharing. Singles R1,030 - R1,150. Price includes breakfast.
Meals: 3-course dinner R240. Lunches on request
Directions: See website for detailed directions.

Steynshoop Lodge

Peter Curle (Owner) & Paulina Banda (manager)

Portion 2 Farm, Steynshoop, Hekpoort
Tel: 014-576-1035
Email: reservations@kashanhouse.co.za Web: www.steynshoop.co.za
Cell: 082-552-4876

The Magaliesberg valley is so tranquil and beautiful it's hard to believe that you're only an hour's drive from the metropolis of Johannesburg. As I got stuck, hypnotized by the view which stretches all the way to the Hartbeespoort dam, Paulina's tour of the property took rather longer than normal! The lodge, set around a rose-filled courtyard, has been thoughtfully designed for the self-caterer who wants something a bit different: the wee cottage for single travellers (whither Peter is banished if the house is full); the delightful Arbour Cottage; two quaint two-story cottages in the gate house; a giant honeymoon suite encompassing three cottages (one room = one cottage!); and The Homestead, a five-bedroom masterpiece. I could have quite happily spent hours admiring the intricate Balinese furniture and that view again… enhanced by two dams and an infinity pool. Steynshoop is all about escapism and for me that means hiking. I woke at 5 a.m, fell into my walking boots and found my stride along the path. Emerging from the indigenous forest onto the rocky plain I disturbed a sleeping troop of baboons; one yawn from me inspired their swift retreat. From the saddle of the mountain, marvelling at the valley, I could see why we - and our hominid ancestors - have chosen to inhabit this valley for two million years… and why I'll be coming back for a two-week stay when I can. *Longer hikes, guides and permits can all be arranged in-house.*

Rooms: 7: 2 Gate House cottages (sleeps 2 - 4); Corner Cottage and Arbour Cottage (sleep 2); McGregor Cottage (sleeps 1); Valley Suite (sleeps 2); Homestead (sleeps 10).
Price: Homestead: R5,150 – R6,000 per night; Valley Suite: R1,150 – R1,350 per night; cottages: R950 – R1,150 per night; McGregor: R450 pn
Meals: Self-catering, but chefs can be arranged for Homestead. Meals can be arranged in Kashan House, the adjoining lodge.
Directions: See website for detailed directions.

Soweto

Introduction by Ross Bowers

Lots of tourists come for the day, but if you really want to get under the skin of the South West Township, then staying over is a must. Soweto is a 50-square-mile labyrinth, so getting lost is a distinct possibility. Your tour guide can drop you off at the guest-house and arrange transport to one of the funky local restaurants where extensive wine lists sit comfortably alongside samp 'n' beans, tripe, mutton curry and other Sowetan favourites. There are, of course, many shanty dwellings and much extreme poverty, but there are also tree-lined streets, impressive houses and bustling wide main roads. As you'd expect in a place crammed with an unofficial total of over four million, there's a lot to see. Our selected trio of B&Bs are within 20 metres of each other in the heart of the Vilikazi district of Orlando West, a vibrant, culturally-rich destination. Simon really wanted me to see the Hector Pieterson Museum and I was moved to tears as the reality of the 'struggle' and extreme injustices of the past glared me straight in the eye. If time permits, get yourself to the Chris Hani Baragwanath Hospital, the largest hospital in the world, as well as the Regina Mundi Church. After a truly eye-opening day, I relaxed over an apéritif in the Rusty Bar at the trendy Soweto Hotel in Freedom Square, Kliptown. I recommend you do likewise.

There are a couple of tour guides that we heartily recommend (see below for their contact details). The gentle and genial Simon Mosikare of Soweto Guided Tours kindly picked me up from Oliver Tambo Airport and drove me straight into Soweto. We've also been with Vhupo Tours, run by David Luthaga, a friendly bear of a man with a laugh that could shake Soweto's infamous power station. "You will see all of Soweto. The good, the bad and the very ugly, nothing will be hidden," was his opening gambit. And, true to his word, David showed us Diepkloof Extension, the millionaire's row also known as Diepkloof Expensive. He then handed us over to Reginald who walked with us around the squatter camp Motsoaldi, a patchwork of corrugated iron and wooden planks that he calls home. David emphasised that wherever we were, especially in the squatter camps, the inhabitants expected us to take photos so that people worldwide could witness their living conditions. This attitude stems from pre-Apartheid days, when images from the Sowetan uprising of 1976 galvanised worldwide outcry and it put paid to any concerns that I had over voyeurism.

Vhupo Tours
David Luthaga
www.vhupo-tours.com
info@vhupo-tours.com
011-936-0411

Soweto Guided Tours
Simon Mosikare
www.sowetoguidedtours.co.za
info@sowetoguidedtours.co.za
011-985-6249
083-324-2096

For more information look out for the Soweto Township Complete Guide, published by Soweto Spaza and sold in the shop outside Nelson Mandela's former house on Vilakazi St. On the way in or out of Soweto, be sure to visit the Apartheid Museum near Gold Reef City in Ormonde.

Vhavenda Hills Bed and Breakfast

Kate Luthaga
11749 Mampuru St, Orlando West, Soweto
Tel: 011-936-4275 Fax: 086-503-0469
Email: vhavendahills@iburst.co.za Web: www.sowetobnb.co.za
Cell: 082-213-1630

Soweto born and bred, Kate lives just down the road from Nelson Mandela's old house in the Vilakazi precinct of Orlando West – one of Soweto's numerous suburbs, better known as "The Wild West" during the apartheid years. The great man himself popped round for tea after his release from Robben Island. Clean, white art deco lines make Vhavenda one of the stand-out properties in the neighbourhood. It is very much a family home with pictures of Kate's children around the TV and friends of various offspring popping in and out. Kate's husband David grew up in the property which they converted into a B&B over 10 years ago. He runs the burgeoning Vhupo Tours from his office in one of the back rooms. The bedrooms are comfortable with magnolia walls, baby-blue hues and multi-coloured coverlets. From 2010 they also have new beds and dazzling custom-made checkered headboards to compliment Kate's dashing decor. Ask for the palatial double room with its bath on a plinth and pair of double beds where I fell asleep to the sound of cicadas and the buzz of Johannesburg traffic in the far distance, before waking to the smell of sizzling bacon. *An easy stroll to the Hector Pieterson museum, Mandela House and the superb Sakhumzi and Nambitha restaurants.*

Rooms: 4: 1 king/ twin with en/s bath & shower, 1 king/ twin with en/s shower over bath and separate loo, 1 twin double beds with en/s bath and shower, 1 queen with en/s shower.
Price: R350 - R400 pp sharing. R500 singles.
Meals: Cooked breakfast, plus yoghurt and cereal included. Dinner on request at R120 - R150 pp.
Directions: Arrange a pick-up from Johannesburg, though directions are available on website.

Dakalo B&B

Dolly Hlophe
6963 Inhlwathi St, Orlando West, Soweto
Tel: 011-936-9328 Fax: 086-661-7282
Email: dakalobandb@iburst.co.za/info@dakalobedandbreakfast.co.za
Web: www.dakalobedandbreakfast.co.za Cell: 082-723-0585

The term 'township chic' was invented for Dolly's B&B. I loved the bathroom tiled with blue-spotted mosaics and the rooms with their red quilts, mini-Zulu shields, strawberry table-cloths and zebra print curtains, hand-made by Dolly. Not only is she a wizard on the sewing-machine, but she is also heavily involved with the local tourism association, setting a high standard with her own guesthouse. She and Kate from nearby Vhavenda were off to a hospitality seminar at one of the Southern Sun hotels on the day I arrived. Not that these ladies need any tips! With opera playing in the background and freshly-cut arum lilies on the front table, the house exudes calm. Outside guests can sit under the lapa or admire Dolly's garden, where geraniums sprout from potjie cooking pots and pink bougainvillaea crawls up the walls. You are right in the heart of where history was made in Soweto, particularly when Dolly can count two Nobel Peace Prize winners (Desmond Tutu and Nelson Mandela) among her neighbours. She has some astonishing stories herself of 'the struggle' and is a short walk away from the fascinating Hector Pieterson Memorial and museum. Or, if you're interested in the latest chapter in this extraordinary area's history, the impressive soccer city stadium, which hosted the 2010 World Cup final, is a fifteen-minute ride on the new bright-red Rea Vaya bus service.

Rooms: 4: 3 king/twins; 1 twin. All with en/s showers.
Price: R350 - R400 pp sharing. R400 - R450 singles.
Meals: Full English breakfast. Evening meals on request for R120 - R150.
Directions: Arrange pick-up in Johannesburg.

Nthateng's B&B

Nthateng Motaung
6991 Inhlwathi St, Orlando West, Soweto
Tel: 011-936-2676 Fax: 086-600-5141
Email: info@nthateng.co.za/nthateng@telkomsa.net
Web: www.nthateng.co.za Cell: 082-335-7956

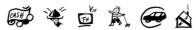

Snappily dressed in tight jeans and gold jewellery, the glamorous Nthateng happily took the time to talk to me about the history of Soweto before insisting that I accompany her to the wedding down the road between a Zulu man and a Swazi woman. "Everyone's invited," she said. Between the tribal colours and shaking dancers, Nthateng sat me down with some fried chicken and samp, washed down with a glass of sparkling ginger (apparently it wouldn't be a proper wedding without it!). Then it was back for a tour of her own place. Optical lighting illuminates the up-to-the-minute, sandy-coloured rooms that boast carved wooden bedheads inlaid with red and gold mosaics. One double room also houses a vast Louis XIV-style dressing table; it's not hard to imagine Marie Antoinette perched on the ornate seat, powdering her wig and applying beauty spots. See Soweto in style – not only is Nthateng's close to the museums and restaurants, but insist that she takes you backstage on Soweto TV. It's a hub of creativity, the crew are really friendly and their studios are located just a couple of blocks up adjacent to a talented seamstress and an inspiring art school for children. With the Hector Pieterson Memorial, Nelson Mandela's house and Soccer City also within easy striking distance Nthateng attests "people must stay in Soweto for two or three nights to get the full experience". Later on, after revelling in an evening of live music and high-energy dancing at the Soweto Beer Festival I'd gladly move in for a week.

Rooms: 5: 2 queens, 1 king and 2 twins. All en/s.
Price: R350 - R400 pp sharing. R450 for singles.
Meals: Full cooked breakfast is included. Evening meals available on request for R120 - R150.
Directions: Arrange a pick-up from Johannesburg. Nthateng can also arrange airport transfers for R450 (daytime) - R550 (at night).

North West Province

Mosetlha Bush Camp and Eco Lodge

Chris, June and Caroline Lucas
Madikwe Game Reserve
Tel: 011-444-9345
Fax: 011-444-9345
Email:
info@thebushcamp.com
Web:
www.thebushcamp.com
Cell: 083-305-7809

Here is a long-standing (since the very first edition) Greenwood Guides favourite! Mosetlha puts the wild into wilderness. No doors or glass here as they would hinder the feel and dust of Africa permeating your very core; no worries either as you leave them at the gate. Facilities are basic but real; guests draw their own hot water from a donkey-boiler before proceeding to the shower. Recently the kitchen was extended and a new thatch and stone lapa has been added for guests to read, relax and compare sightings, but the authenticity remains untainted. The wooden cabins are comfortable, but used only for sleeping - you are here for the wilderness experience of the outdoors. Chris's passion for conservation and his environment shines through and is contagious (which reminds me to say that the area is malaria-free). His guests depart much the wiser, not only because of the game drives, but also (conditions permitting) because of the superb guided wilderness walks. Yes, the Madikwe Game Reserve (75,000 hectares) has the so-called 'Big Five', but a game lodge worth its salt (such as this) will fire your imagination about the whole food chain. A highlight of the reserve for me is the lock system - a maximum of two vehicles per game viewing at any one time - ensuring a more intimate experience for you and less stressful one for the animal. Even the camp itself is an education - all sorts of birds, small mammals and antelopes venture in. Come for a genuine and memorable bush experience. *Children welcome from 6 years old up.*

Rooms: 9 twins sharing 3 shower/toilet complexes.
Price: All-inclusive from R1,795 per person. Gate entrance fee and drinks from the bar extra.
Meals: All meals and refreshments (tea, coffee, fruit juice) included.
Directions: Detailed written directions supplied on request or see website.

The Bush House

Sue and Gordon Morrison

Madikwe Game Reserve
Tel: 076-694-0505 Fax: 086-678-6077
Email: camp@bushhouse.co.za Web: www.bushhouse.co.za
Cell: 083-379-6912

Sue and her husband Gordon stayed here as guests in 2006 and decided they didn't want to leave… so they bought it, along with its history. The Bush House dates back to 1940, when this otherwise barren bushveld afforded no more than cattle farming and citrus fruit orchards. In 1987 it was bought out by the government and incorporated into what became the 75,000 hectare Madikwe Game Reserve. Operation Phoenix, the relocation of 10,000 animals into the reserve, created one of the finest conservation areas in Africa, where rare species occur naturally and over 340 species of birds have been recorded. To complement the wildlife, Sue and Gordon have built an underground hide looking out at mouse-eye level onto the watering-hole - seeing a herd of elephants this close up is really exciting! The lodge retains its structure as a farm building but has been refurbished on the inside. The bedrooms come with your own private patio. Dining is a relaxed affair, with everyone eating together and in downtime guests can explore the grounds' nature trails on foot, leaf through one of the many David Attenborough books in the lounge, indulge in some savoury or sweet nibbles for afternoon tea or hang out on lush lawns overlooking the water-hole, which regularly refreshes all of the big five (plus wild dog). Having practically tickled the trunk of an inquisitive elephant on the afternoon drive we returned to sundowners in the company of four rhinos and three lions quenching their evening thirst. Ah, the magic of Madikwe!

Rooms: 6: 2 double, 4 twins/kings all with en-suite bath and shower.
Price: From R2,750 pp sharing.
Meals: All meals included plus two game drives a day.
Directions: From Pretoria take N4 to Zeerust, then R49/47 towards Madikwe. At Madikwe turn right at the Wonderboom Gate, The Bush House is signposted 1 km from entrance. Federal Air Flight also flies to the reserve daily.

Map Number: 15

Jaci's Lodges

Jan and Jaci van Heteren
Molatedi, Madikwe Game Reserv
Tel: 083-700-2071 or
083-4477-929
Fax: 086-517-5780
Email:
jacisreservations@madikwe.com
Web: www.madikwe.com
Cell: 083-447-7929, reservations
083-700-2071

After hurtling down dusty tracks to Madikwe and negotiating a blockade of elephants I gallivanted across the swing bridge (Indiana Jones eat your heart out) to Jaci's award-winning Safari Lodge. Built on the banks of the Marico River around old leadwood trees and a giant termite mound it could hardly be more stunningly entwined with the bush. My first mission: sundowners by the dam next to Jaci's Tree Lodge (equally striking with its rosewood tree-house suites linked by raised walkways in the canopy of a tamboti forest) where rhinos stopped by for an evening slurp and brown hyenas fought over the remnants of an earlier wild dog kill. Back at the lodge head chef, Matthew, presented a fillet of beef fit for any carnivore (and enough julienne veg to satisfy the most voracious of herbivores), followed by a sumptuous strawberry pana cotta. No scavenging was required. A clap of thunder heralded the season's first rains and a lightning-quick transfer from boma fire to lodge dining table where families and wonderfully attentive staff mingled excitedly. I retired to my opulent thatched suite with hippo-sized stone bath and jungle shower. Awakening to the sweet smell of the dampened bush, we headed out on 'a serious game drive'. A couple of hours tracking revealed a pride of nine lions including a pair of playful cubs. Just another 'day in the life' at Jaci's.

Rooms: Safari Lodge: 8 king/twins, 2 exclusive family suites. Tree Lodge: 8 king/twins. All with outdoor "jungle" shower.
Price: From R4,780 pp sharing per night. Game drives, walking safaris and meals included.
Meals: All meals and game drives included.
Directions: Only 1.5 hours' drive from Sun City or a 3.5 to 4-hour drive from Johannesburg. There are daily flights from Johannesburg to Madikwe Game Reserve with Federal Air. Transfers can also be arranged from Johannesburg. Ask for details when booking.

Mpumalanga

Welgelegen Manor

Amelia Troitzsch

R51 Balfour/Nigel Road, Balfour
Tel: 017-773-9000 Fax: 017-773-9001
Email: info@welgelegenmanor.co.za Web: www.welegelegenmanor.co.za
Cell: 083-281-1706

Entering Welgelegen Manor through its grand white gates, I was whisked back to the year 1913 when the house was born, commissioned by a man named Andries Mostert in honour of his ancestral home that had once stood on the same footprint. Fortunately for Andries and architect Sir Herbert Baker (and ultimately you and I), eighty-eight years later the house fell into the hands of Roger, who went to great lengths to restore its original character. Roger has kindly offered to share this historic treat, leaving it in the managerial hands of Amelia, who also wished to join me in my time travel fantasy. After a 'turn' round the formal garden, in our Edwardian attire (bear with me here!), we glided along the wood-panelled hallway to my enormous suite. Amelia and I mulled for a while over the positioning of the original copper light switches at waist height and concluded this makes much more sense. Such original features, complemented by the modern 'touch', are typical of Welgelegen. After all the 'exercise', an appetite had been earned and was duly and fully rewarded. To wit: grilled salmon and avocado pâté; chicken breast stuffed with spinach, pepperdew and feta; vanilla panacotta with strawberry syrup! Much to my regret, I only stayed one night. Welgelegen is worthy of more with so many activities on offer, such as tennis, croquet, golf (on its own driving range) and archery, as well as a billiard room and a TV theatre to rest weary bones. Sadly for me, all too soon it was time return to the 21st century.

Rooms: 8: 6 king suites & 2 twin suites. All en-s with bath and shower.
Price: R1,500 DBB pppn. R2,000 fully inclusive pppn (extras including lunch, room service and laundry).
Meals: Full breakfast included. Lunch and dinner (4-course set menu) on request. Dietary requirements and preferences catered for.
Directions: From Joburg, take N3 towards Durban. Take exit 59 on R23 twds Standerton. 23.5km. Take Balfour R51 (3rd Balfour turn-off). 1st stop st (DJ Motors) R. 2nd stop st ('Nigel-Devon' sign) L. Tar road veers R. Welgelegen Manor 1.6km on RHS. GPS: S26 38.298' E28 35.650'

Kilmorna Manor

Philip and Laura-ann Keates

Off the N4, Schoemanskloof
Tel: 013-733-6100
Email: laura-ann@kilmornamanor.co.za Web: www.kilmornamanor.co.za
Cell: 083-278-3110

"It's worth it!" reads the sign as I make my way up the gravel drive. Laura-ann, along with husband Philip, left Jo'burg and city life for space and tranquillity in the Schoemanskloof Valley. Kilmorna Manor, sitting in the 600-hectare Greater Kilmorna Conservancy, was built in 1976 by an 'eccentric' Irishman, who, in homage to British history, combined his favourite styles of architecture to create his dream home in the bush. I was encouraged to take advantage of a crisp autumn afternoon, so Laura-ann listed the activities on offer: "if you want to walk in the bush, I will supply you with binoculars, water and walking stick." This would be my morning activity. Stretching my legs along a gentle stroll through the grasslands sounded ideal after a long journey. The grounds are sheltered by an abundance of lush vegetation, home to various plains game including the red and grey duiker that are indigenous to the area; and due to its situation between the low and high veld the cool climate is blissful. The garden path led me to an elevated pool overlooking the valley beneath and this is where my stroll came to an end! Before I could say "wow", I was horizontal on the sun-bed absorbing the warmth of the afternoon rays, only returning at sunset to make sure I did not miss out on a delicious dinner (thank you Portia!) by the open fire, where I sat admiring the couple's museum of colourful trinkets that cover every available surface. Kilmorna Manor is an ideal base to explore Mpumalanga, including The Kruger National Park, and is most definitely worth it!

Rooms: 6: 4 kings en-s shr & bath; 1 king en-s shr; 1 queen en-s shr & bath.
Price: R1,200 pppn B&B. No single supplement charged.
Meals: Full breakfast included. Lunches for residents only (R80). Dinner for residents only: 4-course à la carte (R276), 4-course set menu (R230) or 3-course set menu (R204).
Directions: From Joburg N4 to Witbank & Middleburg. After Machadodorp toll gate take Nelspruit/Lydenburg rd (N4 & R36) signed Nelspruit via Schoemanskloof. After 41km turn L at Matthew Phosa College. Travel on dirt road for 1.5km. L at Sterksruit sign. Kilmorna sign 1.5km on R. Follow dirt rd to main house (passing thro' gate).

Mpumalanga

Torburnlea

Andrew and Kim Hall

Mataffin Macadamia Village, Nr Nelspruit
Fax: 086-516-9960
Email: info@nguniafrica.co.za Cell: 079-578-7677

Torburnlea, situated in Mataffin Macadamia Village on the well-known Hall and Sons farming estate near Nelspruit, is the fourth-generation family homestead of the farming pioneer, H.L. Hall, Andrew's great-grandfather. Andrew, who runs Nguni Africa, a luxury safari and travel business, and his wife Kim, a physiotherapist, began restoring the property in 2012 with the dream of preserving the family heritage. The village, once occupied by the first generation Hall family and farming staff, is centralised around a village green. Since 1917, the year Torburnlea was built, architectural features from subsequent eras have been added to the home, creating an interesting challenge for the Halls in its renovation. All this was absorbed over a glass of wine around the kitchen table - the Halls certainly know how to make a guest feel at home! I was gripped by the story and full of admiration; thought and passion have gone into the finest of details. The next morning, after a scrumptious breakfast prepared by Stanford – a contender to win the "warmest smile in SA" competition - Andrew and I continued to explore the homestead. Ask him to show you the door to an old lift that once transported the village elderly and the piano to the attic room, which doubled up as the local Anglican church on Sundays. Today it has been converted into a beautiful loft apartment. Torburnlea is an ideal gateway to the Kruger National Park, Blyde River Canyon and many other places of interest in the region, but these are just fringe benefits for any guest who chooses to stay in this unique and fascinating heritage home.

Rooms: 5: 2 king/twins en-s bath & shower; 1 king/twin en-s shr; 1 queen en-s shower; 1 open-plan loft, king en-suite bath & shower, kitchenette & living area.
Price: R450 – R650 pp sharing. Singles R675 – R975.
Meals: Full breakfast incl'. Dinner & picnic baskets on request.
Directions: N4 from east, exit 325 Nelspruit, T-jct R, 2nd traffic circle take 2nd exit, next traffic circle take 2nd exit & thro lights/N4 from west, exit 320 Nelspruit, pass Hall's Gateway/Shell, at next lights turn into Mataffin Macadamia Village, follow signs to Torburnlea. GPS S 25° 27' 580" E 030° 55' 560"

umSisi House

Amanda & Paddy Bond Gunning
Portion 38, Farm Peebles 31JU, White River
Tel: 013-750-1520 or 082-479-9700 Fax: 086-548-5686
Email: amanda@umsisihouse.co.za Web: www.umsisihouse.co.za
Cell: 082-479-9700

If you insist on breaking down in South Africa, do so in the White River area and let Amanda and Paddy soothe your psyche in the sumptuous Lowveld home they've created in the mountains of the Jock of the Bushveld Conservancy. The dynamic duo welcomed me into their fabulous life with arms laden with post-traumatic G&T's, ushering me first into the lap pool, then the hilltop woodland jacuzzi, to wash away my strife. And I needn't have worried about other guests invading my bubbles. UmSisi - siSwati for lucky bean tree - invites private groups to be 'at home in Africa': here you have the run of the magnificent country house, the lush gardens, the climb-me mountains and the drinks cabinet, while Amanda, Paddy and their bonkers boxers (dogs not pugilists, thank goodness) pamper you. There is also a divine self-catering cottage under the giant wild fig tree (mind the cheeky, fig-hurling monkeys) and if groups of more than 6 people have filled the house, then extras can stay here. Paddy's home-grown veggies and treats such as game lasagne at supper-time are the norm for guests in the house, but with a bit of prior notice self-catering cottage guests can order evening meals in the cottage too. The English pair have travelled Africa extensively, both as photographers and with their Black Pot Safaris tour company, so can arrange anything for you from Kruger Safaris to Panorama Route tours. At umSisi – where gargantuan showers, African art, deep squishy beds and stylish, light-drenched living spaces are the order of the day - they've taken the chore out of your tour. Here, sit back; let Africa come to you.

Rooms: House (min 4, max 6 pax): 1 king with full en-s & dressing room; 2 kings/twin, both full en-s; Cottage (min 2. max 4 pax) self-catering or if needed for groups of more than 6: 1 king/tw & 1 dble sharing dble sh'r.
Price: R1,342 to R1,788 pp sharing DBB. R1,650 to R2,200 pp sharing full board as required. Cottage R330 to R400 pp sharing on self-catering basis.
Meals: As per rate selected. Cottage self-caterers dinner only provided at separate cost upon prior arrangement.
Directions: 14km from White River on R538 twds Numbi Gate entrance to Kruger Park (15 minutes away). Full directions emailed on confirmation of booking.

Map Number: 17

Entry Number: 230

Plumbago Guest House

Ilara and Robbie Robertson
R40 between White River and Hazyview
Tel: 013-737-8806 Fax: 086-607-5222
Email: plumbagoguesthouse@mweb.co.za
Web: www.plumbagoguesthouse.co.za Cell: 082-954-0467

Through wrought-iron gates at the end of a bougainvillaea-lined drive I found Plumbago, as pretty as the flower that shares its name. Set on an avocado and banana farm, it sits above the plantation watching over it and out to Kruger Park in the distance. When I arrived, 1940s jazz was swinging out from the radio, just the right aural accompaniment to the nostalgic, colonial-inspired setting. In the drawing room and bar, an eclectic collection of antiques, paintings and rugs are interspersed with vases filled with exotic flowers and extravagant palm-leaf fans that stretch up to the ceiling. The rooms have the same casual gracefulness about them with their subtle, natural tones, Jacobean print curtains, mahogany beds and abundance of vased and water-coloured flowers. With a large lived-in verandah, elegant pool and sauna in the beautifully-tended garden there's plenty of opportunity to relax and mull over days gone by. But what really makes this place stand apart are the Robertsons themselves. On my visit, Ilara (who honed her culinary skills cooking for diplomats) was deciding on that evening's dinner menu while Robbie was itching to go flying before being back for waitering duty later on. A young and active bunch, they are often busying about doing their own thing but are more than happy to share their passions with you. *20 mins to Kruger and close to Panorama Route and God's Window. Babysitting available. Activities, game drives, beauty treatments can be arranged with help from Ilara. Small weddings can be arranged in the garden.*

Rooms: 3 garden chalets: 1 king/twin en-s shr; 1 king en-s shr; 1 king extra-length sleigh-bed en-s bath. All rooms air-con heating and cooling.
Price: R750 - R950 pp sharing. Single supplement if staying one night only. Extra beds available on request. Pets & kids by arrangement.
Meals: Full breakfast incl'. Lunch & dinner on request.
Directions: From Jo'burg, take N4 to Nelspruit and then on to White River. Go on R40 to Hazyview, Plumbago is signposted on right 34km out of White River and 10km before Hazyview. A comfortable 4hrs drive from Jo'burg.

Porcupine Ridge Guest House

Janet & John Wills
5 Vanaxe Estate, Hazyview Road, Sabie-Hazyview
Tel: 082-818-0277   Fax: 086-661-4006
Email: info@porcupineridge.co.za Web: www.porcupineridge.co.za
Cell: 073-611-6349

Janet and John are sitting on a gold mine. Literally. Along with nine similar, private homes, Porcupine Ridge B&B forms an old mining village built high upon Vanaxe gold mine. Don't worry, it closed years ago. The only drilling you'll hear these days is the drilling of cuckoo on eucalyptus. After 38 years in residence, the Willses may be more South African than British, but they still chose Sabie as their retirement spot from Durban because, infinitely green and smack bang in the centre of the Panorama Route, it reminded Lancashire-born Janet of the Lake District. Sitting pretty up in the skies, Porcupine Ridge's mountainous doorstep is the active nature-lover's playground. Scenic leg-stretchers sprout from all corners of the sunny yellow house. The climb to the waterfall with deep, refreshing, swimming pools is my favourite and George and Alice, Porcupine Ridge's resident golden retrievers, may even act as your guides. Closer to home, two acres at least of this wilderness have been tamed in the form of a beautiful 50-year-old garden. Barely a lion's roar from Kruger Park or an oar's toss from Blyde River Canyon, you couldn't get bored up here. But if exhaustion sets in, John and Janet (such affable hosts that one returning guest published and gifted them a photography book of their B&B) will be back at your cosy home-from-home, ensuring your snug, comfortably kitted-out rooms are still spic'n'span, plumping sofa cushions in the laid-back lounge, pouring terrace sundowners while you take in dramatic ridge-top views, drawing up tomorrow's itinerary…. *Children over 6 by arrangement.*

Rooms: 5: 3 queens with en-s shower; 2 kings/twin with en-suite shower over bath, one with extra bed.
Price: R430 - R580 pp sharing. Single supplement on request.
Meals: Full breakfast (featuring unique treats such as cheesy potato pancakes, sweetcorn fritters and kedgeree) incl'. Breakfast can be packed if required.
Directions: From Jo'burg N4. L onto R539 to Sabie, L at Rosehaugh T-jct, R at Lydenburg/Sabie T-jct into Sabie. Leave Sabie on R536 Hazyview Rd. After 4km, R at sign for B&B. Follow gravel road up hill for 1km.

Map Number: 17

Entry Number: 232

Blue Jay Lodge

Philip and Margi Nichols

645 – 647 Blue Jay Steeg/Lane/Alley, Hazyview
Tel: 013-737-7546
Email: phil@bluejaylodge.co.za Web: www.bluejaylodge.co.za
Cell: 082-575-1798

I would have been happy enough plonked in a hippo wallow on such a hot and humid day, but Blue Jay Lodge, a cool oasis hidden among lush green, was so much better! And when I say hidden, I really mean it. The neighbours are completely blocked out by the undergrowth, the sycamore figs, fever trees... and many more. In fact, the grounds are home to seventy-three trees indigenous to the lowveld and escarpment ecosystem... and "not planted by humans", Phil adds. Sensing my heat fatigue Phil showed me to my huge room (past blossoming orchids), switched on the air-con and invited me to take a chilled drink from the mini-fridge. A new calmness prevailed as I lay back on the giant bed and gazed up at the high thatched roof. A short walk across the screed floor was my balcony, where the braai area and swimming pool are visible beyond the leaves of an old kiaat tree whose branches reached out to me from under the balustrades. I slept particularly well that night and was only dragged back to consciousness by the irresistible smells of a cooked breakfast with my name on it. Sitting on the verandah, lingering over a second cup of coffee, I watched an African paradise fly-catcher ducking and diving between the leaves. With more than 80 bird species on offer you could easily forget the day's activity and just sit and bird-watch at the lodge. Like I did! *No children under 14. Blue Jay Lodge is 10 minutes from Kruger Park gates. Can organize hot-air ballooning and safari drives.*

Rooms: 5: 4 king/twin with en-suite bath and shower; 1 self-catering unit with king, kitchenette and en-suite bath and shower.
Price: From R695 - R795 pp sharing. R595 - R695 for self-catering.
Meals: Full breakfast included when staying on a B&B basis.
Directions: Five-minute drive from Hazyview centre. See website for detailed directions.

Rissington Inn

Chris Harvie
Hazyview
Tel: 013-737-7700 Fax: 086-246-1370
Email: info@rissington.co.za Web: www.rissington.co.za
Cell: 082-327-6842

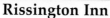

Informality and relaxation dictate at the Rissington Inn; you feel this even as you mount the broad steps to the verandah for the first time. Sun-lounging guests dazily contemplate the flower gardens full of frangipani; the swimming pool is a rectangle of cool aquamarine; the hazy valley shimmers beyond. In the evenings, gourmet, incredibly good-value, candlelit dinners are served by friendly staff. We have eaten with Chris on four separate occasions and never been disappointed, despite much creativity and daring in the dishes. The recent menu follows the 'Ménage a Trois' style of eating, with the selection of three or four smaller dishes for varying taste sensations... perfect for the indecisive like myself! High ceilings put the lid on well-designed rooms. The one I had was enormous with a Victorian bath and its own sitting area. But Rissington isn't the sort of place where you feel like hiding away or watching TV. Owner/maker/shaker Chris actually seems to LIKE seeing his guests doing what they want, dressed how they feel and making friends. When you arrive there is usually a gaggle of guests lined up in his wooden bar and you could easily mistake them for Chris's personal friends. They probably only arrived a few minutes before you. *Hazyview sits at the portals of the Kruger National Park. Rissington Inn is home to 154 species of birds.*

Rooms: 16: 2 queens, 4 with 2 queen beds, 3 queens + single bed, 3 kings + single, 2 kings, all en-s. Garden rooms have outside sh'r & aircon. 2 hillside suites, both king/queen + single, en-s bath & sh'r, outside sh'r, aircon & shared private pool.
Price: R500 - R990 pp sharing B&B.
Meals: Full breakfast included and served till noon. Restaurant on-site for à la carte lunch and dinner.
Directions: 2km south of Hazyview on R40 White River Numbi Gate (KNP) Rd. On right coming from main Hazyview 4-way-stop - see signs for Rissington.

Buckler's Africa

Cheryl and OJ Venter
Ngwenya Rd, Tenbosch, Komatipoort
Tel: 084-400-0703 Fax: 086-524-7107
Email: info@bucklersafrica.co.za Web: www.bucklersafrica.co.za

Cheryl and OJ are two of the most unshakeably laid-back, jolly people I've ever had the good fortune to meet, and when they gave me the official Buckler's tour I could see why: that view for starters. Plonked directly on the high southern bank of the Crocodile River, Buckler's lush lawns (and most of the beds in its thatched, chalet-style rooms) gaze out upon a vast, sloping section of the Kruger National Park: "The Kruger is our back garden" is Cheryl's well-founded boast. It's the sort of view - perfectly angled and complete with natural water-hole - about which pricy private lodges physically inside the Kruger National Park can only dream. "A family of lions lives over there," OJ nods nonchalantly, pouring me an icy cider as we scout for hippos, all wisely buried ear-deep in mud on a smoking hot November afternoon. "And the eles are forever scratching their backs against the pool wall," he tuts, raising a jocular eyebrow. With each idiosyncratic, uncluttered, naturally wood-furnished dwelling arranged around the garden, pool and bush oasis, Buckler's is a half B&B, half self-catering affair. Saying that, guests of the latter often poke sheepish sleepy heads into the breezy outside dining areas when aromas of coffee and croissants sneak through those generous windows. Similarly, OJ will happily give B&Bers a hand with a braai if a day in the park works up an appetite for flame-grilled impala fillet.

Rooms: 6: 3 standard rooms with queens, twins or singles with en/s or private bathrooms with bath/shower; 3 self-catering units: 1, 2 or 3 bedroom queens, twins or singles with en-s bathrooms, some outside showers, all bedrooms air-con.
Price: R520 per person sharing B&B (kitchenettes in all B&B rooms). R520 pp sh in s/c chalets (serviced daily).
Meals: Full breakfast included for B&B guests.
Directions: 11.5km outside Komatipoort. From the N4 take the Komatipoort turning, also signed to Crocodile Bridge Gate. Drive through the town on the R571 and continue for 6km until the wide road on the left signed Buckler's Africa. Drive 3.5km, following signs.

Trees Too

Sue and Martyn Steele

Komatipoort
Tel: 013-793-8262 Fax: 086-688-0177
Email: info@treestoo.com Web: www.treestoo.com

Originally from Blighty and the rains of Manchester, Martyn and Sue have adapted well to the B&B malarkey in lush, sub-tropical Komatipoort. Seven years ago, this "wildlife mad" couple wanted to be near animals and they'd be hard pressed to get much closer. A short drive from Kruger National Park, Trees Too is ideal for budgets that don't quite stretch to top-end lodges inside the park itself. Relaxed, friendly and informal, its rooms surrounding a kidney-shaped pool draped with languid palms and crawling bougainvillaea; Trees Too's atmosphere is more tropical beach than arid savannah. It's unsurprising really, when you consider that Maputo, Mozambique's capital on the Indian Ocean coast, is just one hour away. After a dusty day's game drive, grab a cool sundowner from the bar and submerge yourself in cooling water before sitting down at the friendly poolside restaurant. I found myself happily swapping game-spotting stories with other diners while tucking into topical croc pâté and kudu stew! With a storm brewing it was only a quick skip to bed - terracotta flooring, a soaring thatched roof and comfortable, air-conditioning thankfully keep things cool in the forty degree heat of summer. If you manage to tear yourself from the pool and badminton court and tire of SA's biggest game park, then your hosts have plenty of ideas up their sleeves: elephant-back safaris anyone, or perhaps even a trip to a Mozambique beach or the mountains of Swaziland?

Rooms: 8: 3 doubles, with en/s shower; 2 triple rooms with a double plus 1 single, with en/s bath and shower; 1 twin, with en/s bath/shower; 2 family rooms (one sleeping 4 and one sleeping 6, 1 with 4-poster bed), 1 with shower and 1 with bath/shower.
Price: R300 - R500 pp sharing.
Meals: Breakfast is a cold buffet with cheeses, meats and cereals, plus a full English. A range of delicious dinners available at poolside restaurant.
Directions: Take N4 from Jo'burg. On reaching Komatipoort, L at R571 into Rissik St, go 4km thro 2 stop signs then R into Gilfillan St. Take first right into Furley St. Trees Too is No.11 on L.

Map Number: 17

Notten's Bush Camp

The Nottens
Sabi Sand Game Reserve
Tel: 013-735-5105 Fax: 013-735-5970
Email: nottens@iafrica.com Web: www.nottens.com
Cell: 082-414-2711

I want my enthusiasm for this place to hijack your curiosity, my words to infiltrate your subconscious and somehow or other to get you to sleepwalk to Notten's. Few camps are family-run and it's the kind of place GG loves to be affiliated with. Just ask the regulars who return here year upon year (I expect they'll be a bit miffed I'm singing its praises so publicly). Although Notten's is jealously protected by its stalwart patrons who downplay the lodge as an earthy-sounding 'bush camp', comfort is certainly not in short supply. The chalets, with their gaping doors, white linen, dark woods and private decking, sit within a shaded line of trees overlooking a pastured impala oasis. This territory is known for its game, particularly leopards and rhino. Animals can wander into camp unhindered by fences. If you are skeptical have a close look at the elongated lap pool, where there's a paw-print from a visiting lion that recognised a wet-cement celebrity opportunity when it saw one. Nights are especially wonderful at Notten's. Returning from a G&T bush sundowner, I thought the distant camp looked like an AGM for lazy fireflies, an illusion created by hanging paraffin lamps. While ceiling fans rotate and showers run hot – there is minimal electricity for such necessities - the paraffin lamps encouraged we happy campers one step nearer to a state of nature. I found the Notten's 'feel' addictive; camaraderie flourished and apprehensions melted. Why don't more camps operate like this?

Rooms: 8: 2 family units with 1 king and 2 singles. 6 doubles, all with en-suite bathrooms with baths and indoor and outdoor showers.
Price: R3,250 - R3,550 pp sharing. Includes game drives, bush walks and all meals.
Meals: All included. Full breakfast, lunch, afternoon tea, bush sundowners and dinner.
Directions: From Hazyview, take R536 towards Paul Kruger Gate & Skukuza. After 37km see Notten's sign, L onto dirt road. After 7km reach Sabi Sand Reserve Shaws Gate. Entrance fee R110 per vehicle + R20 per person. Follow Notten's signs.

Cheetah Plains Private Game Reserve

Japie van Niekerk
Sabi Sand Game Reserve,
Tel: 013-751-3270
(reservations) or
079-694-8430 (lodge)
Fax: 086-613-9299
Email:
reservations@cheetahplains.
com (reservations)
or gm@cheetahplains.com
(lodge)
Web: www.cheetahplains.com

As I drove through the Sabi Sand Gate, I had finally come to terms with the fact that I was too late for the afternoon game drive…. But suddenly my guide, named Doctor, and fellow guests came speeding through the camp gate! "Jump in! Wild dogs! Don't worry, we have blankets, ponchos and wine!" My knight in shining armour had come back for me, loaded with all the essential ingredients for an afternoon game drive. And what a game drive not to have missed. I later learnt that, combined with the viewings on their morning game drive, my game drive companions had seen the so-called 'Magnificent Seven' in one day; and for one lady in particular, this was her first-ever safari experience and her birthday. We arrived back at camp, high as kites, reliving the drive around the open fire, interrupted by a hippo crossing through the spotlight in the nearby bush on its way to the camp's dam. Three delicious courses later, I retired to my comfortable, bright, thatched chalet, complete with viewing deck and outdoor shower. At 5 am, my human alarm woke me with a 'knock on the door', fresh milk in hand. The morning game drive was an equal success, the only difference being the change in beverage: Doctor's signature Amarula Coffee Cocktail. After a feast of a breakfast, it was time to wave goodbye to my new friends, who were en route to the pool to view the wildlife from the water's edge. I wish I was Dorothy and Cheetah Plains was my 'home'!

Rooms: 8: 6 standard rooms all en-suite with shower only; 2 luxury rooms both en-suite with bath & outdoor shower.
Price: R2,795 - R2,995 pp sharing. Single: R4,190 - R4,490.
Meals: All meals included. Lodge provides, brunch on return from morning game drive & dinner. Lunch on day of arrival not included, but can be arranged if required.
Directions: Enter at Gowry Gate of the Sabi Sand Game Reserve. See website for detailed directions.

Mpumalanga

Rhino Walking Safaris - Plains Camp

Nikki and Gerrit Meyer (Managers)
Rhino Walking Safaris, Kruger National Park, Skukuza
Tel: 011-467-1886 Fax: 011-467-4758
Email: info@rws.co.za Web: www.isibindiafrica.co.za
Cell: 083-631-4956

This is where I fell for Africa: sitting outside my tent in the Kruger, sipping G&T (for the anti-malarial quinine, you understand) and watching game serenely traverse the Timbitene Plain. This is the only private lodge where you can walk in pristine wilderness - nothing short of a privilege. Here the refined pioneer tents have dark wood furniture with brass hinges and leather straps, bathrooms with copper taps protruding from tree stumps and the largest, softest towels. During the day, you can doze on the chocolate-leather sofa or sip highball cocktails in the plunge pool. Pith helmets, surveying tools, maps and a gramophone add to the bygone feel. Walking on rhino footpaths, the trails let you soak up both the scale and detail of the bush. There's no mad rush to tick off half-glimpsed Big Five. This is all about the quality of the sightings. That said, we encountered glowering buffalo, rampant rhino, lionesses on a hunt and had a pulse-quickening showdown with a bull elephant that I'll dine out on for ages. Afterwards we sent the sun down the sky and, wrapped in rugs, headed toward gas-lamp beacons for a never-ending feast. A safari fantasy come true.

Rooms: 4: all twin-bed African-explorer style tents, each with en-suite loo, shower and overhead fan. Tree-house sleep-out option also available.
Price: R3,260 – R3,860 pp sharing. Ask about 3-, 4- or 5-night packages and single supplement. Minimum 2-night stay.
Meals: All meals, soft drinks, house wines and beer, safari activities (primarily walking) and optional sleep-outs included.
Directions: From the Paul Kruger Gate follow signs to Skukuza Rest Camp & Rhino Walking Safaris. Drive past Skukuza on H1-2 towards Tshokwane and Satara. Cross Sabie and Sand rivers and after second turning to Maroela Loop, turn left signed Rhino Walking Safaris. Meet at Rhino Post Safari Lodge.

Rhino Post Safari Lodge

Nikki and Gerrit Meyer (Managers)

Kruger National Park,
Tel: 011-467-1886 Fax: 011-467-4758
Email: info@rws.co.za Web: www.isibindiafrica.co.za
Cell: 083-631-4956

After 6 hours' drive from Jo'burg it was with a mixture of relief and anticipation that we rolled the last few kilometres through the Kruger Park to Rhino Post Safari Lodge. On arrival our bags were magically transferred to our lovely, luxurious, wood-framed chalet with its big glass windows and deck overlooking a dry river bed (or should I say animal motorway?). Although the chalets have phones and electricity, it still feels as rustic and as open to nature as is safely possible. The camp is not fenced so animals are able to walk through the lodge area (you will be escorted back and forth along the boardwalks after dark). So… first an outdoor shower, then tea up at the lodge, on a deck overlooking a frequently-used waterhole; and then straight out in search of game and adventure. Our thanks to Bernard, our guide and driver, for some wonderful experiences. I don't know if we were lucky or not, but 16 rhino on our first night didn't seem bad! We also saw two prides of lion fighting over a giraffe carcass, with scores of vultures in the trees and a large pack of hyenas watching the action for scavenging opportunities. This sunlit tableau is etched on my memory and it was a sighting to brag about that evening over fireside drinks. All the meals at Rhino Post are exceptional and it does not take long to get into the new schedule of early starts, late breakfasts, siestas, late-afternoon game drives… and finally dinner. It was a proper wrench to leave when the time came.

Rooms: 16: 2 double & 6 twin chalets. All en-s bathrooms, deep free-standing baths, outside shwers, overhead fans, mini bar, phone, safe. hairdryer.
Price: R2,860 – R3,440 pp sharing. Ask about 3-, 4- or 5-night packages and winter rates.
Meals: All meals and safari activities included.
Directions: From the Paul Kruger Gate follow signs to Skukuza Rest Camp & Rhino Walking Safaris. Drive past Skukuza on H1-2 towards Tshokwane and Satara. Cross Sabie and Sand rivers & after second turning to Maroela Loop, turn left signed Rhino Walking Safaris.

Black Leopard Camp

Alan and Lynsey Watson

Farm: Thaba Tholo Wilderness, District of Lydenburg
Email: carol@ontracksafaris.co.uk Web: www.blackleopardcamp.com
Cell: 079-354-8538; (UK) +44 (0)7760-349-820

As we drove through the gates of Thaba Tholo Wilderness Reserve, my jaw may well have dropped a tad. My guide pointed to a rock face in the distance: "the camp is just below in the valley". And between here and there lay pure, uplifting bushveld, home to a wide variety of wildlife, including leopard. Once Alan's family holiday home, 'keys' were handed down to Alan and his wife Lynsey, who opened their six thousand hectares of wildlife heaven to conservationists Will and Carol Fox and supported the construction of a research camp on the property, INGWE Leopard Research, which is well worth a visit. On arrival I was greeted with a glass of sherry and a warm flannel, before Lynsey led me along the elevated walkway, lit by solar-panelled jar lamps, and up a maze of stone paths to my 'tent'. I use inverted commas because the only resemblance to my idea of a tent is the shape and the canvas; here were Julia Montana linen, Persian and Afghan rugs and a monument of antique luggage. After a long soak in my Victorian (bush) bath under the stars, I joined fellow guests and staff for pre-dinner drinks by the open fire, before sitting for Alan's delicious Portuguese-themed dinner. This was quickly consumed; so too the Portuguese wine, which I felt I had to indulge in for the sake of the theme. I woke from my best-ever night's sleep (this was prophesied by Alan and Lynsey) to find a flask of hot water by my door for a morning cuppa…. This is bush glamping in spades!

Rooms: 7: 4 double units, with own en-suite and "bush bathroom" with bath and shower; 3 family units (sleeps 5), each with 2 en-suites and "bush bathroom" with bath and shower.
Price: R997.50 per adult sharing per night. R489.50 per child (under 13 years) sharing with adult per night. Single supplement 25%.
Meals: All meals included.
Directions: Black Leopard Camp arrival area 15km outside Lydenburg on R37 towards 'Burgersfort' where you will be met by a guide at 2pm for a game drive to the lodge.

Iketla Lodge

Albert and Hennielene Botha

off R555, Ohrigstad
Tel: 013-238-8900 Fax: 086-514-5288
Email: relax@iketla.com Web: www.iketla.com

"Be relaxed… be peaceful' is Iketla's poetic English translation from the local Sotho dialect. Appropriately named, as it turns out. Surrounded on all sides by hills and rocky outcrops, Albert and Hennielene greeted me in the shebeen, where the late afternoon sun was gushing through the open sides, flooding the thatched, tiled dining area. For those that don't know, a shebeen is a drinking den and it's to this magnet that guests began to flock as they returned, brimming with exhilaration, from the day's adventures. Some had been exploring the Panorama Route, others had been walking guided trails through Iketla's 540 hectares of wilderness, inspecting all creatures great and small and learning about the impressive range of birdlife and traditional uses of indigenous plants. They regaled us with their new-found knowledge and enthusiasm, with Albert, a bushman at heart, chipping in with many jewels of profounder expertise. A faint drumbeat interrupted the banter to signal supper, though my acute senses had already picked up the aroma of something sensational in the air… ostrich strips in a sherry sauce as it turned out. At daybreak I inspected my chalet, similar in style to the main lodge with rugged stone walls, a thatched roof and a verandah outside sliding glass doors. There I read my book and rested my bones, listening to the morning wildlife bring this African wilderness alive.

Rooms: 8 chalets: 3 doubles and 4 twins, 1 honeymoon suite, all with en-suite showers and outside showers.
Price: R1,140 – R1,200 pppn. Singles R1,450 – R1,510.
Meals: Full breakfast and dinner included.
Directions: From N4 turn off at Belfast and follow R540 through Dullstroom to Lydenburg. Follow R36 through Lydenburg (also known as Mashishing) to Ohrigstad. 4km past Ohrigstad turn left onto R555. Sign to Iketla 6km further on right.

Umlani Bushcamp

Marco Schiess
Timbavati Nature Reserve
Tel: 021-785-5547 Fax: 086-696-8518
Email: info@umlani.com Web: www.umlani.com
Cell: 083-468-2041

Rhino-tracking on foot; a rather exciting experience with a couple of bull elephants; sun-downers as the bush settles for the night... this is what safaris are supposed to be about. Umlani is set on a gentle slope above a dry river course (wet in spring) and only a high elephant fence separates guests from the Big 5. You do not, for example, leave your rondavel at night to investigate snuffling noises and elephants regularly swing around the camp perimeter for a drink at the pool. You sleep in delightful reed-walled rondavels with thatched roofs (no bricks here), hurricane lamps (no electricity either), and you shower *au naturel*, but in complete privacy. Marco and his wife Marie ran the camp by themselves for a decade until the demands of a young family compelled them to find like-minded managers. After the evening game drive everyone sits out on the deck by the bar or in the boma round the fire, mulling over what's just been seen, before sitting down to an excellent and often buzzy dinner at tables of 8. Thoughtful hosts and knowledgeable rangers provide the charming, human face of a full-on bush experience. I had many laughs during my stay, while another guest was in tears when she had to leave! Umlani is exceptionally personal and genuine and you live as close to nature as they dare let you. For the more adventurous a night in the treehouse 2km away is a must! *Umlani Bushcamp is the 14th establishment to receive the prestigious Fair Trade in Tourism South Africa Certification.*

Rooms: 8 huts (3 sleeping 4, 1 sleeping 3 and 4 sleeping 2), all with en-suite outside showers.
Price: R2,750 pp sharing, singles R3,610. Children under 12: R1,375. 3-night special: R7,030 pp sharing, R9,240 singles, R3,515 kids under 12. 7-night special also on offer.
Meals: All meals, drinks and 2 - 3 game activities included.
Directions: You will get a map when you book.

Swaziland

Wide Horizons

Rose Roques

Rosecraft Farm, Egebeni/Malkerns
Tel: +268-250-53915
Email: roseroques@googlemail.com
Cell: +268-7604-1373

Just the drive to Wide Horizons is an adventure in itself and a great way to see the beauty of Swaziland. Down the hill and through the stream, the road all of sudden turned purple. It was as though the jacaranda trees somehow knew I was coming as the purple leaf-confetti swirled around my car. And the fairy tale didn't stop there. Pulling up to the gorgeous Alice in Wonderland-style thatched house I was convinced a crazy white rabbit was going to come running out. Thankfully, I was greeted by the much saner and more tranquil Rose, who has lived on the farm for the better part of 38 years. As well as overseeing the farm and running the B&B, she also runs Rosecraft, a hand-weaving workshop that not only produces magnificent blankets, scarves, curtains and much more, but also provides much-needed employment to the local community. Guests are encouraged to have a look around and watch the ladies working the traditional looms and spinning wheels. After a roam around the garden with its spring that runs through and into the natural rock swimming pool (no chemicals here), we headed down to the ever-popular luxury tent. Sitting on the Makungutsha Mountain and overlooking the Lebombo Mountains the panoramic views over this vast space make the drive worth the effort on their own. You should definitely take a walk along the sculpture trail. Not only is this a wonderful way to experience the natural beauty of the landscape and those jaw-dropping views, but you can also enjoy the fruit of the labours of local sculptors as you go. There is nothing about Wide Horizons I would not recommend.

Rooms: 2: B&B in the house: 1 unit with 2 dble rooms, both en-s shr. Can sleep 6 (4 adults + 2 kids); 1 luxury safari tent (sleeps 2), en-s bathroom & separate kitchen for self-catering.
Price: B&B in house or tent R360 pp; self-catering in luxury tent only R300.
Meals: Breakfast included for B&B guests. Dinner in house extra and on request.
Directions: From Mbabane down Malagwane Hill. At bottom L onto MR103. Past Sundowners Backpackers & 1st R. Follow signs for Rosecraft. Email for detailed directions.

Umdoni B&B

Jane Gilbert
Off MR18, Malkerns
Tel: +2682-528-3009 Fax: +2682-550-4334
Email: umdoni@posix.co.sz Web: www.umdoni.com
Cell: +2687-602-0791

Across a pineapple field, between smartly-aligned fever trees and through a white iron gate, I found Umdoni and what a find it was too. Eagerly awaiting my arrival was Jane, who gave me the warmest welcome and I hadn't even left my driver's seat yet! Jane and her husband, both born and bred in Swaziland, chose Ezulwini Valley to set up home and start a family. Some years on, their children "spread their wings", leaving Jane and her three ladies, Elizabeth, Yenzi and Buhle, with nothing to look after. That was until their Umdoni B&B baby was born. Jane and her team had found their calling and it's all down to "girl power", as Jane calls it. Each cottage has been nurtured with pride and love. So too are the guests. Stunned by the size of one of the beds, I learnt a regular guest had suggested two double beds instead of two singles for a 'twin' and as if by magic...! All members of any party, whether single, a couple or a family, would be well provided for here. I stood envisioning my own family: my father and my younger sister playing tennis (reverting to table tennis in the pool house when temperatures insisted), my older sister jumping between pool and sun-bed, and my mother, sat on our cottage verandah enjoying the "peace and quiet" (aka no husband or children!). I would be exploring the area on an Umdoni bicycle. For those that also wish to venture beyond the Umdoni fence, Jane is wise on all local activities and good-quality restaurants and, being located in Ezulwini Valley, all of these are on your doorstep.

Rooms: 2 cottages/4 rooms (available by cottage or room): 1 queen + single bed w/ en-s and 1 twin (d'ble beds) + single w/ en-s, w/ shared kitchen, dining & sitting area; 1 queen w/ en-s and 1 twin w/ en-s, w/ kitchenette & small sitting area.
Price: R430 pppn sharing. Singles: R550 pppn.
Meals: Full breakfast included. Lunch & dinner on request.
Directions: From Mbabane, take main Mbabane/Manzini highway (MR3). At bottom of hill take 1st exit to Ezulwini onto MR103. Continue 17km. Turn R onto MR18 (Sundowners Pub on L). After 3km turn R (Big Rooster & sign for Umdoni). Drive 100m and turn R. This road will take you to Umdoni's gate.

Limpopo

Shikwari Bush Lodge

The Lawrie Family

Shikwari Bush Lodge, R36 Lydenburg/J.G Strydom Tunnel Road, Hoedspruit
Fax: 086-626-8109
Email: enquiries@shikwari.co.za Web: www.shikwari.co.za
Cell: 073-049-7494

The Drakensberg Mountains and the Limpopo bushveld are two of my favourite things… and Shikwari Lodge is blessed with an ample sufficiency of both! This is a family-run lodge and all the Lawries are instrumental in its smooth and happy management. While Sue prepared lunch, Ian took me off into the bush for a look at the chalets. As we went, he identified the various bird songs that provided a soundtrack for our tour. Entering the suites the first thing I noticed was that wonderful smell of thatch - gets me every time. I inhaled a few times, before I took everything else in: the crisp linens, big beds, fine teas and uninterrupted views of the mountains. Don't be surprised if nyala or kudu are grazing outside your window. Plains game roam freely here. You may even pass a giraffe en route to your outdoor shower (there are indoor ones too if you don't fancy al fresco washing). Returning to the main lodge I avoided the temptations of the bar and the plunge pool and opted instead for a comfortable chair in the shade of the verandah… where I waited for my dinner! Sue used to run a cooking school in Jo'burg so I had high expectations and these were fully met in the form of lamb and veggies. If you can't stay at Shikwari for some reason then I recommend you seek out her students! I was pleasantly full and content and the idea of a postprandial Sunday afternoon snooze was almost impossible to resist… but the road beckoned. Next time, I'll book a few days instead. *A guide is available to accompany guests on activity outings, game drives with breakfast, nature walks on property. Kids over 8 welcome.*

Rooms: 5: 4 doubles with en-suite bathrooms and outdoor showers; 1 family suite.
Price: R1,260 - R2,400 pp sharing. Singles R1,743.
Meals: Full breakfast & 3-course dinner included. Lunch is not usually available.
Directions: From N4 turn off at Belfast and follow R540 through Dullstroom to Lydenburg. Follow R36 through Lydenburg and continue through JG Strydom Tunnel, gate 8km from exit.

Pezulu Tree House Game Lodge

Claude and Lydia Huberty

Guernsey, Hoedspruit
Tel: 015-793-2724 Fax: 015-793-2253
Email: pezlodge@mweb.co.za Web: www.pezulu.co.za
Cell: 083-294-7831

The sorry victim of a treehouse-free childhood, I was intrigued by the concept of Pezulu, eight different reed-and-thatch constructions spread among the trees surrounding the central building, itself entwined around a large marula tree. They are all hidden from view behind branch and leaf. Many have bits of tree growing up through the floor to provide the most natural of towel rails, chairs and loo paper holders. Most 'houses' are named after the trees in which they sit: 'False Thorn' has a magnificent shower with views across Thornybush Reserve – be prepared for inquisitive giraffe. 'Huilboerboom' is a honeymoon suite set five metres above ground (privacy even from the giraffe); while 'Dream Tree House' is the ultimate in canopy living, luxuriously expansive with a king bed that wheels outside so you can sleep within the stars. But it's brand-new 'Mountain View', stretching a whopping seven metres up and affording panoramic eyefuls of the Drakensberg Mountains, that is the real king of the skies. Hearty dining takes place in the boma where I chatted to the Hubertys about their Luxembourg origins. Pezulu is situated in the Guernsey Conservancy on the edge of the Kruger Park. There are no predators, only plains game, so you and the buck can wander around the property in relative safety. The usual morning and afternoon game drives, full day Kruger trips, visits to rehabilitation centres and other activities are easily arranged... assuming you can be persuaded down from the trees.

Rooms: 8: 3 family units (1 double and twins) and 4 doubles (2 standard and 3 luxury), variously with outside shower, and/or bath.
Price: R850 - R1,350 pp sharing, inclusive of all meals. Singles R 1,195. Children under 12 years: R495. Game drives and other activities optional extra.
Meals: Includes full English breakfast, high tea and 3-course dinner in the boma.
Directions: Ask when booking.

Mopane Bush Lodge

Paul and Rosemary Hatty & Andrew and Moira Rae
Mapungubwe, Off the R572, Musina
Tel: 083-633-0765 or 015-534-7906 Fax: 015-534-7906 or 086-610-3410
Email: mopanebushlodge@limpopo.co.za
Web: www.mopanebushlodge.co.za Cell: 083-633-0765

This is a fascinating, under-visited frontier of South Africa and both these facts make this a great destination. Hidden in 6,000 hectares of semi-desert mopane scrub, the lodge itself is an oasis where fine food (either taken in the huge, open-plan dining area or outside in the boma round a fire), a swimming pool and intimate cottage-rooms provide all the trappings of sophistication and luxury you could wish for. The game reserve has plains game only, so walking about is safe and I recommend taking the track to a waterhole to birdwatch before dinner. But during the day I loved my two visits to the Mapungubwe National Park, five minutes down the road. First an early-morning visit to the archaeological site of South Africa's earlier version of Great Zimbabwe. This ancient civilisation took place on and around a gigantic rock in dramatic scenery interspersed with giant other-worldly baobab trees. And then a second visit took us to the lush confluence of the Limpopo and Shashe rivers and to a heavenly sundowner spot where you can look out onto Zimbabwe and Botswana. Paul and Andrew can also show you the amazing San rock art. As for wildlife they have it all up here ('big five' etc), but the birdlife takes the *palme d'or*. You'll find some real rarities, including the broad-billed roller and the collared palm thrush. I have been round and round South Africa, but this area was a real find and I heartily recommend both the lodge and its environment. *Mountain bikes are available for guests to use.*

Rooms: 8 rondavels: all can be dble or twin, with en-suite indoor and outdoor showers.
Price: R1,500 - R1,850 pp. R250 - R505 per person for off-site tours.
Meals: All meals and all activities on Mopane's own private nature reserve are included.
Directions: Take N1 from Joburg to Polokwane (Pietersberg). Follow signs thro town for R521 to Dendron. Travel 140km to Alldays, then R to Pontdrif. 46km and R onto R572 to Musina & Mapungubwe. Mopane Bush Lodge 29km along this road, just past cell phone tower on R. Map on web.

Map Number: 16   Entry Number: 248

Index

Index by town name

For our rural properties, we have listed the nearest town

Index

Index by house name

SWAZILAND

Index of activities

GARDENS
Places with lovely gardens and owners who are enthusiastic gardeners.
1, 3, 4, 5, 7, 8, 9, 11, 12, 13, 14, 16, 17, 18, 24, 25, 26, 27, 29, 30, 31, 32, 33, 34, 39, 40, 42, 44, 47, 49, 51, 52, 53, 54, 55, 56, 57, 58, 59, 61, 63, 64, 65, 66, 67, 68, 73, 74, 75, 76, 78, 79, 80, 82, 83, 85, 87, 89, 94, 95, 96, 97, 98, 99, 101, 102, 103, 105, 106, 107, 108, 109, 111, 112, 113, 114, 115, 116, 117, 118, 119, 120, 123, 125, 126, 127, 129, 130, 132, 133, 134, 135, 136, 137, 138, 139, 140, 143, 145, 146, 147, 148, 149, 150, 151, 154, 157, 158, 160, 161, 162, 163, 164, 165, 166, 167, 169, 170, 172, 173, 174, 177, 178, 181, 182, 183, 184, 186, 189, 190, 191, 197, 198, 199, 200, 201, 203, 204, 207, 208, 209, 210, 211, 214, 215, 216, 219, 220, 222, 225, 227, 228, 229, 230, 231, 232, 233, 235, 244, 245, 248

ROCK ART
Sites found either on the property or guests can be shown/guided to nearby sites.
43, 44, 45, 46, 103, 104, 129, 133, 134, 135, 136, 138, 139, 140, 141, 153, 158, 159, 160, 162, 165, 192, 193, 197, 198, 199, 201, 203, 204, 206, 207, 211, 213, 229, 241, 248

CULTURE
Township visits can be organized by owners or cultural experiences (e.g. Zulu dancing) available on site.
2, 6, 7, 8, 9, 12, 14, 15, 16, 17, 18, 19, 21, 22, 25, 26, 29, 30, 31, 32, 33, 34, 50, 51, 54, 56, 59, 61, 62, 64, 66, 71, 73, 75, 76, 79, 89, 91, 93, 96, 97, 98, 102, 104, 107, 111, 113, 114, 117, 118, 119, 121, 123, 125, 126, 127, 130, 131, 136, 138, 141, 142, 145, 146, 148, 149, 150, 151, 153, 154, 155, 157, 162, 163, 165, 169, 172, 173, 174, 175, 176, 177, 178, 180, 181, 182, 183, 184, 185, 186, 187, 188, 189, 190, 192, 193, 195, 196, 197, 198, 199, 200, 201, 203, 206, 211, 219, 221, 222, 223, 226, 229, 230, 231, 232, 233, 234, 236, 243, 244, 245, 247

WINE-MAKER
Wine made on the property.
50, 51, 52, 53, 55, 56, 59, 61, 62, 63, 64, 72, 78, 81, 82, 102, 116, 124, 136

GOOD AND ORIGINAL CUISINE

8, 25, 27, 38, 39, 45, 48, 50, 51, 52, 56, 57, 59, 64, 65, 73, 74, 76, 80, 85, 87, 94, 95, 97, 99, 102, 104, 107, 108, 117, 125, 127, 128, 132, 134, 135, 136, 142, 144, 147, 149, 150, 151, 153, 157, 161, 163, 166, 170, 175, 183, 185, 186, 187, 188, 191, 192, 193, 195, 197, 198, 199, 203, 207, 209, 210, 212, 213, 214, 215, 216, 219, 220, 226, 227, 228, 229, 230, 231, 234, 236, 237, 240, 243, 247, 248

HORSE-RIDING

Available on site.

5, 6, 7, 8, 16, 32, 35, 37, 38, 39, 41, 44, 50, 51, 53, 55, 56, 57, 64, 66, 75, 81, 89, 95, 96, 98, 104, 116, 118, 120, 126, 128, 133, 136, 142, 148, 154, 155, 156, 160, 161, 163, 165, 171, 175, 177, 178, 179, 180, 184, 185, 186, 189, 192, 195, 197, 198, 199, 201, 203, 205, 206, 207, 209, 211, 216, 230, 231, 232, 233, 244, 245

BOAT CHARTER

Property owns boats or can organise charters.

1, 3, 6, 7, 8, 9, 12, 14, 16, 19, 21, 22, 25, 26, 29, 32, 37, 38, 40, 41, 55, 56, 85, 87, 88, 89, 90, 91, 93, 94, 95, 98, 104, 105, 108, 109, 110, 111, 112, 113, 114, 115, 116, 117, 118, 119, 120, 121, 122, 123, 125, 126, 142, 143, 144, 145, 146, 150, 152, 154, 155, 157, 169, 170, 171, 172, 173, 175, 176, 177, 178, 179, 180, 184, 185, 186, 187, 188, 189, 190, 198, 201, 215, 230, 234

CANOEING

Canoes owned or organised by the property.

2, 3, 8, 12, 16, 19, 21, 25, 33, 34, 35, 36, 37, 38, 39, 40, 44, 45, 48, 51, 53, 55, 56, 57, 59, 62, 84, 85, 87, 88, 89, 90, 91, 93, 96, 97, 98, 103, 104, 105, 107, 108, 109, 110, 111, 112, 113, 114, 115, 116, 117, 118, 119, 120, 121, 122, 123, 125, 126, 127, 130, 131, 135, 143, 144, 146, 150, 152, 154, 156, 157, 159, 162, 163, 167, 169, 170, 172, 173, 176, 177, 178, 180, 185, 186, 187, 188, 189, 200, 201, 206, 216, 230, 231, 232, 233, 234

HISTORIC HOUSE

These places are historic buildings.

15, 17, 26, 27, 35, 50, 55, 56, 59, 61, 63, 64, 67, 81, 89, 96, 97, 98, 99, 100, 102, 126, 130, 134, 135, 137, 138, 141, 150, 153, 161, 162, 163, 164, 165, 166, 167, 168, 178, 198, 201, 203, 207, 208, 209, 212, 214, 225, 227, 229

HISTORY TOURS
Organised here (including battlefields).
6, 7, 12, 16, 21, 22, 26, 29, 30, 33, 34, 40, 51, 59, 66, 67, 71, 75, 78, 111, 113, 130, 131, 135, 136, 138, 146, 149, 151, 153, 157, 160, 161, 162, 163, 165, 175, 179, 181, 182, 183, 189, 191, 192, 193, 194, 195, 196, 197, 198, 200, 201, 202, 203, 205, 206, 207, 209, 210, 212, 219, 221, 222, 223, 228, 229, 231, 248

SELF-CATERING OPTION AVAILABLE HERE.
1, 3, 4, 7, 8, 9, 11, 13, 15, 16, 21, 23, 24, 29, 31, 32, 35, 36, 38, 41, 42, 43, 44, 46, 47, 48, 50, 52, 54, 55, 58, 59, 60, 62, 63, 64, 66, 68, 69, 72, 73, 75, 76, 77, 78, 79, 81, 82, 83, 84, 89, 93, 100, 103, 104, 106, 112, 113, 115, 116, 117, 118, 121, 122, 123, 124, 126, 127, 129, 130, 131, 133, 136, 139, 142, 143, 144, 145, 146, 153, 154, 155, 158, 159, 160, 162, 163, 164, 167, 168, 170, 172, 173, 174, 175, 176, 181, 182, 184, 186, 191, 192, 196, 197, 198, 199, 200, 202, 204, 205, 206, 211, 213, 214, 215, 220, 222, 229, 230, 233, 235, 244, 245

BIRD-WATCHING
Owners are enthusiasts.
1, 3, 4, 7, 8, 29, 31, 32, 34, 35, 36, 37, 38, 39, 40, 41, 42, 44, 45, 46, 47, 48, 50, 51, 52, 53, 54, 55, 56, 57, 58, 59, 60, 61, 62, 63, 64, 65, 66, 67, 68, 72, 73, 75, 76, 78, 79, 80, 81, 82, 83, 85, 87, 88, 88, 89, 90, 91, 94, 95, 96, 97, 98, 99, 100, 101, 102, 103, 104, 105, 106, 107, 108, 109, 110, 113, 115, 116, 117, 118, 119, 120, 122, 123, 125, 126, 127, 128, 129, 130, 131, 132, 133, 134, 135, 136, 137, 138, 139, 141, 142, 143, 144, 145, 147, 148, 149, 150, 151, 152, 154, 156, 157, 158, 159, 160, 161, 163, 165, 166, 167, 169, 170, 171, 172, 174, 176, 177, 178, 179, 180, 181, 182, 183, 184, 185, 186, 187, 188, 189, 190, 191, 192, 193, 194, 195, 196, 197, 198, 199, 200, 201, 202, 203, 204, 205, 206, 207, 208, 209, 210, 212, 213, 215, 216, 219, 220, 224, 225, 226, 227, 228, 229, 230, 231, 232, 233, 234, 235, 237, 238, 239, 241, 242, 243, 244, 245, 247, 248

WHALE-WATCHING
Available from the property or from so nearby that it makes little difference.
1, 2, 3, 4, 5, 6, 7, 8, 9, 11, 37, 38, 39, 40, 41, 42, 84, 85, 87, 88, 89, 91, 92, 93, 94, 100, 119, 121, 127, 142, 143, 155, 156, 157, 169, 170, 172, 176, 177, 179, 180, 187

BEACH HOUSE

36, 37, 38, 41, 42, 84, 85, 87, 88, 89, 91, 92, 93, 121, 142, 143, 155, 157, 169, 172, 176, 187

WHITE-WATER RAFTING

Can be arranged in-house.
22, 45, 85, 88, 98, 114, 125, 142, 162, 197, 198, 200, 201, 203, 206, 230, 245, 247

FULLY CHILD-FRIENDLY

Places where children will be particularly well looked-after.
3, 8, 18, 19, 23, 29, 32, 35, 40, 46, 51, 57, 63, 64, 71, 72, 74, 83, 84, 88, 89, 97, 102, 112, 117, 124, 130, 132, 133, 134, 139, 141, 148, 150, 152, 156, 157, 160, 163, 165, 167, 168, 170, 175, 176, 178, 181, 182, 184, 189, 190, 191, 197, 198, 200, 201, 202, 203, 205, 206, 207, 208, 209, 211, 215, 217, 220, 225, 226, 230, 234, 241, 243, 248

FISHING

Can be arranged.
5, 16, 34, 35, 38, 39, 41, 42, 45, 51, 55, 61, 62, 75, 87, 88, 89, 97, 104, 107, 115, 118, 120, 126, 142, 144, 155, 156, 158, 160, 161, 163, 170, 172, 175, 176, 177, 179, 181, 184, 185, 186, 189, 190, 191, 193, 195, 198, 199, 201, 202, 203, 204, 207, 216, 230, 231, 232, 234, 236, 241, 245